# Careers: Paths to Entrepreneurship

# Careers: Paths to Entrepreneurship

SALEM PRESS
A Division of EBSCO Information Services, Inc.
Ipswich, Massachusetts

**GREY HOUSE PUBLISHING**

Cover photo: iStock



*Careers: Paths to Entrepreneurship*, published by Grey House Publishing, Inc., Amenia, NY, under exclusive license from EBSCO Information Services, Inc.



∞ The paper used in these volumes conforms to the American National Standard for Permanence of Paper for Printed Library Materials, Z39.48 1992 (R2009).

Publisher's Cataloging-In-Publication Data
(Prepared by The Donohue Group, Inc.)

Title: Careers : paths to entrepreneurship.
Other Titles: Paths to entrepreneurship | Careers in—
Description: Ipswich, Massachusetts : Salem Press, a division of EBSCO Information Services, Inc. ; Amenia, NY : Grey House Publishing, [2021] | Includes bibliographical references and index.
Identifiers: ISBN 9781642657746 (print) | ISBN 9781642657753 (ebook)
Subjects: LCSH: Entrepreneurship—Vocational guidance—United States. | Self-employed—United States. | Business—Vocational guidance—United States.
Classification: LCC HB615 .C37 2021 (print) | LCC HB615 (ebook) | DDC 658.421/023—dc23

First Printing

PRINTED IN THE UNITED STATES OF AMERICA

# CONTENTS

# PUBLISHER'S NOTE

The latest volume in our *Careers* series, *Careers: Paths to Entrepreneurship* provides a thorough introduction to the wide range of career opportunities available to those interested in starting their own business or developing a product that fills a need.

The types of careers available to entrepreneurs are virtually endless, from the creative to the technical, bakers to engineers, artists to financial advisors. *Careers: Path to Entrepreneurship* offers insight into how to begin and what to expect. If you like being your own boss, can handle financial risk, and can learn from your mistakes, this book is for you.

At the heart of this volume, like the dozens of previous *Careers* titles, are twenty-five occupation profiles of entrepreneurs or of jobs that lead to entrepreneurship. Each career profile offers details about its specific career:

**Snapshots** offer current data on:

- Median pay
- Job outlook
- Educational and other requirements
- Working conditions
- Recommended areas of interest

**Career Overviews** describe:

- Duties
- Work environment
- Work schedules

In addition, each profile provides important qualities for the job, specific and general job requirements, anticipated rates of growth and why. Also included is a list of related occupations, both in the public and private sectors, and a list of resources for more information includes specific associations or certifying bodies.

Merging scholarship with occupational development, this single comprehensive guidebook provides students who are passionate about becoming an entrepreneur with the necessary insight into the wide array of options available. The book offers guidance regarding what job seekers can expect in terms of training, advancement, earnings, job prospects, working conditions, relevant associations, and more. *Careers: Paths to Entrepreneurship* is specifically designed for a high school and undergraduate audience and is edited to align with secondary or high school curriculum standards.

**Additional Materials**

*Careers: Paths to Entrepreneurship* is enhanced with numerous tables, including projections from the U.S. Bureau of Labor Statistics, and median annual salaries or wages for those occupations profiled. Fast Facts, Famous Firsts, and dozens of photos add depth to the discussion.

A popular and valuable highlight of the *Careers* series are the "Conversations With"—interviews with real-life professionals working in relevant jobs. Those interviewed offer their personal career paths, detail the potential for career advancement, and offer advice for students. From fashion designer to bioengineer, it's all here.

The back matter in this volume includes:

Appendix A: Guide to the Holland Code—John Holland's theory that people and work environments can be classified into six different groups: realistic, investigative, artistic, social, enterprising, and conventional. These interest codes are found at the beginning of each profile.

Appendix B: General Bibliography—a list of suggested readings for those who wish to learn more about becoming an entrepreneur.

Appendix C: List of Organizations and Resources—a list of further resources for education, certification, professional development, and networking.

The volume also includes a comprehensive subject index.

Thanks are due to volume editor Allison Blake who defined the coverage and, with the help of Deborah Funk and Cynthia McCormick, wrote the interviews. Salem Press also thanks the professionals who took the time to share their work experience. Their frank and honest responses provide immeasurable value to *Careers: Paths to Entrepreneurship.*

# INTRODUCTION

If steel magnate Andrew Carnegie threw open the entrepreneurial gates during the late 19th century, Henry Ford drove through them at the dawn of the 20th with his Model T Ford. As the 20th century neared its end, Bill Gates co-invented MS-DOS, which went on to become Windows OS, the foundation of Microsoft, Inc., which he also co-founded. Around the same time, Steve Jobs co-invented the Apple I personal computer, then co-launched Apple, Inc. The new millennium brought Mark Zuckerberg, and social media.

All of these notable entrepreneurs share two significant traits—realizing opportunity and taking big risks. The Microsofts and Apples of the world glamorized entrepreneurship during the tech boom of the late 1990s and early 2000s. Creating a startup company became a common career goal, which is still true today; Babson College reported that one-third of Americans know an entrepreneur, based on 2017 data.

Entrepreneurship takes many forms, and entrepreneurs have different visions: people who want to explore the possibility of being their own boss and making a gazillion bucks; people who want to build a small business doing something they love; and people who have identified a problem or need and have invented a product or service to fix or fill it.

Whatever the path, entrepreneurs both shoulder the financial risks and reap the financial rewards. It takes an innate belief in what they're doing to succeed. It also takes a willingness to fail and to learn from mistakes.

Any number of pathways can lead to entrepreneurship, but there are a few places to start looking and learning.

- In college, would-be entrepreneurs may study business or engineering and technical fields. The former teaches the basic practices such as finance and marketing necessary to succeed in the marketplace. Engineering and technical degrees often appeal to inventors.
- Many entrepreneurs start in industry, rise in the ranks, then spin off on their own with an opportunity they've identified. It might be an engineer who understands how to make a specific piece of equipment valuable to a specific industry, or a sales executive who knows how to market a particular niche service.
- Artists and creative individuals make careers out of their entrepreneurial spirit. A fine painter, for example, might sell his work through a gallery, art market, or website. Posting paintings on social media might draw buyers. Or, the artist might connect with an interior designer who sells the artwork to homeowners who are redecorating or renovating.
- Business incubators, often found at universities, are common entry points to entrepreneurship. They help fledgling companies focus their business plans and strategies. In addition to university incubator executives, we interviewed a contemporary art museum incubator executive who helps the artists of New York City learn business practices to help them succeed. Likewise, we spoke to an entrepreneur who has created an incubator-styled business to help food-related enterprises in need of commercial kitchen space and instruction.

- Franchising is another approach to entrepreneurship. This entails a business owner taking the reins of an established business—fast-food restaurants leap to mind—paying to use their template, including business practices and training opportunities. Likewise, an entrepreneur might franchise their own idea if their own business becomes successful enough for the next step.
- Financing a startup can also take several paths. Some people "bootstrap" their new companies, using money from family or friends. Others finance through small business loans or other bank business financing. Another option is venture capital, through which financial partners invest in a fledgling company with the expectation of a significant payoff—a risky proposition.

Once a business is identified and financing secure, entrepreneurs need to find employees or partners who are willing to go all-in to make the new business work, including navigating whatever legal and governmental process is required in their particular enterprise. For example, marketing a particular piece of technology made by someone else requires a patent license.

We've identified a number of different business sectors entrepreneurs could enter, including agriculture, baking, bioengineering, fashion, finance, food markets, smart home and commercial equipment installation, technical engineering inventions, app and platform development, and interior design. Communications experts incorporate web design into their menu of services. An executive who watched a major corporation downsize decided to open a job training service and launched a non-profit corporation. "Serial entrepreneurs" bring their skills to successive startups, sometimes joining a company that's just getting going, and sometimes founding the company themselves; hopefully a big sale allows the entrepreneur to cash out, ready to begin the next startup.

As technology continues to obliterate the silos professionals once inhabited, opportunities for entrepreneurship expand. The main advice we heard while interviewing entrepreneurs boiled down to this: be passionate about what you are doing and be sure that your idea fills a marketable need. Perhaps most important of all, understand that you will make mistakes, which are valuable learning opportunities.

*—Allison Blake*

# Advertising/Promotions/ Marketing Manager

### Snapshot

**Career Cluster(s):** Business, Management & Administration; Human Services; Marketing

**Interests:** Sales; advertising; marketing; creativity

**Earnings (Yearly Average):** $135,900

**Employment & Outlook:** Faster Than Average Growth Expected

## OVERVIEW

### Sphere of Work

Advertising, promotions, and marketing managers plan programs to generate interest in products or services. They work with art directors, advertising sales agents, and financial staff members. They may work for a firm or agency or be self-employed.

### Work Environment

Advertising, promotions, and marketing managers typically work in an office, and often work closely with the company's top executives. They may regularly travel to meet with clients.

Advertising manager brainstorming ideas with his team. Photo via iStock.com/EmirMemedovski. [Used under license.]

### Occupation Interest

Advertising, promotions, and marketing managers have a keen aptitude for what it takes to sell a product or service to customers, and the creativity to organize campaigns to get that message across. Often faced with deadlines, they thrive under pressure. Self-employed advertising professionals have the further drive to source their clients and build a successful business on their own.

### Profile

**Interests:** Things, Data, People
**Working Conditions:** Both Inside and Outside
**Education Needs:** Bachelor's Degree
**Licensure/Certification:** Usually Not Required
**Opportunities for Experience:** Internship
**Interest Score:** EAC

## A Day in the Life—Duties and Responsibilities

Advertising managers create interest among potential buyers of a product or service. They do this for a department, an entire organization, or on a project basis (referred to as an account). Advertising managers work in advertising agencies that put together advertising campaigns for clients, in media firms that sell advertising space or time, and in organizations that advertise heavily.

Advertising managers work with sales staff and others to generate ideas for an advertising campaign. They oversee the staff that develops the advertising. They work with the finance department to prepare a budget and cost estimates for the campaign.

Often, advertising managers serve as liaisons between the client and the advertising or promotion agency that develops and places the ads. In larger organizations with extensive advertising departments, different advertising managers may oversee in-house accounts and creative and media services departments.

In addition, some advertising managers specialize in a particular field or type of advertising. For example, media directors determine the way in which an advertising campaign reaches customers. They can use any or all media, including radio, television, newspapers, magazines, the Internet, and outdoor signs.

### Duties and Responsibilities

- Working with department heads or staff to discuss topics such as budgets and contracts, marketing plans, and the selection of advertising media
- Planning promotional campaigns such as contests, coupons, or giveaways
- Planning advertising campaigns, including which media to advertise in, such as radio, television, print, online media, and billboards
- Negotiating advertising contracts
- Evaluating the look and feel of websites used in campaigns or layouts, which are sketches or plans for an advertisement
- Initiating market research studies and analyzing their findings to understand customer and market opportunities for businesses
- Developing pricing strategies for products or services marketed to the target customers
- Meeting with clients to provide marketing or related advice
- Directing the hiring of advertising, promotions, and marketing staff and oversee their daily activities

Advertising managers known as account executives manage clients' accounts, but they are not responsible for developing or supervising the creation or presentation of advertising. That task becomes the work of the creative services department.

Promotions managers direct programs that combine advertising with purchasing incentives to increase sales. Often, the programs use direct mail, inserts in newspapers, Internet advertisements, in-store displays, product endorsements, or special events to target customers. Purchasing incentives may include discounts, samples, gifts, rebates, coupons, sweepstakes, or contests.

Marketing managers estimate the demand for products and services that an organization and its competitors offer. They identify potential markets for the organization's products. They also develop pricing strategies to help organizations maximize their profits and market share while ensuring that the organizations' customers are satisfied. They work with sales, public relations, and product development staff. For example, a marketing manager may monitor trends that indicate the need for a new product or service. Then he or she may assist in the development of that product or service and to create a marketing plan for it.

Self-employed advertising and marketing professionals may assume one or more of these duties to maximize their appeal to clients.

## WORK ENVIRONMENT

### Immediate Physical Environment

Most advertising, promotions, and marketing managers work full time in an office setting. Some advertising and promotions managers work more than 40 hours per week. Because the work of advertising, promotions, and marketing managers directly affects a firm's revenue, people in these occupations typically work closely with top executives. The jobs of advertising, promotions, and marketing managers can often be stressful, particularly near deadlines. Additionally, they may travel to meet with clients or media representatives.

### Human Environment

Managers in this field routinely interact with other people during their daily work. This could include team members helping to brainstorm, plan, and execute ad campaigns; clients for whom the campaigns are designed; and top executives to whom the managers answer. Self-employed advertising and marketing professionals have the added responsibility of constantly seeking out new clients—in effect, selling themselves.

### Technological Environment

Advertising, promotions, and marketing managers must keep abreast of the latest advances in marketing technology, from online initiatives such as social media and websites aiding in mass-marketing campaigns, to new forms of ad space, such as video screens on bus shelters. Every technological advance has the potential to yield a memorable ad campaign in the right hands.

## EDUCATION, TRAINING, AND ADVANCEMENT

### High School/Secondary

Managers typically have work experience in advertising, marketing, promotions, or sales, so high school students interested in this field should focus on courses such as English, business, art and design, computer science, and math. It is also advisable to find part-time work in sales, such as a summer job to build experience, skills, and confidence.

**Suggested High School Subjects**

- Algebra
- Biology
- Chemistry
- Civics
- Computer Science
- Earth or Environmental Science
- Economics
- English
- Entrepreneurship
- Geometry
- History
- Physics
- Pre-Calculus
- Psychology
- Statistics
- Trigonometry

#### *Transferable Skills and Abilities*

**Analytical Skills**
- Analyzing industry trends to determine the most promising strategies for the organization

**Communication Skills**
- Communicating effectively with a broad-based team comprising of other managers or staff members during the advertising, promotions, and marketing process
- Communicating persuasively with the public

**Creativity**
- Generating new and imaginative ideas

**Decision-making Skills**
- Choosing between competing advertising and marketing strategies put forward by staff

**Interpersonal Skills**
- Dealing with a range of people in different roles, both inside and outside the organization

**Organizational Skills**
- Managing both time and budget efficiently while directing and motivating staff members

**Fast Fact**

**Here's something you may already know from first-hand experience: 72 percent of people have creative insights in the shower.** Source: fastcompany.com

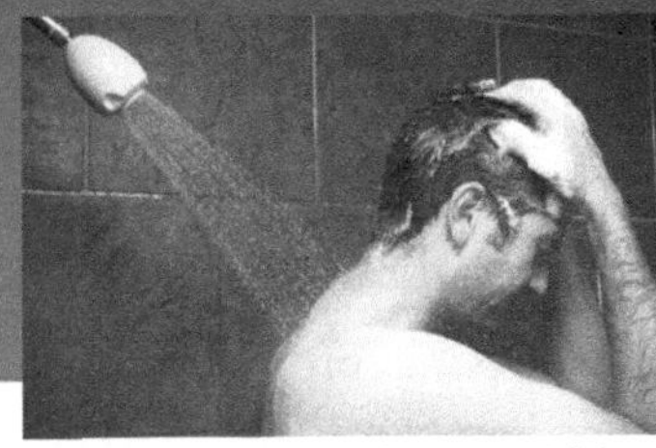

Inspiration can strike anywhere, especially in the shower. Photo via iStock.com/Stacey_ Newman. [Used under license.]

**Related Career Pathways/Majors**

*Business, Management & Administration Career Cluster*

- Business Information Management Pathway
- General Management Pathway

*Human Services Career Cluster*

- Consumer Services Pathway

*Marketing Career Cluster*

- Marketing Communications Pathway
- Marketing Management Pathway
- Marketing Research Pathway
- Professional Sales Pathway

## Postsecondary

A bachelor's degree is required for most advertising, promotions, and marketing management positions. For advertising management positions, some employers prefer a bachelor's degree in advertising or journalism. A relevant course of study might include classes in marketing, consumer behavior, market research, sales, communication methods and technology, visual arts, art history, and photography.

Most marketing manager positions require a bachelor's degree. Courses in business law, management, economics, finance, computer science, mathematics, and statistics are advantageous. For example, courses in computer science are helpful in developing an approach to maximize online traffic, by utilizing online search results, because maximizing such traffic is critical for the success of digital advertisements and promotions. In addition, completing an internship while in school can be useful.

**Related College Majors**

- Advertising
- Communications
- Journalism

- Marketing Research
- Public Relations
- Sales Management

### Adult Job Seekers

Advertising, promotions, and marketing managers typically have work experience in advertising, marketing, promotions, or sales. For example, many managers are former sales representatives; buyers or purchasing agents; or public relations specialists.

## EARNINGS AND ADVANCEMENT

Earnings depend on the experience of the manager, the size firm for which they work, whether they are self-employed, and the caliber of the accounts they manage. Median annual earnings of advertising and promotions managers were $125,510 in 2019. The lowest 10 percent earned less than $61,930, and the highest 10 percent earned more than $208,000. Median annual earnings of marketing managers were $136,850 in 2019. The lowest 10 percent earned less than $71,010, and the highest 10 percent earned more than $208,000.

Advertising, promotions, and marketing managers may receive paid vacations, holidays, and sick days; life and health insurance; and retirement benefits. These are usually paid by an employer if not self-employed. An employer may also cover travel expenses.

## EMPLOYMENT AND OUTLOOK

Advertising, promotions, and marketing managers held 314,900 jobs in 2019. Eleven percent were self-employed. Employment is expected to grow faster than the average for all occupations through the year 2029, at a rate of 6 percent, varying by occupation.

Marketing managers will continue to be in demand as organizations use marketing campaigns to maintain and expand their market share. These managers will be sought after for their advice on crafting pricing strategies and finding new ways to reach customers.

The continued rise of electronic media will result in decreasing demand for print advertisements. The newspaper publishing industry, which employs many advertising and promotions managers, is projected to lose jobs over the next 10 years. Despite overall employment declines for advertising and promotions managers, there may be some growth in industries that rely on these workers to create digital media campaigns that target customers using websites, social media, or live chats.

Advertising, promotions, and marketing manager positions are highly desirable and are often sought by other managers and experienced professionals. With Internet-based advertising becoming more important, advertising managers who can navigate the digital world should have the best prospects.

### Related Occupations

- Advertising Sales Agent
- Art Director
- Editor
- Financial Manager
- Graphic Designer
- Market Research Analyst
- Public Relations/Fundraising Manager
- Public Relations Specialist
- Sales Manager

## MORE INFORMATION

**American Advertising Federation (AAF)**
1101 K Street NW, Suite 420
Washington DC 20005
202.898.0089
www.aaf.org

**American Association of Advertising Agencies (4A's)**
1065 Avenue of the Americas, 16th Floor
New York, NY 10018
212.682.2500
www.aaaa.org

**American Marketing Association (AMA)**
130 E Randolph Street
Chicago, IL 60601
800.262.1150
customersupport@ama.org
www.ana.net

**Association of National Advertisers (ANA)**
155 E 44th Street
New York, NY 10017
212.697.5950
info@ana.net
www.ana.net
ANA Business Marketing:
www.marketing.org

**International Advertising Association (IAA)**
511 Avenue of Americas, Suite 4017
New York, NY 10011
646.849.9908
iaa@iaaglobal.org
www.iaaglobal.org

**Out of Home Advertising Association of America (OAAA)**
1850 M Street, NW, Suite 1040
Washington, DC 20036
202.833.5566
oaaa.org

**Promotional Products Association International (PPAI)**
3125 Skyway Circle North
Irving, TX 75038
888.426.7724
webmaster@ppai.org
www.ppai.org

---

*Stuart Paterson*

## *Conversation With...*
## TODD HARVEY

Co-founder and Principal
Mission Media, LLC, Baltimore, MD
Years in Field, 21

**What was your individual career path in terms of education/training, entry-level job, or other significant opportunity?**

Joe Loverde and I started Mission in 2000 when we were young and naïve. I was twenty-four, and Joe was twenty-seven. It was a lot of trial and error and intuition. Joe has a Bachelor of Communications from Towson University. He'd worked in a couple [of] startups; so, he had much more technical and business savvy. I was more vision and creative. We each were at a point where our jobs and career paths were changing.

I'd gone to the Baltimore School for the Arts for high school and have my Bachelor of Fine Art from the Maryland Institute College of Art. I got into set design and interned at a Christmas design shop where I met a set designer who hired me to work for his small studio. I loved set design and thought I was going to do it forever. I worked for another small studio in Washington, DC that was working on a project for the Smithsonian Institution. It was a one-year contract and when it was over, I wasn't sure what I was going to do.

Joe and I have known each other all our lives. As I was starting the idea of Mission, the company Joe had been working for as a developer was sold. It was a good time for him to jump ship, and he saw the potential of our partnership.

I learned a lot about entrepreneurship when I worked at the small art studios, and I wasn't intimidated. My bosses always showed this well, you just do it mentality. If you mess up, try again. I learned to take the high road, don't burn bridges—all those clichés—and realize you don't always know where your network will lead.

Mission's growth has always been about referrals and relationship building. We didn't set out to create an advertising and digital agency. It started as a co-operative. We had an art space and a performance space. We had a recording studio called Mission Studio. The Gallery was called Mission Space. One project led to the next, and we started hiring. The recording studio wasn't profitable and closed. Every time we shifted and pivoted, we broadened ourselves. Now we're a medium-sized agency and serve clients across the country in sports, food and beverage, and education industries. We've worked with STX, Wilson, Louisville Slugger, and

Nike; Johns Hopkins University, George Mason University, and Towson University; and Sunkist to Pabst. We worked with DreamWorks on marketing events. Most recently we worked with NASA on a project called Home and City, which is basically NASA's initiative to have the world understand how important NASA is, and how products it creates are in everyone's homes. It's a lot of fun.

We also do a lot of nonprofit and cause-related work centered in the community where we live and work.

We're in sort of our post-COVID rebuild period so right now we have 30 employees. Before COVID, we had 36. We fared pretty well, considering. Our industry was hit hard, and the industries we work with were hit hard.

**What are the most important skills and/or qualities for someone in your profession?**
You need to be genuine and interested in what the client does. You have to be open-minded, listen, and get in the mindset of someone who would buy your client's product or service. The best work always comes through collaboration with the client, and it takes charisma to have a friendly relationship with them. A lot of it is the soft skills, the human skills.

You need to care about your employees—not just the job they do, but who they are. You are working with people who have lives and opinions and aren't just cogs in a wheel.

The very first person we hired and every person since, we hired because they were better at something than we were. I have so much respect for them.

**What do you wish you had known going into this profession?**
I don't like to think about that because the journey, process, and failures of the lessons learned are better than having a playbook. Those learning opportunities are more powerful than a step-by-step. There have also been some really scary moments, the scariest over the last year during the COVID pandemic. If you had known that was coming or a possibility, you probably wouldn't have started a business. There will be ups and downs, but it's better to just not know and then deal with it when it comes, because it will come. It's not an easy path to choose because the buck always stops at you. That could scare a lot of people off from trying.

**Are there many job opportunities in your profession? In what specific areas?**
Design agencies offer a lot of job opportunities for account managers, project managers, designers, copywriters, programmers, systems architects, and digital marketers. There are a lot of different roles and a lot of different ways in. Our staff comes from all sorts of different backgrounds: finance degrees, writing degrees, video production degrees, no degrees, and everything in between. It's an industry where you can jump between lanes pretty easily, especially at a smaller or midsize agency where you wear a lot of different hats. Make yourself invaluable and suddenly you have a lot of accountability. You can forge your own path.

**How do you see your profession changing in the next 5 years? How will technology impact that change, and what skills will be required?**
Technology is pervasive in the industry already but how we use data to tell a story and reach the audience, down to the personalized email or text message, is an evolving process. HTML,

java script, programming, and database management aren't so much a computer science pathway as a partnership with the creative aspects.

There are hard skills related to software that can be honed and advanced, but there are also levels of taste, sensibility, and talent. The tone of society impacts messaging and forces us to evolve. When things are good, humor plays really well. When things are bad, there's a somber tone. You have to be sensitive to that. Besides knowing the software and being a technician, you need to infuse the human aspect as well.

**What do you enjoy most about your job? What do you enjoy least about your job?**

There are things that are challenging, but the job is the sum of its parts. I love the process and the journey. I love the people I work with and watching these kernels of ideas through trial and error come out on the other end to serve the client. There's still a thrill driving somewhere or someone pointing out to you a major brand's ad, and you're like, hey we did that. Or having your kid say, "You did that?"

I wish the whole world operated on the barter system because I hate the money side of business. Money determines whether a client hires us, whether or not we work on a project, whether a campaign is successful. You want every project to be perfect, but everything has a budget; everything has a scope. Money makes the world go round, but it's ugly. At the same time, Joe and I have been able to give a livelihood to a lot of people. It just feels it gets in the way of the true passion part.

**Can you suggest a valuable "try this" for students considering a career in your profession?**

Start with a product, place, or organization you love. Then, write down all the reasons you would use to get someone else to love it. Think about who that person is and what about your own passion might relate to them. Keep simplifying the message until you have it down to 8 words. Extra credit would be putting those words with a visual (drawing, photograph, collage, video). Then show that person and be prepared to do 10 more versions until it works.

# Animal Care/Service Worker

### Snapshot

**Career Cluster(s):** Agriculture, Food & Natural Resources; Hospitality & Tourism

**Interests:** Training and grooming animals; spending time outdoors; solving problems; communicating with people

**Earnings (Yearly Average):** $24,990

**Employment & Outlook:** Much Faster Than Average Growth Expected

## OVERVIEW

### Sphere of Work

Animal care and service workers tend to the needs of mammals, birds, fish, amphibians, and reptiles for various nonprofit organizations, research facilities, and private businesses, as well as individuals. Animal caretaking encompasses many job titles and occupational specialties, including trainers, groomers, pet sitters, aquarists, zookeepers or animal keepers, veterinary assistants, and attendants in animal shelters, pet shops, and kennels. Being an animal caretaker of any stripe can also lend itself to crossover into fields such as humane education, which aims to instill in children a respect for animals, the environment, and other people. There are opportunities

Keeper feeding a kangaroo. Photo via iStock.com/AzmanL. [Used under license.]

for entrepreneurship in this area, as pet ownership is at an all-time high, and animal owners need qualified individuals to tend to them.

### Profile

**Interests:** Animals, People, Things
**Working Conditions:** Both Inside and Outside
**Physical Strength:** Medium Work, Heavy Work
**Education Needs:** On-the-Job Training, High School Diploma with G.E.D., High School Diploma with Technical Education, Apprenticeship
**Licensure/Certification:** Usually Not Required
**Opportunities for Experience:** Apprenticeship, Volunteer Work, Part-Time Work
**Interest Score:** RC

## Work Environment

Animal caretakers work in kennels, zoos, pet stores, shelters, animal hospitals, wildlife sanctuaries, horse stables, grooming salons, and animal laboratories. Pet sitters usually attend to animals in private residences. Some caretakers travel between client homes or with their animals to special shows. Although some caretakers are limited to working either outside or inside, most divide their time between indoor and outdoor locations. Flexible schedules are common, and hours might include nights, evenings, weekends, and/or holiday shifts. Humane educators may travel to schools and learning centers to engage with children in group settings.

## Occupation Interest

Animal caretaker positions attract people who respect animals and understand their specific needs and abilities. In exchange for performing hard physical labor and sometimes unpleasant tasks, animal caretakers gain insight into the unique behavior of animals. They need to be patient and kind, yet firm, in their treatment of animals. Prospective animal caretakers should be good at following schedules and directions, reading animal behavior, solving problems, and communicating with people-especially children when in an educational setting.

### Duties and Responsibilities

- Giving food and water to animals
- Cleaning equipment and the living spaces of animals
- Monitoring animals and recording details of their diet, physical condition, and behavior
- Examining animals for signs of illness or injury
- Exercising animals
- Bathing animals, trimming nails, clipping hair, and attending to other grooming needs
- Training animals to obey or to behave in a specific manner

## A Day in the Life—Duties and Responsibilities

The two most common responsibilities of animal caregivers are feeding animals and cleaning their living environments. They feed animals according to guidelines set by veterinarians or other professionals, or the animals' owners. Most animals are given prepackaged, formulated food, although some may be fed live prey such as rodents, insects, or other small animals. Some baby mammals must be fed by a bottle or dropper. Before cleaning a cage, stall, aquarium, or other enclosure, the animal caretaker typically removes the animal and places it in another safe location. The habitat is then emptied of debris and sprayed, wiped, mopped, or scrubbed with a strong disinfectant and/or detergent. After rinsing and drying, the caretaker applies a fresh layer of bedding and/or replaces heat lamps, lights, toys, water bottles, and other equipment. In addition to cages, animal caretakers must clean carriers, dog runs, quarantine areas, medical treatment areas, and other supplies and rooms that may become contaminated.

Bathing, grooming, exercising, and socializing are also typical components of animal care. Caretakers may walk dogs, ride horses, or observe mice scurrying through special mazes, which are often among the greatest rewards of the work.

Some animal caretakers assist professional trainers or train animals themselves for educational, entertainment, security, and medical purposes. They also transport animals to shows, animal hospitals, and other locations. Depending on training and work setting, animal caretakers may perform healthcare tasks, such as dressing wounds and administering medications. They are also sometimes involved with the death of animals or assist with euthanasia.

When not working directly with animals, animal caretakers often keep records, maintain inventories of food and supplies, and greet customers or give educational presentations.

## OCCUPATION SPECIALTIES

### Animal Shelter Attendant

Animal shelter attendants typically work with cats and dogs in animal shelters or rescue leagues. These attendants take care of the animals' basic needs and may have administrative duties, such as keeping records, answering questions from the public, educating visitors about pet health, and screening people who want to adopt an animal. Experienced attendants may have more responsibilities, such as helping to vaccinate or euthanize animals alongside a veterinarian.

### Animal Trainer

Animal trainers teach animals a variety of skills, such as obedience, performance, riding, security, and assisting people with disabilities. They familiarize animals with human voices and contact, and they teach animals to respond to commands. Most animal trainers work with dogs and horses, but some work with marine mammals, such as dolphins. Trainers teach a variety of skills. For example, some train dogs to guide people with disabilities, or they may train animals for a competition.

**Fast Fact**

**Not only do 55 percent of startups begin at home, they stay there. Fifty-nine percent of established small businesses operate from their owners' homes.**
Source: fortunly.com.

Many established small businesses operate out of their owner's homes. Photo via iStock.com/ijeab. [Used under license.]

### Groom

Grooms work at stables, caring for horses and maintaining equipment. Responsibilities include feeding, grooming, and exercising horses; cleaning stalls; polishing saddles; and organizing the tack room, which stores harnesses, saddles, and bridles. Experienced grooms sometimes help train horses.

### Groomer

Groomers specialize in maintaining a pet's appearance. They typically groom dogs and cats, which may include cutting, trimming, shampooing, and styling fur; clipping nails; and cleaning ears. Groomers also schedule appointments, sell products to pet owners, and identify problems that may require veterinary attention. Groomers may work in or operate a grooming salon, kennel, veterinary clinic, pet supply store, or mobile grooming service, a self-contained business that travels to clients' homes.

### Kennel Attendant

Kennel attendants care for pets, often overnight, in place of owners. They clean cages and dog runs and feed, exercise, and play with animals. Experienced attendants also may provide basic healthcare, bathe animals, and attend to other basic grooming needs.

### Pet Sitter

Pet sitters look after animals while the pet owner is away. Most pet sitters feed, walk, and play with pets daily. They go to the pet owner's home, allowing the pet to stay in its familiar surroundings and follow its routine. Experienced pet sitters also may bathe, groom, or train pets. Pet sitters typically watch over dogs, but some also take care of cats and other pets.

### Zookeeper

Zookeepers care for animals in zoos. They plan diets, feed animals, and monitor the animals' eating patterns. They also clean the animals' enclosures and monitor behavior for signs of illness or injury. Depending on the size of the zoo, they may work with one species or multiple species of animals. Zookeepers may help raise young animals, and they often spend time answering questions from the public.

## WORK ENVIRONMENT

### Immediate Physical Environment

Animals and their environments often come with strong odors or noises. Animal caretakers are at some risk for diseases, bites, scratches, or kicks from animals, and they can be exposed to harsh cleaning chemicals, germicides, and insecticides. The work may be physically demanding, requiring heavy lifting, standing for long periods, and regular bending and kneeling. Some caretakers might also find the work emotionally difficult at times.

### Human Environment

Many animal caretakers spend as much time working with humans as they do animals. Most report to a supervisor, director, or manager, and interact with volunteers and various staff members, such as veterinarians, research scientists, and professional groomers or trainers. Self-employed pet sitters interact with their clients and household staff. Caretakers who work in animal shelters and commercial settings also interact with the public. Humane educators must coordinate with schools and learning centers and spend the bulk of their time preparing for and delivering presentations to children of varying ages. They may also host children at a facility such as a shelter.

### Technological Environment

The level of technological sophistication varies with the type of facility. Some caretakers work in fully equipped offices with computerized feeding schedules and high-tech security systems. Many caretakers also use hand and power tools to maintain cages or other animal environments. Some animal caretakers drive wagons, trucks, vans, or cars to transport animals. Humane educators may use distance-learning tools such as video-conferencing apps to engage with children, although in-person lessons are still preferred where possible. Caretakers who are self-employed or run a business with staff must be familiar with standard business software programs such as accounting and payroll.

## EDUCATION, TRAINING, AND ADVANCEMENT

### High School/Secondary

A high school diploma or its equivalent is required for most jobs. A vocational course in animal science, usually offered through agricultural education programs, will provide a suitable foundation for some animal caretaker jobs; however, students interested in becoming a zookeeper, aquarist, or veterinary technician must follow a college-preparatory program. Important courses include biology, health, math, English, and speech communication. Volunteer or part-time work in an animal shelter, veterinary office, pet store, kennel, or farm, or pet sitting for friends and neighbors will provide the experience desired by many employers. Students should also consider 4-H and similar extracurricular opportunities that build familiarity with animals and their care.

**Suggested High School Subjects**

- Algebra
- Biology
- Chemistry
- Civics
- Earth or Environmental Science
- English
- Geography
- Geometry
- History
- Physics
- Psychology
- Trigonometry

**Related Career Pathways/Majors**

*Agriculture, Food & Natural Resources Career Cluster*

- Animal Systems Pathway

*Hospitality & Tourism Career Cluster*

- Recreation, Amusements & Attractions Pathway

***Transferable Skills and Abilities***

**Compassion**

- Showing compassion when dealing with animals and their owners
- Showing kindness to animals

**Customer-service Skills**

- Understanding pet owners' needs

**Detail-oriented**

- Maintaining records and monitoring changes in animals' behavior

**Patience**

- Maintaining patience when working with animals

**Physical Stamina**

- Kneeling, crawling, and lifting heavy supplies, such as bags of food

**Problem-solving Skills**

- Assessing whether animals are responding to teaching methods and identifying which methods are successful

**Reliability**

- Caring for animals on schedule and in a timely manner

### Postsecondary

Although pet groomers typically learn by working under the guidance of an experienced groomer, they can also attend grooming schools. Animal trainers usually need a high school diploma or equivalent, although some positions may require a bachelor's degree. For example, marine mammal trainers usually need a bachelor's degree in marine biology, animal science, biology, or a related field. Dog trainers and horse trainers may take courses at community colleges or vocational and private training schools. Most zoos require zookeepers to have a bachelor's degree in biology, animal science, or a related field.

**Related College Majors**

- Animal Behavior
- Animal Science
- Environmental Science
- Equine Studies
- Marine Biology
- Pre-Veterinary Studies
- Veterinary Nursing
- Veterinary Technology
- Zoology

## Adult Job Seekers

Adults with the appropriate educational background and firsthand experience as pet owners, animal foster caretakers, or volunteers in pet shelters or rehabilitation centers may be qualified for many animal caretaker jobs. Pet sitting and grooming may offer the most flexible schedules. Interested landowners might be in a good position to establish a kennel or boarding stables as an entrepreneurial opportunity. The necessary skills and knowledge for animal care can be learned from online courses, as well as evening or weekend continuing education courses. Qualified animal caretakers should apply directly to companies and organizations that have posted open positions.

New animal caretakers are often limited to cleaning cages and feeding animals but are given additional responsibilities after gaining experience. Animal caretakers can move into supervisory or management positions with additional experience or education.

## Professional Certification and Licensure

There are no licenses required for animal caretakers, although the owners of kennels, laboratories, and rescue shelters are regulated. Professional certification is available from the National Association of Professional Pet Sitters (NAPPS), American Association for Laboratory Animal Science (AALAS), and other professional associations. Most certifications require completion of an exam, which in some cases includes a practical section.

### Additional Requirements

A driver's license is required for many jobs. Animal caretakers also need to be in good health, with good eyesight and hearing. Familiarity with the Animal Welfare Act (AWA) is also beneficial.

## EARNINGS AND ADVANCEMENT

Earnings depend on the employer, size and geographic location of the facility, and the individual's education and experience. Earnings are also dependent on whether the caretaker is self-employed.

Animal caretakers earned a median annual salary of $24,780 in 2019. The lowest 10 percent earned less than $18,630, and the highest 10 percent earned more than $38,630.

Animal trainers earned a median annual salary of $30,430 in 2019. The lowest 10 percent earned less than $20,810, and the highest 10 percent earned more than $59,110.

Animal care and service workers may receive paid vacations, holidays, and sick days; life and health insurance; and retirement benefits. These are usually paid by an employer.

## EMPLOYMENT AND OUTLOOK

There were approximately 300,700 animal caretakers employed nationally in 2019. Most were employed by boarding kennels, animal shelters, stables, grooming shops, animal hospitals, and veterinary offices. Twenty-six percent of animal caretakers in 2019 were self-employed.

There were approximately 50,200 animal trainers employed nationally in 2019. Thirty-five percent were self-employed, and the rest were employed in agriculture and forestry, animal production and aquaculture, arts and entertainment, and retail trade.

Employment of animal care and service workers is expected to grow much faster than the average for all occupations through the year 2029, with employment projected to increase 22 percent. This is due to the continual growth of the pet population. Many people consider their pets to be a part of their family and are willing to pay more for pet care than pet owners have in the past. As more households include companion pets, employment of animal care and service workers in the pet services industry will continue to grow. Employment of animal care and service workers in kennels, grooming shops, and pet stores is projected to increase to keep up with the growing demand for animal care.

Many of those openings are expected to result from the need to replace workers who transfer to different occupations or exit the labor force, such as to retire.

### Related Occupations

- Agricultural Worker
- Farmer/Rancher/Other Agricultural Manager
- Veterinarian
- Veterinary Assistant/Laboratory Animal Caretaker
- Veterinary Technologist/Technician
- Zoologist/Wildlife Biologist

## MORE INFORMATION

**Academy of Prosocial Learning (APL)**
860.262.1807
info@prosocialacademy.org
www.prosocialacademy.org

**American Association for Laboratory Animal Science (AALAS)**
9190 Crestwyn Hills Drive
Memphis, TN 38125
901.754.8620
info@aalas.org
www.aalas.org
Offers testing and certification for animal technicians
www.aalas.org/certification/technician-certification

**American Humane Association**
1400 16th Street NW, Suite 360
Washington, DC 20036
800.227.4645
info@americanhumane.org
www.americanhumane.org

**American Society for the Prevention of Cruelty to Animals (ASPCA)**
424 East 92nd Street
New York, NY 10128-6804
212.876.7700
outreach@aspca.org
www.aspca.org

**Association of Zoos and Aquariums**
8403 Colesville Road, Suite 710
Silver Spring, MD 20910-3314
301.562.0777
generalinquiry@aza.org
www.aza.org
Sponsors professional development training and scholarships to attend training
www.aza.org/scholarships

**Humane Education Advocates Reaching Teachers (HEART)**
P.O. Box 738
Mamaroneck, NY 10543
347.766.7650
email@teachheart.org
teachheart.org

**Humane Education Coalition**
432 S. Juliana Street
Bedford, PA 15522
info@hecoalition.org
www.hecoalition.org

**Humane Education Network (HEN)**
650.851.8735
hen@hennet.org
www.hennet.org

**Humane Society of the United States**
Companion Animals Division
1255 23rd Street NW, Suite 450
Washington, DC 20037
202.452.1100
www.humanesociety.org

**Institute for Humane Education**
P.O. Box 260
Surry, ME 04684
info@humaneeducation.org
humaneeducation.org

**Latham Foundation for the Promotion of Humane Education**
1320 Harbor Bay Parkway, Suite 200
Alameda, CA 94502
510.521.0920
www.latham.org

**National Association of Animal Breeders (NAAB)**
8413 Excelsior Drive, Suite 140
Madison, WI 53717
608.827.0277
naab-css@naab-css.org
www.naab-css.org

**National Association of Professional Pet Sitters (NAPPS)**
P.O. Box 362
Huron, OH 44839
856.439.0324
NAPPS@petsitters.org
www.petsitters.org
Offers online course that leads to certification:
petsitters.org/page/NAPPSCertificationCourse

**Maddie's Fund**
6150 Stoneridge Mall Road, Suite 125
Pleasanton, CA 94588
925.310.5450
info@maddiesfund.org
www.maddiesfund.org

Maddie's Tail Wag activities for children:
www.maddiesfund.org/maddies-tail-wag.htm

**RedRover**
P.O. Box 188890
Sacramento, CA 95818
916.429.2457
info@redrover.org
redrover.org
Readers program:
redrover.org/readers

---

*Sally Driscoll; updated by Stuart Paterson*

# *Conversation With...*
# AUDREY REICHARDT

Co-owner, Dogwood Acres Pet Resort
Davidsonville, MD, 23 years

**What was your individual career path in terms of education/training, entry-level job, or other significant opportunity?**

My husband Kurt and I do this together, and we're a really good team. He has a background in architecture. So much of what we do involves the design of buildings and facilities, and he has a really good understanding of how buildings are made and how they work. My background is human resources and organizational development.

Kurt got his architecture degree from Clemson University and after one year, he realized an office career was not for him. I graduated from Davidson College with a degree in industrial organizational psychology and went on to get a Master's in human resources and organizational development from Johns Hopkins University, which is just incredibly useful.

We both love animals. We found this property, which is in an affluent, semi-agricultural area near Washington, DC. It was just dumb luck there was a kennel here, and Kurt started boarding animals as a side business.

We sold everything and moved onto the property, into an existing apartment. My husband's father is a retired veterinarian in the area, and Kurt had a lot of exposure to small business and caring for animals. My parents were looking for an investment and invested in this property. We turned a profit very quickly, and it became clear the business would grow. So, I quit my job as a national recruiter for a big international company called Goldwell Cosmetics and came to work for us and applied all my skills. My job is hiring, performing assessments, marketing, strategic planning, and business development.

Zoning, however, was impossible. It took five years for us to make improvements and expand. At that time, the pet industry had not yet exploded. The banks weren't sure they wanted to invest in two young people. But we knew the demand. Business was begging by the time we opened the doors on our expansion, and we went from 30 to 50 pets overnight and 30 in daycare to tripling that.

Unfortunately, due to zoning, many pet hotels are in industrial areas and have to be indoors. We were able to create huge playgrounds here. We created outdoor space for dogs, who are all about interaction and energy. We built separate, unique cat rooms and suites with individually ventilated cat condos because cats get respiratory diseases. It's quiet. We have activities that suit whatever the pet needs or the owners want. We have a lot of flexibility. The only thing we can't accommodate is putting a cat and dog together unless it's a small dog. This year, after a long property search, we opened a similar, second pet resort across the Chesapeake Bay Bridge from Annapolis in a well-traveled location.

Day care is the bread and butter of our business; it's most profitable and most resistant to recession and change. People who bring their dogs rely on it, especially if they have an energetic or destructive dog. Our staffing rule of thumb is one caretaker for every 15 dogs. We take care of an animal, but we also are taking care of an entire family.

We benefit from being close to Washington, DC, which is relatively recession-proof. We generate business through word of mouth, of course, but also through veterinarians, pet retail, hotels, and realtors who refer people who are moving or have to show their house.

**What are the most important skills and/or qualities for someone in your profession?**
When you're dealing with pet care, patience is extremely important. It's a very physically demanding job, and you do a lot of cleaning. On a very hot day or very cold day, you're out there with the dogs. I also look for people with high integrity.

**What do you wish you had known going into this profession?**
If you want your business to be successful, you don't really do what you went into the business to do, which is to care for the animals. You need basic business and finance skills, and there's no avoiding it.

**Are there many jobs opportunities in your profession? In what specific areas?**
No. The most traditional path in pet care is to become a veterinarian, but those are medical jobs. People might decide to be a vet tech, then decide, "I don't want to do euthanasia or see blood. I want to play with animals." I think entering this industry is easy but getting an actual opportunity is difficult. Very few places make enough money to hire a lot of staff.

**How do you see your profession changing in the next five years, how will technology shift, and what skills will be required?**
As with everything else, technology constantly impacts our business. We're eventually expecting simple things like using technology to catalog when a dog goes in and out of a room. A lot of the time and effort that goes into managing that process won't be needed in the future. However, you can't do this work without humans because you need someone who is paying attention to what's going on, whether you're dealing with a problem or supervising play.

**What do you enjoy most about your job? What do you enjoy least about your job?**
As a business owner, I most enjoy developing talent. I'm also lucky to be in such a joyous field and to be around the animals. I least enjoy the disciplinary side of dealing with employees. And on the pet care side, unfortunately sad things do happen. A pet may get injured or pass away, such as a dog who died of congestive heart failure without any forewarning. We've had injuries that were our fault and that, technically, were not. These kinds of things will happen, and you have to be prepared. On the other hand, we have saved dogs' lives due to issues the owners had overlooked and that's really satisfying.

**Can you suggest a valuable "try this" for students considering a career in your profession?**

Volunteer at a shelter. People may love animals but it's very different when you are taking care of someone else's animal—an animal you don't know. In a shelter, there is barking, a dog will jump on you, an animal will be terrified and bite you. You will not like every dog, and every dog will not like you. These are not your pets at home who are not under stress. Also, it's a physical job. You clean up a lot.

# Baker

## Snapshot

**Career Cluster(s):** Business, Management & Administration; Hospitality & Tourism

**Interests:** Food; baked goods & desserts; baking; customer service

**Earnings (Yearly Average):** $27,700

**Employment & Outlook:** Faster Than Average Growth Expected

## OVERVIEW

### Sphere of Work

Bakers mix ingredients according to recipes to make breads, pastries, and other baked goods. They may be employed at a grocery store, café, or manufacturing facility. Alternately, entrepreneurial bakers run their own cafés or bake shops.

### Work Environment

Bakers must follow daily production schedules to bake products in sufficient quantities while maintaining consistent quality. Depending on where a baker works, he or she might be required to work early mornings or late nights. Part-time work is also common. Bakers who own their own business may work long, irregular hours to maintain production while overseeing other business elements such as staffing, payroll, and inventory.

Bakers preparing cupcakes for icing. Photo via iStock.com/ xavierarnau. [Used under license.]

### Occupation Interest

Bakers are creative individuals who not only have a love for baked goods, but for the finely tuned process that goes into making those items. They are skilled in their craft and are excited to try new ideas and tools to bring customers the best baked goods possible. They monitor trends in the industry and on social media and try to stay with or ahead of the curve. They also enjoy interacting with customers when in a retail setting.

### Profile

**Interests:** Things, People
**Working Conditions:** Inside
**Physical Strength:** Medium Work, Heavy Work
**Education Needs:** On-the-Job Training, High School Diploma with Technical Education, Junior/Technical/Community College, Apprenticeship
**Licensure/Certification:** Usually Not Required
**Opportunities for Experience:** Internship, Apprenticeship, Part-Time Work
**Interest Score:** RC

## A Day in the Life—Duties and Responsibilities

Bakers produce various types and quantities of breads, pastries, and other baked goods sold by grocers, wholesalers, restaurants, and institutional food services.

Commercial bakers, also called production bakers, work in manufacturing facilities that produce breads, pastries, and other baked products. In these facilities, bakers use high-volume mixing machines, ovens, and other equipment, which may be automated, to mass-produce standardized baked goods. They carefully follow instructions for production schedules and recipes.

Retail bakers work primarily in grocery stores and specialty shops, including bakeries. In these settings, they produce smaller quantities of baked goods for people to eat in the shop or for sale as specialty baked goods. Retail bakers may take orders from customers, prepare baked products to order, and occasionally serve customers. Although the quantities prepared and sold in these stores are often small, they usually come in a wide variety of flavors and sizes. Most retail bakers are also responsible for cleaning their work area and equipment and unloading supplies.

### Duties and Responsibilities

- Checking the quality of baking ingredients
- Preparing equipment for baking
- Measuring or weighing ingredients
- Combining measured ingredients in mixers or blenders
- Kneading, rolling, cutting, and shaping dough
- Placing dough into pans, into molds, or onto baking sheets
- Setting oven temperatures and place items into ovens or onto grills

Some retail bakers own bakery shops where they make and sell breads, pastries, pies, and other baked goods. In addition to preparing the baked goods and overseeing the entire baking process, they are also responsible for hiring, training, and supervising their staff. They must budget for and order supplies, set prices, and decide how much to produce each day.

Grocery stores and restaurants sell freshly baked goods throughout the day. As a result, bakers are often scheduled to work shifts during early mornings, late evenings, weekends, and holidays. Bakers who work in commercial bakeries that bake continuously may have to work late evenings and weekends. Some bakers work part-time.

## WORK ENVIRONMENT

### Immediate Physical Environment

The work can be stressful because bakers follow time-sensitive baking procedures and often work under strict deadlines. For example, bakers must follow daily production schedules to bake products in sufficient quantities while maintaining consistent quality. In manufacturing facilities, they often work with other production workers, such as helpers and maintenance staff, so that equipment is cleaned and ready.

Bakers are exposed to high temperatures when working around hot ovens. They stand for hours at a time while observing the baking process, making the dough, or cleaning the baking equipment. Bakeries, especially large manufacturing facilities, are filled with potential dangers such as hot ovens, mixing machines, and dough cutters. Bakers must take precautions to avoid injury.

Although their work is generally safe, bakers may endure back strains caused by lifting or moving heavy bags of flour or other products. Other common risks include cuts, scrapes, and burns. To reduce these risks, bakers often wear back supports, aprons, and gloves.

### Human Environment

Human interaction differs by duty. Some bakers may be involved solely in production, and, therefore, will be limited in contact to their coworkers and supervisors. Others who work in retail may interact with customers daily, taking special orders, and providing the finished product. Bakery owners deal with customers, staff, and suppliers, including resolving disputes.

### Technological Environment

Bakers must be adept at using all the tools of the trade in order to produce consistent, quality products, including large and powerful appliances such as mixers and ovens. They must be safety conscious to avoid injury. Ongoing on-the-job training may be required as new tools and equipment are introduced.

## EDUCATION, TRAINING, AND ADVANCEMENT

### High School/Secondary

No formal education is required to become a baker, but students wishing to attend postsecondary technical or culinary programs must have a high school diploma. Students should focus on math, science, and English courses, as well as courses such as accounting and economics if a long-term goal is to own a business. Seeking part-time work in the field is also beneficial, as is practicing home baking.

**Suggested High School Subjects**

- Accounting
- Algebra
- Biology
- Chemistry
- Civics
- Earth or Life or Physical Science
- Economics
- English
- Entrepreneurship
- Geography
- Geometry
- History
- Physics
- Psychology
- Statistics

#### *Transferable Skills and Abilities*

**Communication Skills**
- Dealing effectively with customers in a retail setting

**Detail-oriented**
- Monitoring products in the oven to keep them from burning
- Having an eye for detail because many pastries and cakes require intricate decorations

**Math Skills**
- Possessing basic math skills, especially knowledge of fractions, in order to precisely mix recipes, weigh ingredients, or adjust mixes.

**Physical Stamina**
- Standing for extended periods while preparing dough, monitoring baking, and packaging baked goods

**Physical Strength**
- Lifting and carrying heavy bags of flour and other ingredients, which may weigh up to 50 pounds

**Related Career Pathways/Majors**

*Business, Management & Administration Career Cluster*

- General Management Pathway

*Hospitality & Tourism Administration Career Cluster*

- Restaurants & Food/Beverage Services Pathway

### Postsecondary

Although there are no formal education requirements to become a baker, some candidates attend a technical or culinary school. Programs generally last from 1 to 2 years and cover nutrition, food safety, and basic math. To enter these programs, candidates may be required to have a high school diploma or equivalent.

## Fast Fact

**It doesn't take a degree to launch your own business: only about 44 percent of entrepreneurs have a college degree.** Source: whattobecome.com

No degree necessary. Photo via iStock.com/Ivan-balvan. [Used under license.]

### Related College Majors

- Baking & Pastry Arts
- Culinary Arts
- Food Science
- Nutrition
- Professional Cooking

### Adult Job Seekers

As no formal education is required to be a baker, adults with an interest in and a skill for baking stand a good chance of transitioning into the field. Coming from a related field such as culinary or baking supply sales is an asset. Coursework is recommended to become familiar with standard techniques and concepts such as food safety.

### Professional Certification and Licensure

Certification is voluntary and shows that a baker has the skills and knowledge to work at a retail baking establishment.

The Retail Bakers of America (RBA) offers certification in four levels of competence, with a focus on several topics, including baking sanitation, management, retail sales, and staff training. Those who wish to become certified must satisfy a combination of education and experience requirements before taking an exam.

The education and experience requirements vary by the level of certification desired. For example, a Certified Journey Baker (CJB) requires no education but must have at least 1 year of work experience. A Certified Baker must have 4 years of work experience and 30 hours of sanitation coursework, and a Certified Master Baker (CMB) must have 8 years of work experience, 30 hours of sanitation coursework, and 30 hours of professional development education.

### Additional Requirements

Most bakers learn their skills through long-term on-the-job training, typically lasting 1 to 3 years. Some employers may provide apprenticeship programs for aspiring bakers. Bakers in specialty bakery shops and grocery stores often start as apprentices or trainees and learn the basics of baking, icing, and decorating. They usually study topics such as nutrition, sanitation procedures, and basic baking. Some participate in correspondence study and may work toward a certificate in baking.

Some bakers learn their skills through work experience related to baking. For example, they may start as a baker's assistant and progress into a full-fledged baker as they learn baking techniques.

## EARNINGS AND ADVANCEMENT

Earnings depend on many factors such as employer, location, and nature of work (i.e., retail or commercial). Median annual earnings of bakers were $27,700 in 2019. The lowest 10 percent earned less than $20,310, and the highest 10 percent earned more than $41,640.

Bakers may receive paid vacations, holidays, and sick days; life and health insurance; and retirement benefits. These are usually paid by an employer if the business is not self-owned.

## EMPLOYMENT AND OUTLOOK

Bakers held 199,300 jobs in 2019. Six percent were self-employed. Employment is expected to grow faster than average for all occupations through the year 2029, at a rate of 5 percent. Population and income growth are expected to result in greater demand for specialty baked goods, such as cupcakes, pies, and cakes, from grocery stores, retail bakeries, and restaurants. However, employment of bakers in food manufacturing may be limited as these facilities increasingly use automated machines and equipment to mass-produce baked goods.

Job opportunities are expected to be good because of the need to replace workers who leave the occupation every year.

### Related Occupations

- Chef/Head Cook
- Cook
- Food/Tobacco Processing Worker
- Food Preparation Worker

## MORE INFORMATION

**AIB International**
P.O. Box 3999
1213 Bakers Way
Manhattan, KS 66505-3999
www.aibinternational.com

**American Bakers Association (ABA)**
601 Pennsylvania Avenue NW, Suite 230
Washington, DC 20004
202.789.0300
info@AmericanBakers.org
americanbakers.org

**Cookie and Snack Bakers Association (CASBA)**
jnewell@batoryfoods.com
mike@aecdierolls.com
casba.us

**Home Baking Association (HBA)**
2931 SW Gainsboro Road
Topeka, KS 66614-4413
785.478.3283
hbapatton@aol.com
www.homebaking.org

**Independent Bakers Association (IBA)**
316 F Street NE, Suite 206
Washington, DC 20002
202.333.8190
www.ibabaker.com/

**International Dairy Deli Bakery Association (IDDBA)**
8317 Elderberry Road
Madison, WI 53717-2603
608.310.5000
iddba@iddba.org
www.iddba.org

**Retail Bakers of America (RBA)**
15941 S Harlem Avenue, Suite 347
Tinley Park, IL 60477
800.638.0924
info@retailbakersofamerica.org
retailbakersofamerica.org

**RPIA Group**
P.O. Box 803
Westfield, IN 46074
800.746.6551
rick.crawford@rpiausa.org
www.rpiausa.org

---

*Stuart Paterson*

# Bioengineer/ Biomedical Engineer

## Snapshot

**Career Cluster(s):** Business, Management & Administration; Science, Technology, Engineering & Mathematics

**Interests:** Inventing; science; medicine; engineering

**Earnings (Yearly Average):** $91,410

**Employment & Outlook:** Faster Than Average Growth Expected

## OVERVIEW

### Sphere of Work

Bioengineers and biomedical engineers combine engineering principles with sciences to design and create equipment, devices, computer systems, and software. This can include brand-new inventions, and some engineers may own businesses focused on designing and creating equipment for specialized segments of the market.

### Work Environment

Bioengineers and biomedical engineers typically work on teams with scientists, healthcare workers, or other engineers, depending on the project. Engineers may be required to travel to locations where their creations are put into use in order to gauge their effectiveness and note opportunities for improvement.

Two female medical engineers examining a piece of equipment. Photo via iStock.com/SolStock. [Used under license.]

Most bioengineers and biomedical engineers work full-time, and some work more than 40 hours per week.

### Profile

**Interests:** Things, Data, People
**Working Conditions:** Inside
**Education Needs:** Bachelor's Degree; Graduate Degree
**Licensure/Certification:** Usually Not Required
**Opportunities for Experience:** Internship, Co-op
**Interest Score:** IR

## Occupation Interest

Bioengineers and biomedical engineers are creative, science-oriented individuals who have a desire to contribute to the scientific and medical field through the creation of new tools and systems. They are able to identify gaps in the current market and have the technical expertise to design new equipment or software to fill those voids. They are eager to apply the latest technological advances towards new creations that will make scientific and medical work faster, safer, and more efficient.

## A Day in the Life—Duties and Responsibilities

Bioengineers and biomedical engineers often work in research and development (R&D) or quality assurance.

The work of bioengineers spans many fields. For example, although their expertise is in engineering and biology, they often design computer software to run complicated instruments, such as 3D x-ray machines. Others use their knowledge of chemistry and biology to develop new drug therapies. Still others draw on math and statistics to understand signals transmitted by the brain or heart. Some are involved in sales.

Biomedical engineers focus on advances in technology and medicine to develop new devices and equipment for improving human health. For example, they might design software to run medical equipment or computer simulations to test new drug therapies. In addition, they design and build artificial body parts, such as hip and knee joints, or develop materials to make replacement parts. They also design rehabilitative exercise equipment.

### Duties and Responsibilities

- Designing equipment and devices, such as artificial internal organs, replacements for body parts, and machines for diagnosing medical problems
- Installing, maintaining, or providing technical support for biomedical equipment
- Collaborating with manufacturing staff on the safety and effectiveness of biomedical equipment
- Working with scientists to research how engineering principles apply to biological systems
- Developing statistical models or simulations using statistical or modeling software
- Preparing procedures and write technical reports and research papers
- Presenting research findings to a variety of audiences, including scientists, clinicians, managers, other engineers, and the public
- Designing or conducting follow-up experiments as needed

## OCCUPATION SPECIALTIES

**Biochemical Engineer**
Biochemical engineers focus on cell structures and microscopic systems to create products for bioremediation, biological waste treatment, and other uses.

**Bioinstrumentation Engineer**
Bioinstrumentation engineers use electronics, computer science, and measurement principles to develop tools for diagnosing and treating medical problems.

**Biomaterials Engineer**
Biomaterials engineers study naturally occurring or laboratory-designed substances for use in medical devices or implants.

**Biomechanics Engineer**
Biomechanics engineers study thermodynamics and other systems to solve biological or medical problems.

**Clinical Engineer**
Clinical engineers apply medical technology to improve healthcare.

**Genetic Engineer**
Genetic engineers alter the genetic makeup of organism using recombinant deoxyribonucleic acid (rDNA) technology, such as in developing vitamin-fortified food crops to prevent disease in humans.

**Rehabilitation Engineer**
Rehabilitation engineers develop devices that aid people who are recovering from or adapting to physical or cognitive impairments.

**Systems Physiologist**
Systems physiologists use engineering tools to understand how biological systems function and respond to changes in their environment.

## WORK ENVIRONMENT

### Immediate Physical Environment

Bioengineers and biomedical engineers work on teams with scientists, healthcare workers, or other engineers. Where and how they work depends on the project. For example, a biomedical engineer who has developed a new device might spend hours in a hospital to ensure that the device works as planned. If the device needs adjusting, the engineer might need to suggest alterations in the manufacturing process.

### Human Environment

As engineering work is usually a team effort, bioengineers and biomedical engineers must be prepared to collaborate during most projects, and, therefore, must be able to work with colleagues, sometimes from varying disciplines. They may also interact with clients and patients during the design and implementation stages, including on-site testing of equipment. Engineers that own their own businesses have the added responsibility of overseeing their employees in a managerial capacity.

### Technological Environment

Engineers must be able to incorporate the latest technological advances into their work, to further their own creations and better the scientific and medical communities. Nanotechnology, smartphone technology, three-dimensional printing, and artificial intelligence (AI) are all examples of constantly evolving technologies that can play a role in bioengineering. Engineers who own their own businesses must also be well-acquainted with standard business software used for accounting and payroll, for example.

## EDUCATION, TRAINING, AND ADVANCEMENT

### High School/Secondary

In high school, students interested in becoming bioengineers or biomedical engineers should take classes in sciences such as chemistry, physics, and biology. They should also study math, including algebra, geometry, trigonometry, and calculus. If available, classes in drafting, mechanical drawing, and computer programming are also useful.

**Suggested High School Subjects**

- Algebra
- Biology
- Chemistry
- Civics
- Computer Science
- Drafting

- Earth or Environmental Science
- Economics
- English
- Entrepreneurship
- Geometry
- History
- Physics
- Pre-Calculus
- Psychology
- Statistics
- Trigonometry

**Related Career Pathways/Majors**

*Business, Management & Administration Career Cluster*

- General Management Pathway

*Science, Technology, Engineering & Mathematics Career Cluster*

- Engineering & Technology Pathway
- Science & Mathematics Pathway

### Transferable Skills and Abilities

**Analytical Skills**

- Assessing the needs of patients and customers prior to designing products

**Communication Skills**

- Working with patients and customers and often working on teams
- Writing reports and research papers

**Creativity**

- Coming up with innovations in healthcare equipment and devices

**Math Skills**

- Using calculus and other advanced math and statistics for analysis, design, and troubleshooting in their work

**Mechanical Skills**

- Operating complex machinery and occasionally performing routine maintenance

**Problem-solving Skills**

- Dealing with intricate biological systems
- Working independently and with others to incorporate ideas into the complex problem-solving process

## Postsecondary

At the bachelor's degree level, prospective bioengineers should enter bioengineering or traditional engineering programs, such as mechanical and electrical. Students who pursue traditional engineering degrees may benefit from taking biological science courses.

Bachelor's degree programs in bioengineering and biomedical engineering focus on engineering and biological sciences. These programs typically include laboratory- and classroom-based courses in biological sciences and subjects such as fluid and solid mechanics, circuit design, and biomaterials.

These programs also include substantial training in engineering design. As part of their study, students may have an opportunity to participate in co-ops or internships with hospitals and medical device and pharmaceutical manufacturing companies. Bioengineering and biomedical engineering programs are accredited by the Accreditation Board for Engineering and Technology, Inc. (ABET).

**Fast Fact**

**Rowland Macy, founder of the department store Macy's, was a serial entrepreneur who failed at seven business ventures before hitting paydirt with his landmark store.** Source: lifehack.org

Rowland Macy. Photo via Wikimedia Commons. [Public Domain.]

**Related College Majors**

- Biochemical Engineering
- Biological Engineering
- Chemical Engineering
- Computer Engineering
- Electrical Engineering
- Engineering Science
- Materials Engineering
- Mechanical Engineering
- Polymer & Plastics Engineering
- Robotics Engineering

### Adult Job Seekers

Some bioengineers attend medical or dental school to specialize in techniques such as using electric impulses in new ways to get muscles moving again. Others earn law degrees and work as patent attorneys. Still others pursue a master's degree in business administration (MBA) and move into managerial positions.

## EARNINGS AND ADVANCEMENT

Earnings depend on whether the engineer works for or owns the business, and the type and scale of projects undertaken. Median annual earnings of bioengineers or biomedical engineers were $91,410 in 2019. The lowest 10 percent earned less than $55,280, and the highest 10 percent earned more than $148,210.

Bioengineers or biomedical engineers may receive paid vacations, holidays, and sick days; life and health insurance; and retirement benefits. These are usually paid by an employer if the business is not self-owned. Bioengineers or biomedical engineers may also be able to expense travel to on-site locations for product testing.

Bioengineers and biomedical engineers may increase their responsibilities as they gain experience or advanced degrees. To lead a research team, a bioengineer or biomedical engineer typically needs a graduate degree. Those who are interested in basic research may become medical scientists.

## EMPLOYMENT AND OUTLOOK

Bioengineers and biomedical engineers held 21,200 jobs in 2019. Employment is expected to grow faster than average for all occupations through the year 2029, at a rate of 5 percent, because of increasing technologies and their applications to medical equipment and devices. Smartphone technology and three-dimensional printing are examples of technology being applied to biomedical advances.

As the baby-boom generation lives longer and stays active, the demand for bioengineers and biomedical devices and procedures, such as hip and knee replacements, is expected to increase. In addition, as the public awareness of medical advances continues, increasing numbers of people will seek biomedical solutions to their health problems from their physicians.

Bioengineers and biomedical engineers work with scientists, other medical researchers, and manufacturers to address a range of injuries and physical disabilities. The ability of these engineers to collaborate on activities with workers from other fields is enlarging the range of applications for biomedical engineering products and services.

### Related Occupations

- Agricultural Engineer
- Architectural/Engineering Manager
- Biochemist/Biophysicist
- Chemical Engineer
- Electrical/Electronics Engineer
- Materials Engineer
- Mechanical Engineer
- Medical Scientist
- Physician/Surgeon
- Sales Engineer

## MORE INFORMATION

**Accreditation Board for Engineering and Technology, Inc. (ABET)**
415 North Charles Street
Baltimore, MD 21201
410.347.7700
www.abet.org

**American Association of Engineering Societies (AAES)**
1801 Alexander Bell Drive
Reston, VA 20191
202.296.2237
orders@aaes.org
www.aaes.org

**American Institute for Medical and Biological Engineering (AIMBE)**
1400 I Street NW, Suite 235
Washington, DC 20005
202.496.9660
info@aimbe.org
aimbe.org

**American Society for Engineering Education (ASEE)**
1818 N Street NW, Suite 600
Washington, DC 20036
202.331.3500
www.asee.org

**American Society of Agricultural and Biological Engineers (ASABE)**
2950 Niles Road
St. Joseph, MI 49085
269.429.0300
www.asabe.org

**American Society of Mechanical Engineers (ASME)**
Two Park Avenue
New York, NY 10016-5990
800.843.2763
CustomerCare@asme.org
www.asme.org

**Biomedical Engineering Society (BMES)**
8201 Corporate Drive, Suite 1125
Landover, MD 20785
membership@bmes.org
301.459.1999
www.bmes.org

**Engineering Education Service Center (EESC)**
1411 Old Hardman Btms Road
Clarkesville, GA 30523
706.499.5011
www.engineeringedu.com

**IEEE Engineering in Medicine and Biology Society (EMBS)**
445 Hoes Lane
Piscataway, NJ 08854
732.981.3433
www.embs.org

**Institute of Biological Engineering (IBE)**
446 East High Street, Suite 10
Lexington, KY 40507
859.977.7450
info@ibe.org
www.ibe.org

**Society of Biological Engineers (SBE)**
c/o American Institute of Chemical Engineers (AIChE)
120 Wall Street, FL 23
New York, NY 10005-4020
800.242.4363
www.aiche.org/sbe

**Technology Student Association (TSA)**
1904 Association Drive
Reston, VA 20191-1540
703.860.9000
general@tsaweb.org
tsaweb.org

---

*Stuart Paterson*

## *Conversation With...*
# RICHARD COTE

President and Founder, Avidien Technologies, Inc., Hudson, MA
Product design and development, development management, business management, 26 years

**What was your individual career path in terms of education/training, entry-level job, or other significant opportunity?**

My father worked as a technical instructor at Massachusetts Institute of Technology, and we had an extensive shop in the basement. So, I was exposed to machine shops and how to put things together. After high school, I spent about 18 months doing different jobs like working on a commercial fishing boat. I also got to the point I could not only take apart a car engine but understand the technical side of it. That led me to want to study mechanical engineering.

While studying mechanical engineering at Northeastern University in the early 1990s, I took advantage of their cooperative education program. In my final co-op assignment, I worked for a company called Costar in Cambridge, Massachusetts, that made life science laboratory equipment and disposable labware.

The exposure in that initial job was the start of my career developing new products used in life science labs around the world. The guy I worked for during my last co-op session offered me a job, and I worked for him or with him for 20 years. He and I moved from one company to another, founded a company, and he is still a good friend.

I was at Costar for about 6 years, then moved to Matrix Technologies. Due to a merger, our parent company was bought. Five of us decided to start a new company, Viaflow Integra. That company is now very successful, but it was both challenging and exciting in the beginning. That experience led me to start my own company, Avidien Technologies Inc. I spent a couple of years doing product development in my spare time while working for another company before launching Avidien full-time.

If you work in chemistry or life sciences, you have to be able to transfer liquids precisely. We make the smallest of a type of automated pipette that is really easy and intuitive to use. Automation reduces mistakes. There are competitors out there, but we developed many concepts that allow these instruments to be small.

We spent 5 years creating the company and designing our product, the first of which was released in 2017. Our clients include pharmaceutical and diagnostic companies, as well as university labs.

Many entrepreneurs have an idea and then go find their funding first. Avidien was bootstrapped, meaning that the company was self-funded through savings, family, and friends. The main reason I was able to afford to bootstrap the company is because I could do a lot of the engineering work myself.

There are many paths that can lead to entrepreneurial pursuits, but for me the cooperative education model followed by direct exposure to the startup environment was the course that led me to where I am today. In addition, most new companies are built around new products, so being an engineer involved in the new product development process before starting Avidien gave me a good foundation on which to build a company.

**What are the most important skills and/or qualities for someone in your profession?**
As an entrepreneur, you have to be willing to take risks and push yourself to keep trying when failure is always a possibility. Above all, the main quality an entrepreneur has to possess is a deep belief in themselves and their ideas.

**What do you wish you had known going into this profession?**
Starting a business requires the founders and early employees to wear many hats—marketing, sales, human resources, accounting, etc. In most jobs people tend to stay in their professional lanes and not pay much attention to the other business functions around them. Through my career I wish that I had paid more attention and asked more questions that in retrospect would have helped me while starting Avidien.

Also, given hindsight, I would tell somebody thinking about entrepreneurship to try it early on. Not so early you don't have enough work experience, but early enough so you're not deep into a mortgage and family. The risk is lower. Also, accept you may fail once or twice but you learn from the failure.

**Are there many job opportunities in your profession? In what specific areas?**
Anyone with the right drive and determination can choose to be an entrepreneur; so, it is not really about job opportunity. However, the key to being a successful entrepreneur is choosing a specific area that is a fit for your skills and your passions, and that is also a marketable endeavor, whether a service, product, or other enterprise.

**How do you see your profession changing in the next 5 years? How will technology impact that change, and what skills will be required?**
In the next five years it will continue to become easier to be a successful entrepreneur. For example, finding your customers is a key aspect to starting a business. As technology advances, reaching potential customers worldwide will continue to evolve into something you can do simply through your computer and internet connection. Success will go to those who develop skills marketing products through the constantly evolving social media platforms and are able to take advantage of that access.

**What do you enjoy most about your job? What do you enjoy least about your job?**

The aspect I enjoy most about being an entrepreneur in a company that develops products for laboratory use is hearing positive feedback about our company's products and service from our customers. Fortunately, this happens frequently. Hearing about a problem a customer is having with one of our products is something I enjoy least. On the positive side, it is also how we learn to improve our products.

**Can you suggest a valuable "try this" for students considering a career in your profession?**

If a student is interested in pursuing a life as an entrepreneur, I would recommend that they work or spend some time in a young startup company to get a flavor for the environment and its challenges. There are also many online and print periodicals dedicated to the aspects of becoming a successful entrepreneur that will paint a bigger picture of what it means to start a company. I also think the show Shark Tank is great for understanding the fundraising component and how investors think about a new venture.

# Childcare Worker

**Snapshot**

**Career Cluster(s):** Business, Management & Administration; Human Services

**Interests:** Children; childcare; community services

**Earnings (Yearly Average):** $24,230

**Employment & Outlook:** Slower Than Average Growth Expected

## OVERVIEW

### Sphere of Work

Childcare workers attend to children's needs while helping to foster early development. They may help younger children prepare for kindergarten or assist older children with homework.

### Work Environment

Family childcare workers care for children in their own homes. They may convert a portion of their living space into a dedicated space for the children. Nannies usually work in their employers' homes. Childcare workers' schedules vary, and part-time work is common.

### Occupation Interest

Individuals involved in childcare enjoy working with children and caring for them when their parents cannot. They are able to multitask and handle multiple children at once, providing a clean and safe environment in which they can play and develop.

Childcare workers at play with their young charges. Photo via iStock.com/Rawpixel. [Used under license.]

### A Day in the Life—Duties and Responsibilities

Childcare workers read and play with babies and toddlers to introduce basic concepts. For example, they teach them how to share and take turns by playing games with other children.

Childcare workers help preschool-age children prepare for kindergarten. Young children learn from playing, questioning, and experimenting. Childcare workers use play and other instructional techniques to help children's development. For example, they may use storytelling and rhyming games to teach language and vocabulary. They may help improve children's social skills by having them work together to build something in a sandbox. Or they may teach about numbers by having children count when building with blocks. They also involve children in creative activities, such as art, dance, and music.

Childcare workers may also watch school-age children before and after school. They often help these children with their homework and may take them to after-school activities, such as sports practices and club meetings.

During the summer, when children are out of school, childcare workers may watch older children as well as younger ones while the parents are at work.

### *Profile*

**Interests:** People, Things, Data
**Working Conditions:** Inside
**Physical Strength:** Medium Work
**Education Needs:** Varies By State, High School Diploma Usually Required
**Licensure/Certification:** Varies By State
**Opportunities for Experience:** Training, Part-Time Work
**Interest Score:** SA

## OCCUPATION SPECIALTIES

### Childcare Center Worker

Childcare center workers work in facilities that include programs offering Head Start and Early Head Start. They often take a team-based approach and may work with preschool teachers and teacher assistants to teach children through a structured curriculum. They prepare daily and long-term schedules of activities to stimulate and educate the children in their care. They also monitor and keep records of the children's progress.

### Family Childcare Provider

Family childcare providers run a business out of their own homes to care for children during standard working hours. They need to ensure that their homes and all staff they employ meet the regulations for family childcare providers. They also

## Duties and Responsibilities

- Supervising and monitoring the safety of children
- Preparing and organizing mealtimes and snacks for children
- Helping children keep good hygiene
- Changing the diapers of infants and toddlers
- Organizing activities or implementing a curriculum that allows children to learn about the world and explore their interests
- Developing schedules and routines to ensure that children have enough physical activity, rest, and playtime
- Watching for signs of emotional or developmental problems in children and bringing potential problems to the attention of parents or guardians
- Keeping records of children's progress, routines, and interests

prepare contracts that set rates of pay, when payment can be expected, and the number of hours children can be in care. Furthermore, they establish policies such as whether sick children can be in their care, who can pick children up, and how behavioral issues will be dealt with. Family childcare providers may market their services to prospective families.

**Nanny**

Nannies work in the homes of the families whose children they care for. Most often, they work full-time for one family. They may be responsible for driving children to school, appointments, or afterschool activities. Some live in the homes of the families employing them.

## WORK ENVIRONMENT

### Immediate Physical Environment

Many states limit the number of children that each staff member is responsible for by regulating the ratio of staff to children. Ratios vary with the age of the children. Childcare workers are responsible for relatively few babies and toddlers. However, workers may be responsible for greater numbers of older children.

Childcare centers usually are open year-round, with long hours so that parents or guardians can drop off and pick up their children before and after work. Some centers employ full-time and part-time staff with staggered shifts to cover the entire day.

Family childcare providers may work long or irregular hours to fit parents' work schedules. In some cases, these childcare providers offer evening and overnight care to meet the needs of families. After the children go home, family childcare providers often have more responsibilities, such as shopping for food or supplies, keeping records, and cleaning.

Nannies work either full- or part-time. Full-time nannies may work more than 40 hours a week to cover parents' time commuting to and from work.

### Human Environment

By definition, childcare workers interact with people, especially children, on a daily basis and as part of their jobs. They also interact with parents and guardians, as well as other staff. Childcare workers who run their own business must be prepared to handle any issues that arise, including emergencies, and settle disputes with parents and guardians, and staff members. Nannies interact with family members of their employers, as well as outside individuals such as teachers, tutors, and doctors. Nannies who live with their employers form a unique bond with their employers and their children.

### Technological Environment

Childcare workers should be proficient in basic computer software such as word processors, email, and spreadsheets. They may also incorporate the latest educational technology into their activities, including software and mobile apps.

## EDUCATION, TRAINING, AND ADVANCEMENT

### High School/Secondary

Childcare workers' education requirements vary. Some states require these workers to have a high school diploma or equivalent, but others do not have any education requirements for entry-level positions. Employers often prefer to hire workers who have at least a high school diploma. However, workers with postsecondary education or an early childhood education credential may qualify for higher-level positions.

Childcare workers in Head Start and Early Head Start programs must meet specific education and certification requirements, which vary by work setting and job title.

States do not regulate educational requirements for nannies. However, some employers may prefer to hire workers with at least some formal instruction in childhood education or a related field, particularly when they will be hired as full-time nannies.

**Suggested High School Subjects**

- Algebra

- Biology
- Chemistry
- Civics
- Earth or Life or Physical Science
- Economics
- English
- Entrepreneurship
- Geometry
- History
- Personal Finance
- Physics
- Pre-Calculus
- Psychology
- Statistics
- Trigonometry

**Related Career Pathways/Majors**

*Business, Management & Administration Career Cluster*

- General Management Pathway

*Human Services Career Cluster*

- Early Childhood Development & Services Pathway

### Transferable Skills and Abilities

**Communication Skills**

- Providing direction or information effectively and good listening skills to understand parents' instructions

**Decision-making Skills**

- Responding to emergencies or difficult situations

**Interpersonal Skills**

- Working well with people to develop good relationships with parents, children, and colleagues

**Patience**

- Needing to be able to respond calmly to overwhelming and difficult situations

**Mechanical Skills**

- Operating complex machinery and occasionally performing routine maintenance

**Physical Stamina**

- Working with children can be physically demanding, so childcare workers should have a lot of energy

## Postsecondary

With a couple of years of experience and a bachelor's degree, childcare workers may advance to become a preschool or childcare center director.

**Related College Majors**

- Arts Education
- Childcare Provider/Assistant
- Early Childhood Education
- Elementary Education
- Social Work
- Special Education

## Adult Job Seekers

Adults with experience working with or caring for children in a developmental setting stand a good chance of transitioning into childcare work, especially as educational requirements are quite minimal.

### Professional Certification and Licensure

Many states require childcare centers, including those in private homes, to be licensed. To qualify for licensure, staff often must pass a background check, have a complete record of immunizations, and meet a minimum training requirement. Some states require staff to have certifications in cardiopulmonary resuscitation (CPR) and first aid.

Some states and employers require childcare workers to have a nationally recognized credential. Most often, states require the Child Development Associate (CDA) credential offered by the Council for Professional Recognition. Obtaining the CDA credential requires coursework, experience in the field, and a period during which the applicant is observed while working with children. The CDA credential must be renewed every 3 years.

Other organizations, such as The National Association for Family Child Care (NAFCC) may also offer optional accreditation.

### Additional Requirements

Many states and employers require providers to complete some training before beginning work. Also, many states require staff in childcare centers to complete a minimum number of training hours annually. Training may include information about topics such as safe sleep practices for infants.

## EARNINGS AND ADVANCEMENT

Pay varies with the worker's education level and work setting. Those in formal childcare settings and those with more education usually earn higher wages. Median annual earnings of childcare workers were $24,230 in 2019.

Pay for self-employed workers is based on the number of hours they work and the number and ages of children in their care.

## EMPLOYMENT AND OUTLOOK

Childcare workers held 1,146,400 jobs in 2019. Twenty-three percent were self-employed. Employment is expected to grow slower than the average for all occupations through the year 2029, at a rate of 2 percent. Parents or guardians who work will continue to need the assistance of childcare workers. In addition, the demand for preschools and childcare facilities, and consequently childcare

**Fast Fact**

**Most people who start small businesses are between ages 40 and 60.** Source: smallbizgenius.com

An older couple at their self-owned coffee business. Photo via iStock.com/pixelfit. [Used under license.]

workers, should remain strong because early childhood education is widely recognized as important for a child's intellectual and emotional development. However, the increasing cost of childcare may reduce demand for childcare workers.

Despite limited employment growth, about 160,200 openings for childcare workers are projected each year, on average, over the decade.

Most of those openings are expected to result from the need to replace workers who transfer to different occupations or exit the labor force, such as to retire.

Workers who attain the Child Development Associate credential should have the best job prospects.

## Related Occupations

- Kindergarten/Elementary School Teacher
- Preschool/Childcare Center Director
- Preschool Teacher
- Special Education Teacher
- Teacher Assistant

## MORE INFORMATION

**Child Care Aware of America**
703.341.4100
membership@usa.childcareaware.org
www.childcareaware.org

**Council for Professional Recognition**
2460 16th Street NW
Washington, DC 20009-3547
800.424.4310
www.cdacouncil.org

**International Nanny Association**
P.O Box 70496
Milwaukee, WI 53207
888.878.1477
info@nanny.org
nanny.org

**National Association for the Education of Young Children (NAEYC)**
1401 H Street NW, Suite 600
Washington, DC 20005
800.424.2460
help@naeyc.org
www.naeyc.org

**National Association of Family Child Care (NAFCC)**
700 12 Street NW
Suite 700
Washington, DC 20005
202.796.5700
nafcc@nafcc.org
nafcc.org

**National Child Care Association (NCCA)**
P.O. Box 2948
Merrifield, VA 22116
877.537.6222
ncca@necpa.net
nationalchildcare.org

---

*Stuart Paterson*

# Craft/Fine Artist

### Snapshot

**Career Cluster(s):** Arts, A/V Technology & Communications; Business Management & Administration

**Interests:** Art; creativity; design

**Earnings (Yearly Average):** $48,760

**Employment & Outlook:** Little or No Change Expected

## OVERVIEW

### Sphere of Work

Craft and fine artists use a variety of materials and techniques to create original works of art for sale and exhibition. Craft artists create objects, such as pottery, glassware, and textiles, that are designed to be functional. Fine artists, including painters, sculptors, and illustrators, create pieces of art more for aesthetics than for function.

### Work Environment

Many artists work in fine- or commercial-art studios located in office buildings, warehouses, or lofts. Others work in private studios in their homes. Some artists share studio space, where they also may exhibit their work. Artists may also choose to work outdoors, depending on their medium and artistic intent.

Young artist making a clay bowl on a potter's wheel. Photo via iStock.com/Sladic. [Used under license.]

Most craft and fine artists work full-time, although part-time and variable schedules are also common. Many hold another job in addition to their work as an artist. During busy periods, artists may work additional hours to meet deadlines. Those who are self-employed usually determine their own schedules.

### Profile

**Interests:** Things, People
**Working Conditions:** Both Inside and Outside
**Physical Strength:** Medium Work, Varies
**Education Needs:** On-the-Job Training, Bachelor's Degree
**Licensure/Certification:** Usually Not Required
**Opportunities for Experience:** Internship, Apprenticeship, Volunteer Work, Part-Time Work
**Interest Score:** ARE

## Occupation Interest

Professional craft and fine artists are creative individuals by nature and have a desire to not only share their creations, but to turn their passion into a source of income. Over half of all craft and fine artists are self-employed, meaning these individuals must have a drive to succeed in a crowded and highly entrepreneurial field. In many cases, they should expect to work another job to make a living wage.

## A Day in the Life—Duties and Responsibilities

Artists create objects that are beautiful, thought provoking, and sometimes shocking. They often strive to communicate ideas or feelings through their art.

Craft artists work with many different materials, including ceramics, glass, textiles, wood, metal, and paper. They use these materials to create unique pieces of art, such as pottery, quilts, stained glass, furniture, jewelry, and clothing. Many craft artists also use fine art techniques—for example, painting, sketching, and printing—to add finishing touches to their products.

Fine artists typically display their work in museums, in commercial or nonprofit art galleries, at craft fairs, in corporate collections, on the Internet, and in private homes. Some of their artwork may be commissioned (requested by a client), but most is sold by the artist or through private art galleries or dealers. The artist, gallery, and dealer together decide in advance how much of the proceeds from the sale each will keep.

### Duties and Responsibilities

- Using techniques such as knitting, weaving, glassblowing, painting, drawing, and sculpting
- Developing creative ideas or new methods for making art
- Creating sketches, templates, or models to guide work
- Selecting which materials to use based on color, texture, strength, and other criteria
- Shaping, joining, or cutting materials for a final product
- Using visual techniques, such as composition, color, space, and perspective, to produce desired artistic effects
- Developing a portfolio that highlights artistic style and ability to show to gallery owners and others
- Displaying work at auctions, craft fairs, galleries, museums, and online marketplaces
- Completing grant proposals and applications to obtain financial support for projects

Most craft and fine artists spend their time and effort selling their artwork to potential customers and building a reputation. This can include in-person showings and online sales through marketplaces designed specifically for selling one's own art. In addition to selling their artwork, many artists have at least one other job to support their craft or art careers.

Some artists work in museums or art galleries as art directors or as archivists, curators, or museum workers, planning and setting up exhibits. Others teach craft or art classes or conduct workshops in schools or in their own studios.

## OCCUPATION SPECIALTIES

**Cartoonist**

Cartoonists create simplified or exaggerated drawings to visually convey political, advertising, comic, or sports concepts. Some cartoonists work with others who create the idea or story and write captions. Others create plots and write captions themselves. Most cartoonists have humorous, critical, or dramatic talent, in addition to drawing skills.

**Ceramic Artist**

Ceramic artists shape, form, and mold artworks out of clay, often using a potter's wheel and other tools. They glaze and fire pieces in kilns, which are large, special furnaces that dry and harden the clay.

**Digital Artist**

Digital artists use design and production software to create interactive art online. The digital imagery may then be transferred to paper or some other form of printmaking or made available directly on web-accessible devices.

**Fiber Artist**

Fiber artists use fabric, yarn, or other natural and synthetic materials to weave, knit, crochet, or sew textile art. They may use a loom to weave fabric, needles to knit or crochet yarn, or a sewing machine to join pieces of fabric for quilts or other handicrafts.

**Fine-art Painter**

Fine-art painters paint landscapes, portraits, and other subjects in a variety of styles, ranging from realistic to abstract. They may work in a variety of media, such as watercolors, oil paints, and acrylics.

**Furniture Maker**

Furniture makers cut, sand, join, and finish wood and other materials to make handcrafted furnishings. For information about other workers who assemble wood furniture, see the profile on woodworkers.

**Glass Artist**

Glass artists process glass in a variety of ways—such as by blowing, shaping, staining, or joining it—to create artistic pieces. Some processes require the use of kilns, ovens, and other equipment and tools that bend glass at high temperatures. These workers also decorate glass objects, such as by etching or painting.

**Illustrator**

Illustrators create pictures for books, magazines, and other publications and for commercial products, such as textiles, wrapping paper, stationery, greeting cards, and calendars. Illustrators increasingly use computers in their work. They might draw in pen or pencil and then scan the image, using software to add color, or they might use a special pen to draw images directly onto the computer.

**Jewelry Artist**

Jewelry artists use metals, stones, beads, and other materials to make objects for personal adornment, such as earrings or necklaces. For more information about other workers who create jewelry, see the profile on jewelers and precious stone and metal workers.

**Medical/Scientific Illustrator**

Medical and scientific illustrators combine drawing skills with knowledge of biology or other sciences. Medical illustrators work with computers or with pen and paper to create images, three-dimensional models, and animations of human anatomy and surgical procedures. Scientific illustrators draw animal and plant life, atomic and molecular structures, and geologic and planetary formations. These illustrations are used in medical and scientific publications and in audiovisual presentations for teaching purposes. Some medical and scientific illustrators work for lawyers, producing exhibits for court cases.

**Printmaker**

Printmakers create images on a silk screen, woodblock, lithography stone, metal etching plate, or other types of matrices. A hand printing press then creates the final work of art, inking and transferring the matrix to a piece of paper.

**Public Artist**
Public artists create large paintings, sculptures, and displays called "installations" that are meant to be seen in open spaces. These works are typically displayed in parks, museum grounds, train stations, and other public areas.

**Sculptor**
Sculptors design and shape three-dimensional works of art, either by molding and joining materials such as clay, glass, plastic, and metal or by cutting and carving forms from a block of plaster, wood, or stone. Some sculptors combine various materials to create mixed-media installations, such as by incorporating light, sound, and motion into their work.

**Sketch Artist**
Sketch artists are a type of illustrator who often use pencil, charcoal, or pastels to create likenesses of subjects. Their sketches are used by law enforcement agencies to help identify suspects, by the news media to show courtroom scenes, and by individual customers for their own enjoyment.

**Tattoo Artist**
Tattoo artists use stencils and draw by hand to create original images and text on skin. With specialized needles, these artists use a variety of styles and colors based on their clients' preferences.

**Video Artist**
Video artists record avant-garde, moving imagery that is typically shown in a loop in art galleries, museums, or performance spaces. These artists sometimes use multiple monitors or create unusual spaces for the video to be shown.

## WORK ENVIRONMENT

### Immediate Physical Environment

Work settings for artists vary depending on the person and the type of art being created. Artists may also desire to have particular surroundings in order to inspire and stimulate creativity.

Artists' studios are usually well lit and ventilated. However, artists may be exposed to fumes from glue, paint, ink, and other materials. They may also have to deal with dust or other residue from filings, splattered paint, or spilled cleaning and other fluids. Artists often wear protective gear, such as breathing masks and goggles, to remain safe from exposure to harmful materials. Ceramic and glass artists must use caution in working with materials that may break into sharp pieces and in using equipment that can get extremely hot, such as kilns. Artists and related workers have one of the highest rates of injuries and illnesses of all occupations.

### Human Environment

Depending on the person and nature of their art, human interaction during working hours may be limited. However, artists commonly share their studios with like-minded individuals to help cover rental and other costs, and possibly to share ideas and techniques. Artists also must be comfortable interacting with the public when selling their art, be it in person or online, and must be able to cope with criticism of their work. When selling or showing art in public, artists must also interact with gallery owners.

### Technological Environment

Technological requirements vary widely in the field of craft and fine art. Much depends on the type of art being created and the medium being used. Most artists work with their hands and must be familiar with the tools and techniques required to accomplish what they envision. A painter must know the benefits and limitations of certain canvases, paints, and brushes, for example, while a sculptor must understand the properties of the material being used to sculpt. Painters may also become skilled at framing. Artists increasingly also use computer technology, including advances in areas such as 3D printing, in novel ways to create new forms of art. From a business standpoint, artists who sell their work to the public should be familiar with the internet platforms available, as well as record keeping software for organizational purposes.

## EDUCATION, TRAINING, AND ADVANCEMENT

### High School/Secondary

High school art classes can teach prospective craft artists the basic drawing skills they need. Craft and fine artists improve their skills through practice and repetition. English classes are also important for improving communication skills. High school students interested in pursuing art as a business should also take fundamental business classes and be comfortable with practical math.

**Suggested High School Subjects**

- Algebra
- Art/Design

- Biology
- Earth or Life or Physical Science
- Economics
- English
- Entrepreneurship
- Geometry
- History
- Physics
- Political Science
- Psychology
- Trigonometry

**Related Career Pathways/Majors**

*Arts, A/V Technology & Communications*

- Visual Arts Pathway

*Business, Management & Administration Career Cluster*

- Business Information Management Pathway
- General Management Pathway
- Operations Management Pathway

## Transferable Skills and Abilities

**Artistic Ability**

- Creating artwork and other objects that are visually appealing or thought provoking

**Business Skills**

- Self-promotion in order to build a reputation
- Studying the market to increase understanding of what prospective customers might want
- Developing an online presence as an important part of art sales

**Creativity**

- Developing new and original ideas

**Customer-service Skills**

- Dealing with customers and prospective buyers

**Dexterity**

- Manipulating tools and materials to create art

**Interpersonal Skills**

- Interacting with people, including customers, gallery owners, and the public

### Postsecondary

Most fine artists pursue postsecondary education to improve their skills and job prospects. A formal educational credential is typically not needed to be a craft artist. However, it is difficult to gain adequate artistic skills without some formal education.

A number of colleges and universities offer bachelor's and master's degrees in subjects related to fine arts. In addition to studio art and art history, postsecondary programs may include core subjects, such as English, marketing, social science, and natural science. Independent schools of art and design also offer postsecondary education programs, which can lead to a certificate in an art-related specialty or to an associate, bachelor's, or master's degree in fine arts.

The National Association of Schools of Art and Design (NASAD) accredits more than 360 postsecondary institutions with programs in art and design. Most of these schools award a degree in art.

**Fast Fact**

**Learning and practicing art strongly correlates with higher achievement in reading and math.**

Source: theoldjailartcenter.org

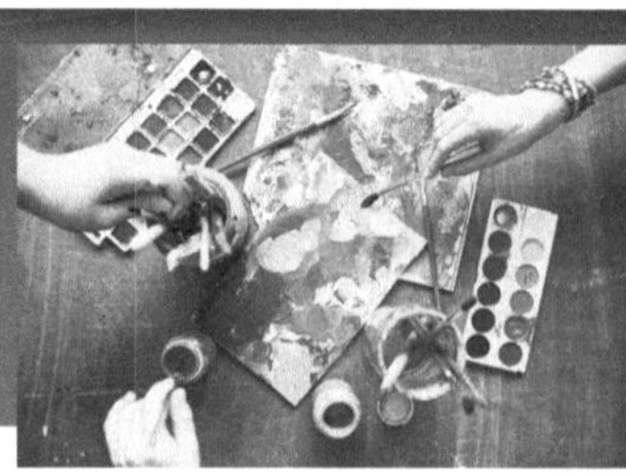

Painting can be a key to achievement in other disciplines. Photo via iStock.com/mediaphotos. [Used under license.]

Education gives artists an opportunity to develop their portfolio, which is a collection of an artist's work that demonstrates his or her styles and abilities. Portfolios are essential, because art directors, clients, and others look at them when deciding whether to hire an artist or to buy the artist's work. In addition to compiling a physical portfolio, many artists choose to create a portfolio online.

**Related College Majors**

- Architecture
- Art Design
- Digital Media
- Drawing & Painting
- Printmaking
- Sculpture
- Studio Arts

## Adult Job Seekers

Adults who are looking to turn their artistic passion into a business should become familiar with art currently on the market in their chosen niche and start to build an online presence. Doing so can simultaneously help curate a portfolio, which is vital so an artist can show examples of their work to prospective buyers. Adults can also attend continuing education courses, such as night school, to improve techniques or learn new methods.

## Professional Certification and Licensure

Those who want to teach fine arts at public elementary or secondary schools usually must have a teaching certificate in addition to a bachelor's degree.

## Additional Requirements

Craft and fine artists improve their skills through practice and repetition. They can train in several ways other than, or in addition to, formal schooling. Craft and fine artists may train with simpler projects before attempting something more ambitious.

Some artists learn on the job from more experienced artists. Others attend noncredit classes or workshops or take private lessons, which may be offered in artists' studios or at community colleges, art centers, galleries, museums, or other art-related institutions.

## EARNINGS AND ADVANCEMENT

Earnings depend on the nature of the art being produced, the clientele, the stature of the artist, and whether the artist is self-employed or works for a company. Median annual earnings of craft and fine artists were $48,760 in 2019. The lowest 10 percent earned less than $22,290, and the highest 10 percent earned more than $106,000.

It is unlikely that craft and fine artists will receive benefits such as paid vacations, holidays, and sick days; life and health insurance; and retirement benefits, unless the artist works for a company.

Competition for jobs as craft and fine artists is expected to be strong because there are more qualified candidates than available jobs. Competition is likely to grow among independent or self-employed artists, given that many of them sell their work in the same online marketplaces. In addition, competition among artists for the privilege of having their work shown in galleries is expected to remain intense.

Because the demand for artwork depends on consumers having extra income to spend, many of these artists will find that their income changes alongside changes in the overall economy. Only the most successful craft and fine artists receive major commissions for their work.

Despite the competition, studios, galleries, and individual clients are always on the lookout for artists who display outstanding talent, creativity, and style. Talented individuals who have developed a mastery of artistic techniques and marketing skills are likely to have the best job prospects.

## EMPLOYMENT AND OUTLOOK

Craft and fine artists held 51,900 jobs in 2019. Fifty-one percent were self-employed. Employment is expected to show little or no change through the year 2029. Employment growth for artists depends largely on the overall state of the economy and whether people are willing to spend money on art, because people usually buy art when they can afford to do so. During good economic times, people and businesses are interested in buying more artwork; during economic downturns, they generally buy less. However, there is always some demand for art by private collectors and museums.

Job growth for craft and fine artists may be limited by the sale of inexpensive, machine-produced items designed to look like handmade crafts. A continued interest in locally made products and crafted goods will likely offset some of these employment losses.

Illustrators and cartoonists who work in publishing may see their job opportunities decline as traditional print publications lose ground to other media forms. However, new opportunities are expected to arise as the number of electronic magazines and other Internet-based publications continue to grow.

### Related Occupations

- Archivist/Curator/Museum Worker
- Art Director
- Fashion Designer
- Graphic Designer
- Industrial Designer
- Jewelers/Precious Stone and Metal Workers
- Multimedia Artists/Animators
- Photographers
- Woodworkers

## MORE INFORMATION

**Accrediting Commission for Community and Precollegiate Arts Schools (ACCPAS)**
11250 Roger Bacon Drive, Suite 21
Reston, VA 20190-5248

703.437.0700
info@arts-accredit.org
accpas.arts-accredit.org

**American Craft Council (ACC)**
1224 Marshall Street NE, Suite 200
Minneapolis, MN 55413
612.206.3100
council@craftcouncil.org
www.craftcouncil.org

**Art Dealers Association of America (ADAA)**
205 Lexington Avenue, Suite #901
New York, NY 10016
212.488.5550
adaa@artdealers.org
artdealers.org

**Association of Medical Illustrators (AMI)**
201 E. Main Street, Ste. 1405
Lexington, KY 40507
866.393.4264
hq@ami.org
ami.org

**College Art Association of America (CAAA)**
50 Broadway, 21st Floor
New York, NY 10004
212.691.1051
nyoffice@collegeart.org
www.collegeart.org

**Council of Arts Accrediting Associations (CAAA)**
11250 Roger Bacon Drive, Suite 21
Reston, VA 20190-5248
703.437.0700
info@arts-accredit.org
www.arts-accredit.org
National Office for Arts Accreditation (NOAA):
www.arts-accredit.org/national-office-for-arts-accreditation

**National Assembly of State Arts Agencies (NASAA)**
1200 18th Street NW, Suite 1100
Washington, DC 20036
202.347.6352
nasaa@nasaa-arts.org
nasaa-arts.org

**National Association of Schools of Art and Design (NASAD)**
11250 Roger Bacon Drive, Suite 21
Reston, VA 20190-5248
703.437.0700
info@arts-accredit.org
nasad.arts-accredit.org

**National Endowment for the Arts**
400 7th Street SW
Washington, DC 20506
202.682.5400
www.arts.gov

**New York Foundation for the Arts (NYFA)**
20 Jay Street, Suite 740
Brooklyn, NY 11201
212.366.6900
help@nyfa.org
www.nyfa.org

---

*Stuart Paterson*

## *Conversation With...*

# SCOTT MOORE

Fine Artist, specializing in landscape paintings
Stockton Springs, ME
Years in field, 45 years

**What was your individual career path in terms of education/training, entry-level job, or other significant opportunity?**

I have a Bachelor of Fine Arts in Painting from Maine College of Art. My parents were artists when I was growing up. We lived near Washington, DC. My mother was a fashion illustrator for all the major department stores there, and my father was the art director at the Institute of Heraldry, which designed flags, medals, and seals for the US Army. They gave me the idea that an art career was a normal thing to do. I had materials and direction available right at home, which was helpful. We used to go to the National Gallery of Art fairly frequently, and the Hirshhorn Museum. So, there was good art to be seen and creativity there, and I could see the possible modes of expression.

I paint landscapes because I enjoy working outdoors. I've always responded to landscape. A portrait painter has to be somewhat of a courtier, and I'm a little more self-contained.

The first painting I sold was at a sidewalk art show in Portland, Maine, when I was a college student. One of my professors thought I was too inexperienced to be out selling paintings. I was always more geared to try to make a living at it, and I wanted to be self-directed. The only other thing I ever wanted to do was to be an archeologist, and there are fewer jobs for that. So, it was either this, or that.

After college I got a job at a friend's parents' shop as a picture framer. That's a good skill for a painter to have because framing is expensive. I started showing when I was 25, at the frame shop where I worked in a little space there, and then at a co-op gallery, which is a good place when you're just starting out.

It was a gradual process to paint full-time. I've worked in restaurants from time to time, at night so I had the daylight hours to paint. I've pounded nails. I tended to take jobs that didn't absorb too much of my energy, in general, because I wanted it for painting and that's where my focus was. For a lot of my career, I worked six and a half days a week.

I was fortunate enough to be in the right place at the right time. In 1992, there was a big CEO who bought an armload of my paintings and continued to do so. I was making frames then for a gallery that also showed my work. I cut back to working one day a week in framing, but the gallery didn't mind because they were also selling my paintings. Word got around that this CEO was buying a lot of my work, and other people got the idea that maybe they should, too. That's what helped my business the most. There was a period of 6 years where I was making almost all of my income from painting. But up until 1998, for a predictable income, I still worked a few hours a week making frames. Cutting loose of the predictable world entirely was something I was reluctant to do, and only did so at the urging of my wife.

I usually exhibit at between four and six galleries at any one time. I gravitated toward places where I had constant exposure because that's the best way to be seen. I've also been in juried and invitational shows. Some of the significant shows were at the Harvard Club and at the Attleboro Museum. I try to be in the studio from 9 to 5 on weekdays. I generally produce at least one painting a week. But in my 40s, when I was going like gangbusters, I made 100 paintings a year. I'm not quite as vigorous as I was then.

This is a high wire act without a net and no set time limits. It's an exciting way to make a living.

**What are the most important skills and/or qualities for someone in your profession?**
Persistence is first. You really have to have a lot of desire and a need to do it. A secondary thing is you need to be a reasonable diplomat, good at dealing with patrons and galleries. It's important to pick galleries where people are actually your friends.

**What do you wish you had known going into this profession?**
The ability to do the art is ultimately what's important. It's not necessarily the degree.

Also, most artists get burned once or twice, where the painting will get sold by a gallery and the check never comes to you. That happened to me twice. There's always a certain element of risk-taking on a gallery because there are fly-by-night galleries out there. Young artists are most likely to be victimized. Since then, I tend to scout out the gallery, and if I know any of the artists, I'll talk to them about their experience there.

**Are there many job opportunities in your profession? In what specific areas?**
As a painter, you really are starting every day from scratch—to a certain extent. If you're an illustrator, certainly there are jobs available. But commercial artists tend to work for someone else, like advertising agencies, newspapers, or magazines.

**How do you see your profession changing in the next 5 years? How will technology impact that change, and what skills will be required?**
Technology already has changed art quite a bit already. My daughter is an artist who is embarking on her career. A lot of people are using computers as drafting aids. I haven't done that, but she does rather frequently. More computer literacy will be required for that than I possess.

There probably will be more online sales. I've sold a few things to people who have bought my paintings before, so they know what they are getting. But I've never sold a big painting online to anyone who hadn't bought one face-to-face. Generally online sales are small paintings, on the low end of prices.

The business side is also changing from the traditional gallery exhibiting. Typically, a gallery selects the artists it wants to exhibit and shares a percentage of the art sales. There are some pay-to-play galleries now where artists pay the gallery to let the artists exhibit. This is something that started recently, and I'm sad to see it because it doesn't mean the art is good. It just means the artist can afford to pay for exposure.

**What do you enjoy most about your job? What do you enjoy least about your job?**
Independence is both the blessing and the curse of it. It's a blessing because I like doing what I do. It's a curse because I don't always know what I should do. Do you need another gallery to exhibit my work? Do you need more outlets? Where should you go? What towns would be good?

The thing that's hardest about it is it's an uncertain trade. If there's a severe economic downturn, one of the first things people stop buying is paintings. I've had a year where I sold more than 100 paintings and a year where I sold 20.

**Can you suggest a valuable “”try this" for students considering a career in your profession?**
Find other painters that are perhaps more schooled than you are and tag along with them if you can. Find someone who teaches and does demonstrations. You don't need to ape their style but it's instructive to see how others deal with creative issues. You can see that there is this process, and that can spark something in you. It's like becoming a better chess player: you want to play with someone better than you are if you can.

# Delivery Truck Driver/ Driver/Sales Worker

## Snapshot

**Career Cluster(s):** Business, Management & Administration; Transportation, Distribution & Logistics

**Interests:** Driving; delivery

**Earnings (Yearly Average):** $32,020

**Employment & Outlook:** Faster Than Average Growth Expected

## OVERVIEW

### Sphere of Work

Delivery truck drivers and driver/sales workers pick up, transport, and drop off packages and small shipments within a local region or urban area. They drive trucks weighing less than 26,001 pounds total for vehicle, passengers, and cargo. Delivery truck drivers usually transport merchandise from a distribution center to businesses and households.

### Work Environment

A delivery worker with boxes ready to be sent out. Photo via iStock.com/PIKSEL [Used under license.]

Delivery drivers spend much of their day on the road, driving between pickup and dropoff locations. Most drivers work full-time, and some work more than 40 hours per week. Those who have regular routes sometimes must begin work exceedingly early in the morning or work late at night. For example, a driver who delivers bread to a deli every day must arrive before the deli opens. Drivers often work weekends and holidays, and their schedules may vary. Drivers must operate in varying weather conditions.

### Profile

**Interests:** Things, People, Data
**Working Conditions:** Both Inside and Outside
**Physical Strength:** Medium Work, Heavy Work
**Education Needs:** On-the-Job Training, High School Diploma
**Licensure/Certification:** Driver's License
**Opportunities for Experience:** Apprenticeship, Part-Time Work
**Interest Score:** RE

## Occupation Interest

Individuals attracted to delivery services prefer to be on the go most of the time and enjoy the challenge of delivering their cargo to different locations, usually within the same city or surrounding area. They are confident drivers with the stamina to perform their jobs at odd hours and in all types of weather. They take satisfaction from delivering goods safely and on time. Drivers who also engage in sales have strong people skills and enjoy interacting with others. Most drivers need to be well-organized to manage the necessary paperwork that comes with the job.

## A Day in the Life—Duties and Responsibilities

Most drivers generally receive instructions to go to a delivery location at a particular time, and it is up to them to determine the best route. Other drivers have a regular daily or weekly delivery schedule. All drivers must understand an area's street grid and know which roads allow trucks and which do not.

Driver/sales workers are delivery drivers who also have sales responsibilities. They recommend products to businesses and solicit new customers. These drivers may have a regular delivery route and may be responsible for adding clients who are located along their route. For example, they may make regular deliveries to a hardware store and encourage the store's manager to offer a new product.

Some driver/sales workers use their own vehicles to deliver goods to customers, such as takeout food, and accept payment for those goods. Freelance or independent driver/sales workers may use smartphone apps to find specific delivery jobs.

### Duties and Responsibilities

- Loading and unloading cargo
- Communicating with customers to determine pickup and delivery needs
- Reporting incidents on the road to a dispatcher
- Following applicable traffic laws
- Reporting mechanical problems to the appropriate personnel
- Keeping their truck and associated equipment clean and in working order
- Accepting payments for delivery
- Handling paperwork, such as receipts or delivery confirmation notices

Light truck drivers, often called pickup and delivery or P&D drivers, are the most common type of delivery driver. They drive small trucks or vans from distribution centers to delivery locations. Drivers make deliveries based on a set schedule. Some drivers stop at the distribution center once only, in the morning, and make many stops throughout the day. Others make multiple trips between the distribution center and delivery locations. Some drivers make deliveries from a retail location to customers.

## WORK ENVIRONMENT

### Immediate Physical Environment

Delivery truck drivers and driver/sales workers have physically demanding jobs. When loading and unloading cargo, drivers do a lot of lifting, carrying, and walking. Driving in congested traffic or adhering to strict delivery timelines can also be stressful.

Light truck drivers have one of the highest rates of injuries and illnesses of all occupations. Injuries can result from workers lifting and moving heavy objects, as well as from automobile accidents.

### Human Environment

Drivers routinely interact with personnel at the warehouse from which their goods originate, as well as clients on the delivery end. Driver/sales workers must also recommend products to the businesses they serve and try to add new clients to their roster.

### Technological Environment

Delivery drivers must be confident and knowledgeable behind the wheel. An understanding of truck mechanics, even rudimentary, can be an asset if their vehicle encounters problems on the road. Self-employed drivers who use smartphone apps to facilitate their services must be able to use mobile technology to their advantage to maximize profits. Familiarity with Global Positioning System (GPS) and navigation software is also an asset. Some drivers may also use spreadsheets or logistics software to organize their deliveries and plan routes.

## EDUCATION, TRAINING, AND ADVANCEMENT

### High School/Secondary

Delivery truck drivers and driver/sales workers typically need a high school diploma or equivalent to enter these occupations. However, some opportunities exist for those without a high school diploma. Workers undergo 1 month or less of on-the-job training. They must have a driver's license from the state in which they work and have a clean driving record.

**Suggested High School Subjects**

- Algebra
- Biology
- Chemistry
- Civics
- Economics
- English
- Entrepreneurship
- Geometry
- History
- Physics
- Pre-Calculus
- Statistics
- Trigonometry

**Related Career Pathways/Majors**

*Business, Management & Administration Career Cluster*

- General Management Pathway

*Transportation, Distribution & Logistics Career Cluster*

- Logistics Planning & Management Services Pathway
- Sales & Service Pathway
- Transportation Operations Pathway
- Warehousing & Distribution Center Operations Pathway

#### Transferable Skills and Abilities

**Customer-service Skills**

- Interacting with customers and making a good impression to ensure repeat business

**Hand-eye Coordination**

- Observing surroundings at all times while operating a vehicle

**Math Skills**

- Counting cash and making change quickly and accurately when handling payments

**Patience**

- Remaining calm and composed when driving through heavy traffic congestion

**Sales Skills**

- Persuading customers to purchase new or different products

**Visual Ability**

- Delivery truck drivers and driver/sales workers must be able to pass a state vision test

### Adult Job Seekers

Some delivery drivers begin as package loaders at warehouse facilities, especially if the driver works for a large company.

## Fast Fact

**Food delivery is big business, accelerated by the pandemic. Delivery sales could rise to $365 billion worldwide by 2030, up from $35 billion in 2018.**
Source: upserve.com.

Food delivery services are on the rise. Photo via iStock.com/RichLegg. [Used under license.]

### Professional Certification and Licensure

All delivery drivers need a driver's license.

### Additional Requirements

Companies train new delivery truck drivers and driver/sales workers on the job. This may include training from a driver-mentor who rides along with a new employee to make sure that the driver is able to operate a truck safely on crowded streets.

New-driver training also covers company policies about package dropoffs and returns, taking payment, and what to do with damaged goods.

Driver/sales workers must learn detailed information about the products they offer. Their company also may teach them proper sales techniques, such as how to approach new customers.

## EARNINGS AND ADVANCEMENT

Earnings depend on location, the nature of the goods being delivered, whether the driver is self-employed, and whether he or she also engages in sales activities.

Median annual earnings of driver/sales workers were $25,860 in 2019. The lowest 10 percent earned less than $18,060, and the highest 10 percent earned more than $48,970.

Median annual earnings of light truck drivers were $34,730 in 2019. The lowest 10 percent earned less than $21,060, and the highest 10 percent earned more than $65,400.

Delivery truck drivers may receive paid vacations, holidays, and sick days; insurance; and retirement benefits. These are usually paid by an employer if the driver is not self-employed. Drivers may also be able to expense the costs of being on the road, such as fuel and maintenance.

## EMPLOYMENT AND OUTLOOK

Delivery truck drivers and driver/sales workers held 1,506,000 jobs in 2019. Eight percent were self-employed. Employment is expected to grow faster than average for all occupations through the year 2029, at a rate of 8 percent, varying by occupation.

Continued growth of e-commerce should increase demand for package delivery services, especially for the large and regional shipping companies. More light truck drivers will be needed to fulfill the growing number of e-commerce transactions.

Self-employed or independent contractors, who sign up with smartphone-based food delivery companies, may be needed to deliver food from grocery stores and from restaurants that previously provided only takeout services. In addition, robotic driverless vehicles may replace some workers in food delivery.

About 163,100 openings for delivery truck drivers and driver/sales workers are projected each year, on average, over the decade. Many of those openings are expected to result from the need to replace workers who transfer to different occupations or exit the labor force, such as to retire.

Job applicants with experience and a clean driving record should have the best job prospects.

### Related Occupations

- Hand Laborer/Material Mover
- Heavy/Tractor-trailer Truck Driver
- Material Recording Clerk
- Passenger Vehicle Driver
- Postal Service Worker
- Railroad Worker
- Water Transportation Worker

## MORE INFORMATION

**American Drivers Association**
P.O. Box 178
Winona, TX 75792
800.944.4948
americandriversassociation@gmail.com
americandriversassociation.com

**American Trucking Associations (ATA)**
950 North Glebe Road, Suite 210
Arlington, VA 22203-4181
atamembership@trucking.org
www.trucking.org

**Association for Delivery Drivers (A4DD)**
P.O. Box 123
Gaylordsville, CT 06755
877.264.2433
a4ddteam@a4dd.org
www.a4dd.org

**Express Carriers Association (ECA)**
9532 Liberia Avenue, Suite 752
Manassas, VA 20110
703.361.1058
eca@expresscarriers.org
www.ecadeliveryindustry.org

**Federal Motor Carrier Safety Administration (FMCSA)**
United States Department of Transportation
1200 New Jersey Avenue SE
Washington, DC 20590
800.832.5660
cdlcompliance@dot.gov
www.fmcsa.dot.gov

**Logistics & Transportation Association of North America (LTNA)**
P.O. Box 426
Union, WA 98592
360.898.3344
www.ltna.org

**National Ground Delivery Association (NGDA)**
833.347.6863
info@grounddelivery.org
www.grounddelivery.org

**National Home Delivery Association (NHDA)**
P.O. Box 4141
Falls Church, VA 22044
703.931.6324
blecos@lecosandassociates.com
www.nationalhomedeliveryassociation.com

**National Motorists Association (NMA)**
1001 Arboretum Drive, Suite 120
Waunakee, WI 53597
nma@motorists.org
www.motorists.org

**NorthAmerican Transportation Association (NTA)**
9120 Double Diamond Parkway, Suite 346
Reno, NV 89521-4842
800.805.0040
www.ntassoc.com

**Women In Trucking Association (WIT)**
P.O. Box 400
Plover, WI 54467-0400
888.464.9482
WIT@womenintrucking.org

---

*Stuart Paterson*

# Electrical/ Electronics Engineer

## Snapshot

**Career Cluster(s):** Business, Management & Administration; Science, Technology, Engineering & Mathematics

**Interests:** Electronics; electrical systems; technology; design; creativity

**Earnings (Yearly Average):** $101,250

**Employment & Outlook:** As Fast As Average Growth Expected

## OVERVIEW

### Sphere of Work

Electrical engineers design, develop, test, and supervise the manufacture of electrical equipment, such as electric motors, radar and navigation systems, communications systems, or power generation equipment. Electrical engineers also design the electrical systems of automobiles and aircraft.

Electronics engineers design and develop electronic equipment, including broadcast and communications systems, such as portable music players and Global Positioning System (GPS) devices. Many also work in areas closely related to computer hardware.

A team of engineers at work. Photo via iStock.com/gorodenkoff [Used under license.]

### Work Environment

Electrical and electronics engineers typically work in offices of various sizes, although travel may be necessary to visit sites where their equipment is being installed and operated.

**Profile**

**Interests:** Things, Data
**Working Conditions:** Both Inside and Outside
**Education Needs:** Bachelor's Degree
**Licensure/Certification:** Usually Not Required
**Opportunities for Experience:** Internship, Co-op
**Interest Score:** IR

### Occupation Interest

Electrical and electronics engineers are creative, math- and science-oriented individuals who want to apply their knowledge to the creation of new electrical and electronic systems, components, and equipment. Applications in this field are wide-ranging, and many engineers can transition into entrepreneurial activities when they identify areas they can improve upon or in which they can innovate.

**Duties and Responsibilities**

**Electrical Engineer**

- Designing new ways to use electrical power to develop or improve products
- Performing detailed calculations to develop manufacturing, construction, and installation standards and specifications
- Directing the manufacture, installation, and testing of electrical equipment to ensure that products meet specifications and codes
- Investigating complaints from customers or the public, evaluating problems, and recommending solutions
- Working with project managers on production efforts to ensure that projects are completed satisfactorily, on time, and within budget

### A Day in the Life—Duties and Responsibilities

The work of electrical engineers and electronics engineers is often similar. Both use engineering and design software and equipment to do engineering tasks. Both types of engineers also must work with other engineers to discuss existing products and possibilities for engineering projects.

Electronics engineers who work for the federal government research, develop, and evaluate electronic devices used in a variety of areas, such as aviation, computing, transportation, and manufacturing. They work on federal electronic devices and systems, including satellites, flight systems, radar and sonar systems, and communications systems.

## WORK ENVIRONMENT

### Immediate Physical Environment

Electrical and electronics engineers generally work indoors in offices. However, they may visit sites to observe a problem or a piece of complex equipment. Most electrical and electronics engineers work full-time.

### Human Environment

Electrical and electronics engineers may conduct solitary office and laboratory work, but team efforts are common, and engineers must be prepared to work with manufacturers, visit sites, interact with customers and the public, and troubleshoot issues. They also must report to superiors unless their business is self-owned. Entrepreneurial engineers are responsible for their own staffing, and, therefore, must handle all employment matters, including conflicts. They will likely also need to interact with financial backers to get their products or businesses off the ground.

### Duties and Responsibilities

**Electronics Engineer**

- Designing electronic components, software, products, or systems for commercial, industrial, medical, military, or scientific applications
- Analyzing customer needs and determining the requirements, capacity, and cost for developing an electrical system plan
- Developing maintenance and testing procedures for electronic components and equipment
- Evaluating systems and recommending design modifications or equipment repair
- Inspecting electronic equipment, instruments, and systems to make sure they meet safety standards and applicable regulations
- Planning and developing applications and modifications for electronic properties used in parts and systems to improve technical performance

### Technological Environment

By their nature, electrical and electronics engineers must be intimately familiar with the equipment necessary to carry out their work and must stay apprised of new developments in their field. Computer-aided design (CAD) software is commonly used, as is analytical or scientific software, development environment software, and object- or component-oriented development software. Those who own their own businesses must also be familiar with standard applications such as accounting and payroll software and platforms.

## EDUCATION, TRAINING, AND ADVANCEMENT

### High School/Secondary

High school students interested in studying electrical or electronics engineering benefit from taking courses in physics and math, including algebra, trigonometry, and calculus. Courses in drafting are also helpful, because electrical and electronics engineers often are required to prepare technical drawings. During high school, students can attend engineering summer camps to see what these and other engineers do. Attending these camps can help students plan their coursework for the remainder of their time in high school. The Engineering Education Service Center (EESC) has a directory of engineering summer camps.

### Suggested High School Subjects

- Algebra
- Biology
- Chemistry
- Civics
- Computer Science
- Drafting
- Earth or Environmental Science
- Economics
- English
- Entrepreneurship
- Geometry
- History
- Physics
- Pre-Calculus
- Psychology
- Statistics
- Trigonometry

### Related Career Pathways/Majors

*Business, Management & Administration Career Cluster*

- General Management Pathway

*Science, Technology, Engineering & Mathematics Career Cluster*

- Engineering & Technology Pathway
- Science & Mathematics Pathway

### Transferable Skills and Abilities

**Concentration**

- Designing and developing complex electrical systems and electronic components and products
- Keeping track of multiple design elements and technical characteristics when performing these tasks

**Initiative**

- Applying knowledge to new tasks in every project undertaken
- Engaging in continuing education to keep up with changes in technology

**Interpersonal Skills**

- Working with others during the manufacturing process to ensure that plans are implemented correctly
- Monitoring technicians and devising remedies to problems as they arise

**Math Skills**

- Using the principles of calculus and other advanced math to analyze, design, and troubleshoot equipment

**Speaking Skills**

- Working closely with other engineers and technicians
- Explaining designs and reasoning clearly and relaying instructions during product development and production
- Explaining complex issues to customers who have little or no technical expertise

**Writing Skills**

- Developing technical publications related to equipment they develop, including maintenance manuals, operation manuals, parts lists, product proposals, and design methods documents

## Postsecondary

To enter the occupation, prospective electrical and electronics engineers need a bachelor's degree in electrical engineering, electronics engineering, electrical engineering technology, or a related engineering field. Programs include classroom, laboratory, and field studies. Courses include digital systems design, differential equations, and electrical circuit theory. Programs in electrical engineering, electronics engineering, or electrical engineering technology should be accredited by the Accreditation Board for Engineering and Technology, Inc. (ABET).

## Famous First

**We know about Benjamin Franklin flying his kite to discover electricity. But did you know he also invented bifocals?**
Source: nbcnews.com

Portrait of Benjamin Franklin (1783), by Joseph Siffred Duplessis (1725-1802), National Portrait Gallery, Smithsonian Institution, via Wikimedia Commons.

Some colleges and universities offer cooperative programs in which students gain practical experience while completing their education. Cooperative programs combine classroom study with practical work. Internships provide similar experience and are growing in number.

At some universities, students can enroll in a 5-year program that leads to both a bachelor's degree and a master's degree. A graduate degree allows an engineer to work as an instructor at some universities, or in research and development.

**Related College Majors**

- Agricultural Business & Management
- Agricultural Production Workers & Managers
- Agricultural Supplies Retailing & Wholesaling
- Farm & Ranch Management
- Horticulture Science
- Horticulture Services Operations & Management
- International Agriculture
- Plant Sciences

## Professional Certification and Licensure

Licensure is not required for entry-level positions as electrical and electronics engineers. A Professional Engineering (PE) license, which allows for higher levels of leadership and independence, can be acquired later in one's career. Licensed engineers are called professional engineers (PEs). A PE can oversee the work of other engineers, sign off on projects, and provide services directly to the public. State licensure generally requires:

- A degree from an ABET-accredited engineering program
- A passing score on the Fundamentals of Engineering (FE) exam
- Relevant work experience, typically at least 4 years
- A passing score on the Professional Engineering (PE) exam

The initial FE exam can be taken after earning a bachelor's degree. Engineers who pass this exam commonly are called engineers in training (EITs) or engineer interns (EIs). After meeting work experience requirements, EITs and EIs can take the second exam, called the Principles and Practice of Engineering (PE).

Each state issues its own licenses. Most states recognize licensure from other states if the licensing state's requirements meet or exceed their own licensure requirements. Several states require continuing education for engineers to keep their licenses.

## EARNINGS AND ADVANCEMENT

Earnings depend on industry, experience, and project scope and scale. Median annual earnings of electrical engineers were $98,530 in 2019. The lowest 10 percent earned less than $63,020, and the highest 10 percent earned more than $155,880. Median annual earnings of electrical engineers were $105,570 in 2019. The lowest 10 percent earned less than $66,620, and the highest 10 percent earned more than $164,210.

Electrical and electronics engineers may receive paid vacations, holidays, and sick days; life and health insurance; and retirement benefits. These are usually paid by an employer if the business is not self-owned. Engineers who are required to travel may be able to recoup these expenses by their employer.

Electrical and electronic engineers may advance to supervisory positions in which they lead a team of engineers and technicians. Some may move to management positions, working as engineering or program managers. Preparation for managerial positions usually requires working under the guidance of a more experienced engineer.

For sales work, an engineering background enables engineers to discuss a product's technical aspects and assist in product planning and use.

## EMPLOYMENT AND OUTLOOK

Electrical and electronic engineers held 328,100 jobs in 2019. Employment is expected to grow as fast as average for all occupations through the year 2029, at a rate of 3 percent. Employment growth is expected to be tempered by slow growth or decline in some industries, such as manufacturing and utilities.

Job growth for electrical and electronics engineers is projected to occur largely in professional, scientific, and technical services firms, as more companies are expected to tap the expertise of engineers for projects involving electronic devices and systems. These engineers also will be needed to develop sophisticated consumer electronics.

The rapid pace of technological innovation will create some demand for electrical and electronics engineers in research and development, an area in which engineering expertise will be needed to design distribution systems related to new technologies. These engineers will play key roles in new developments with solar arrays, semiconductors, and communications technologies.

### Related Occupations

- Aerospace Engineer
- Architectural/Engineering Manager
- Bioengineer/Biomedical Engineer
- Computer Hardware Engineer
- Electrical/Electronics Engineering Technician
- Electrical/Electronics Installer/Repairer
- Electrician
- Electro-mechanical Technician
- Network/Computer Systems Administrator
- Sales Engineer

## MORE INFORMATION

**Accreditation Board for Engineering and Technology, Inc. (ABET)**
415 North Charles Street
Baltimore, MD 21201
410.347.7700
www.abet.org

**American Association of Engineering Societies (AAES)**
1801 Alexander Bell Drive
Reston, VA 20191
202.296.2237
orders@aaes.org
www.aaes.org

**American Society for Engineering Education (ASEE)**
1818 N Street NW, Suite 600
Washington, DC 20036
202.331.3500
www.asee.org

**Engineering Education Service Center (EESC)**
1411 Old Hardman Btms Road
Clarkesville, GA 30523
706.499.5011
www.engineeringedu.com

**International Society of Automation (ISA)**
67 T.W. Alexander Drive
Research Triangle Park, NC 27709
919.549.8411
www.isa.org

**National Association of Power Engineers (NAPE)**
1 Springfield Street, Suite 1
Chicopee, MA 01013
413.592.9273
www.powerengineers.com

**National Council of Examiners for Engineering and Surveying (NCEES)**
200 Verdae Boulevard
Greenville, SC 29607
800.250.3196
ncees.org

**National Society of Professional Engineers (NSPE)**
1420 King Street
Alexandria, VA 22314
888.285.6773
www.nspe.org

**Technology Student Association (TSA)**
1904 Association Drive
Reston, VA 20191-1540
703.860.9000
tsaweb.org

---

*Stuart Paterson*

# *Conversation With...*
# THOMAS SLOWE

Entrepreneur in Residence
Buffalo University, Buffalo, NY
Entrepreneur, 33 years

**What was your individual career path in terms of education/training, entry-level job, or other significant opportunity?**

Both of my parents were entrepreneurs, so I had a lot of guidance in terms of understanding the basic questions involved: what can you make, and how do you sell it? How do you identify what is going to be something people are interested in obtaining, what are they actually going to cough up money for, how much, and how much time, energy, and what materials do you need to produce that thing?

I started my first company when I was fourteen, and my family lived in Rochester, New York. At that time, neckties were conservative in style. I decided I wanted to make ties. My mom had been running a quilt-making business and had the sewing machines and fabric. My dad was involved in the arts community, and they had art shows. I used all sorts of flashy eighties and nineties colors and sold my completely wild ties at shows and made several thousand dollars.

I'm from a family of engineers and went on to earn my BS in electrical engineering and computer science from Rutgers University, then went straight to Massachusetts Institute of Technology and earned an MS in media arts and sciences from their Media Lab. This was during the dotcom boom of 1996-1998.

At Rutgers, I worked on making automated recognition systems to find things in video and images, and I graduated with published work. I also did a lot of artwork during school. I carried that research to MIT, where the Media Lab is all about the integration of art and science.

After graduating, I moved to Stockholm, Sweden, for 2 years to work for Ericsson Telecom, a company that had been a Media Lab sponsor. I enjoyed my time there and set up a lab for them but, overall, that experience validated that big companies were not for me.

I returned and got a job at a startup company called ObjectVideo in Reston, Virginia, outside Washington, DC. We worked with the intelligence community, and I was a senior scientist there for several years, although during this time I realized that I was not only interested in engineering. After a while I decided to start my own company and moved back to my hometown of Buffalo.

I've been involved with a number of startup companies, but Nervve was the biggest one that was cleanly founded by me. It centered on my experience working with the US intelligence community. I saw that they have and continue to acquire huge volumes of video and imagery. The published data point we had at the time showed that less than 2 percent of that video was ever seen by a human. The use of video for defense and intelligence was largely relegated to understanding what happened after the bomb already had gone off.

We essentially invented the core algorithm that made it possible to scan—very, very efficiently—a huge volume of video 1000 times faster than the competing technology at the time. We got investment from the intelligence community alongside a bunch of other people. We worked with foreign and domestic spy agencies, and then branched into sports media and worked with many major league teams. We were able to use the technology to measure the output of branding in an entire season's worth of games and combine that with viewership data to put a value on in-screen advertising. The company was sold in 2017.

I've always got five or six side hustles. I've built furniture. I've done designs for construction projects. I've got a few entrepreneurial ventures now with high hopes things will be solidified over the next 3 months. I'm also an Entrepreneur-in-Residence at Buffalo University and work with 10 to 12 companies—or embryonic ideas for companies—at any one time.

**What are the most important skills and/or qualities for someone in your profession?**
Risk tolerance, self-generated motivation, broad interests, and a willingness to constantly acquire new skills. You need an ability to withdraw from the situation from time to time to look at the big picture so you can validate whether what you're doing or who you are collaborating with makes sense. You need to be willing to try new things.

**What do you wish you had known going into this profession?**
I wish I had known to much more strictly judge individuals I do business with. As the stakes get higher, that tends to attract a higher percentage of bad players. My perceptions going in have been far more optimistic than they should have been because a lot of people are pretty Machiavellian.

**Are there many job opportunities in your profession? In what specific areas?**
There are an infinite number of job opportunities. It's all about you creating it and taking responsibility for it.

**How do you see your profession changing in the next 5 years? How will technology impact that change, and what skills will be required?**
I think that integration between traditionally siloed knowledge spaces is going to accelerate significantly. When I was a kid, lawyers did their thing, accountants did theirs. Now all that has changed. If you're a super geek who wants to go to engineering school, stretch yourself and do different things. Learn to cook. Take a class in fashion design.

**What do you like most about your job? What do you like least about your job?**

I love the feeling you get when you sell something you spent time working on. I love working with smart, motivated people. I really detest working with people who are not motivated and don't finish their work, or their work is of poor quality.

**Can you suggest a "try this" for a student who may be considering a career in your field?**

I would advise coming up with an idea and then figuring out what you can make or produce. That really is the crux of it. If you can get an internship or work with a small company, that's going to help you.

# Farmer/Rancher/ Agricultural Manager

**Snapshot**

**Career Cluster(s):** Agriculture, Food & Natural Resources; Business, Management & Administration

**Interests:** Agriculture; business practices; being outside; working independently

**Earnings (Yearly Average):** $71,160

**Employment & Outlook:** Decline Expected

## OVERVIEW

### Sphere of Work

Farmers, ranchers, and other agricultural managers grow food for personal consumption and for wholesale and retail consumers. Farmers and farm managers oversee agricultural production and financial operations at farms, nurseries, ranches, and greenhouses. Farmers, ranchers, and other agricultural managers grow crops and tend to livestock, poultry, or aquatic animals. Although specific tasks vary by type of agricultural work, all farmers and farm managers are responsible for ensuring the care of crops and animals from conception to market. Farmers often perform the hands-on labor of planting, cultivating, operating farm machinery, harvesting crops and raising animals. They also engage in the business side of the operation and may have a personal stake in the opera-

Dairy farmers must ensure the proper care of milk cows. Photo via iStock.com/torwai. [Used under license.]

tion's finances, such as having inherited it as a family business, or having built it from the ground up. As such, the manager may be involved in the marketing and selling of crops and animals, as well as hiring, training, and supervising farm staff to complete daily tasks.

**Profile**

**Interests:** Data, People, Things, Animals
**Working Conditions:** Both Inside and Outside
**Physical Strength:** Medium Work, Heavy Work
**Education Needs:** On-the-Job Training, High School Diploma with Technical Education, Junior/Technical/Community College, Apprenticeship, Bachelor's Degree
**Licensure/Certification:** Usually Not Required
**Opportunities for Experience:** Internship, Apprenticeship, Volunteer Work, Part-Time Work
**Interest Score:** ERC

## Work Environment

Farmers, ranchers, and other agricultural managers work in farms, nurseries, ranches, and greenhouses that they own or lease. Farmers and farm managers do not have set work hours and instead must work until tasks are complete. Crop farm work is seasonal. During nongrowing seasons, crop farmers and farm managers focus on repairing farm machinery, planning next year's crops, and marketing and selling efforts. They also interact with financial professionals who may be involved in the operation's backing, such as lenders or investment managers, and landholders if the land is leased. Animal farmers and farm managers work steadily throughout the year to care for their livestock, poultry, and aquatic animals.

## Occupation Interest

Individuals attracted to the farming profession tend to be physically strong and detail-oriented people. Successful farmers and farm managers exhibit stamina, resilience, organizational abilities, integrity and ethics, independence, and effective time management. Business acumen and familiarity with computer technology is advantageous. Farmers and farm managers should enjoy physical labor and have a strong background in agriculture and business. Entrepreneurial farmers must have a desire to steadily grow their business and turn a profit—such farms may become legacies and be passed down to future generations.

## A Day in the Life—Duties and Responsibilities

Farmers and farm managers perform different daily occupational duties and responsibilities depending on their specialization and work environment. They may specialize in the production of crops, beef, poultry, pork, dairy, or aquaculture.

On crop farms, farmers and farm managers oversee activities related to the planting, tending, and harvesting of crops. These tasks may include preparing soil and managing its nutrient levels, using natural or chemical methods to eliminate

## Duties and Responsibilities

- Supervising all steps of crop production or ranging, including planting, fertilizing, harvesting, and herding
- Making decisions about crops or livestock by evaluating factors such as market conditions, disease, soil conditions, and the availability of federal programs
- Choosing and buying supplies, such as seed, fertilizer, and farm machinery
- Maintaining farming equipment
- Maintaining farm facilities, such as water pipes, fences, and animal shelters
- Serving as the sales agent for crops, livestock, and dairy products
- Recording financial, tax, production, and employee information

pests, irrigating and draining fields, weather forecasting, and storing fuels and chemicals. Crop farmers and farm managers promote and sell crops to distributors and food-processing companies, retail customers in farmers markets or farm stands, or shareholders in a Community Supported Agriculture (CSA) program.

Animal farmers and farm managers oversee meat production operations. They raise beef cattle, chickens, turkeys, ducks, game birds, goats, or pigs. Animal farmers and farm managers must ensure proper breeding and birthing and feeding, housing, transportation, and slaughtering. Those who work with beef cattle and pigs medicate and vaccinate the animals as needed. On poultry farms, they also manage the hatchery, establish egg or meat-bird production effort, adjust the lighting in poultry buildings to promote molting or egg laying, and match stock size to seasonal demand. All animal farmers and farm managers are responsible for promoting and selling meat products.

Dairy farmers and farm managers direct tasks related to the production, collection, and sale of milk. They must ensure the proper care for milk cows. These farmers and farm managers oversee the establishment of a feed storage system for corn silage, alfalfa, hay, cottonseed, and soybeans. They also supervise the construction and maintenance of a milking parlor, a milking and milk storage system, and a manure management system. Dairy farmers and farm managers promote, transport, and sell dairy products.

Aquaculture farmers and farm managers oversee aquaculture production tasks. They or their staff stock ponds or floating nets with eggs, shellfish, or juvenile fish, feed fish stock, and protect fish stock from predators and contamination. Like their meat and dairy counterparts, these farmers and farm managers are responsible for the promotion and sale of their products.

In addition, all farmers and farm managers are responsible for purchasing supplies, maintaining farm machinery, ensuring the cleanliness of farm facilities, and educating themselves about government regulations and business trends affecting their industry. Recordkeeping abilities are paramount, to ensure smooth day-to-day business operations.

## OCCUPATION SPECIALTIES

**Farm General Manager**
Farm General Managers operate farms for corporations, cooperatives, or other owners.

**Fish Farmers**
Fish Farmers spawn and raise fish for commercial purposes.

**Fur Farmer**
Fur Farmers feed and raise mink, fox, chinchilla, rabbits, and other fur-bearing animals for sale on the fur market.

**Horse Trainer**
Horse Trainers train horses for riding or harness.

**Livestock Rancher**
Livestock Ranchers breed and raise livestock such as beef cattle, dairy cattle, goats, horses, sheep, and swine to sell meat, dairy products, wool, and hair.

**Nursery Manager**
Nursery Managers supervise plant nurseries that produce plants for sale to wholesale or retail customers.

**Organic Farmer/Farm Manager**
Organic Farmers/Farm Managers grow crops, control pests, and maintain soil health without the use, or the limited use, of synthetic fertilizers and pesticides.

**Poultry Farmer**
Poultry Farmers raise chickens, turkeys, or other fowl for meat or egg production.

**Shellfish Grower**
Shellfish Growers cultivate and harvest beds of shellfish, such as clams and oysters.

**Tree-Fruit-and-Nut Crop Farmers**
Tree-Fruit-And-Nut Crop Farmers plant and cultivate fruit producing trees.

**Vegetable Farmers**
Vegetable Farmers plan and plant vegetables according to weather, type of soil, and size and location of the farm.

## WORK ENVIRONMENT

### Immediate Physical Environment

Farmers and farm managers work in farms, nurseries, ranches, and greenhouses. Farming tends to be very physical and requires extensive hard labor, walking, lifting, and bending. Farmers and farm managers are at high risk for back strain, pesticide exposure, and machine accidents.

### Human Environment

Farms, nurseries, ranches, and greenhouses tend to be remotely located and isolated. However, farmers and farm managers interact with farm workers, families, customers, landholders, bankers, veterinarians, and government inspectors. The amount of human interaction often depends on the scale and business model of the farm operation. If the farm is not self-owned, farm managers typically report to a farmer or corporation.

### Technological Environment

In the course of their work, farmers and farm managers use farm machinery and equipment such as animal feeders, hay balers, mowers, trucks, irrigation systems, tractors, chain saws, and milking machines. In addition, farmers and farm managers use computers, Internet communication tools, accounting and farm management software, and spreadsheets to assist them with the important business tasks of farming.

## EDUCATION, TRAINING, AND ADVANCEMENT

### High School/Secondary

High school-level study of mathematics, agricultural science, biology, chemistry, and business can provide a strong foundation for work as a farmer or college-level study in the field. High school students interested in this career path may benefit from internships, apprenticeships, or part-time work with local farms that expose them to the diversity and challenges of farming responsibilities. Work experience is required to reach the managerial level.

**Suggested High School Subjects**

- Algebra
- Biology
- Chemistry

- Civics
- Earth or Environmental Science
- Economics
- English
- Entrepreneurship
- Geometry
- History
- Physics
- Pre-Calculus
- Psychology
- Statistics
- Trigonometry

**Transferable Skills and Abilities**

**Analytical Skills**
- Monitoring and assessing the quality of land or livestock

**Critical-thinking Skills**
- Determining how to improve harvest and livestock while reacting to conditions that may affect short- or long-term plans

**Initiative**
- Being self-motivated in order to maximize crop or livestock production

**Interpersonal Skills**
- Supervising laborers and other workers

**Mechanical Skills**
- Operating complex machinery and occasionally performing routine maintenance

**Physical Stamina**
- Physically strenuous, repetitive tasks, such as bending, stooping, and lifting

**Related Career Pathways/Majors**

*Agriculture, Food & Natural Resources Career Cluster*
- Agribusiness Systems Pathway
- Animal Systems Pathway
- Natural Resources Systems Pathway
- Plant Systems Pathway
- Power, Structural & Technical Systems Pathway

*Business, Management & Administration Career Cluster*
- General Management Pathway

## Postsecondary

Although a postsecondary degree is not strictly necessary for farm work, aspiring farmers or farm managers should pursue the associate degree or bachelor's degree in agriculture, farm management, agronomy, and dairy science. Formal postsecondary studies afford students a better understanding of the work and industry and provide greater opportunities for advancement. Postsecondary students can gain work experience and potential advantage in their future job searches by securing internships or part-time employment with local farms.

**Related College Majors**
- Agricultural Business & Management
- Agricultural Production Workers & Managers
- Agricultural Supplies Retailing & Wholesaling
- Farm & Ranch Management
- Horticulture Science

## Fast Fact

**Agriculture has its own entrepreneurial name: agripreneurship. This refers to businesses that support and manage ag-focused businesses from manufacturing and production to marketing.**
Source: 101entrepreneurship.org.

Sheep farming is one entrepreneurial path for animal lovers. Photo by fir002/Flagstaffotos, GFDL 1.2 <http://www.gnu.org/licenses/old-licenses/fdl-1.2.html>, via Wikimedia Commons.

- Horticulture Services Operations & Management
- International Agriculture
- Plant Sciences

### Adult Job Seekers

Adults seeking employment as farmers or farm managers should have, at a minimum, a high school diploma or associate degree. Some farm manager jobs require experience, on-the-job training, and a bachelor's or master's degree. Those seeking farm manager positions should educate themselves about the educational and professional requirements of their prospective employers.

Adult job seekers may benefit from joining professional associations to help with networking and job searching. Professional farming and agricultural associations, such as the American Farm Bureau Federation (AFBF), the American Society of Agronomy (ASA), and the American Society of Farm Managers & Rural Appraisers (ASFMRA), generally offer job-finding workshops and maintain lists and forums of available jobs.

Becoming an entrepreneurial farm owner without previous experience can be extremely challenging. It is highly recommended to gain firsthand experience by working in the industry, while attaining the relevant education and contacts through networking.

### Professional Certification and Licensure

Certification and licensure are not required for farmers but may be required of farm managers as a condition of employment, salary increase, or promotion. The Accredited Farm Manager (AFM) certification, offered by ASFMRA, is the leading option for voluntary farm manager certification. The AFM certification requires a minimum of 4 years of farm management experience, a 4-year college degree or equivalent, a sample farm management plan, the successful completion of coursework, and an exam.

### Additional Requirements

Successful farmers and farm managers will be knowledgeable about the profession's requirements, responsibilities, and opportunities. The US Environmental Protection Agency (EPA) requires farmers and farm workers to be trained in agricultural pesticide safe practices. Operating licenses for farm vehicles may be required for some types of agricultural work.

## EARNINGS AND ADVANCEMENT

Earnings depend on the size of the farm, type of crops grown or animals raised, the weather during the growing season, market prices, cost of materials, labor costs, and management ability. Median annual earnings of farmers and farm managers were $71,160 in 2019. The lowest 10 percent earned less than $37,530, and the highest 10 percent earned more than $132,760.

Farmers and farm managers may receive paid vacations, holidays, and sick days; life and health insurance; and retirement benefits. These are usually paid by an employer if the business is not self-owned. Farmers and farm managers may also receive free housing, transportation, and farm products.

## EMPLOYMENT AND OUTLOOK

Farmers and farm managers held 952,300 jobs in 2019. Sixty-seven percent were self-employed. Employment is expected to decline 6 percent through the year 2029, due to the long-term trend toward the consolidation of farms into fewer and larger farms. Most job openings will result from the need to replace farmers who retire or leave the occupation for economic or other reasons.

### Related Occupations

- Agricultural Engineer
- Agricultural/Food Science Technician
- Agricultural/Food Scientist
- Agricultural Worker
- Animal Care/Service Worker

- Construction Equipment Operator
- Grounds Maintenance Worker
- Purchasing Manager/Buyer/Purchasing Agent

## MORE INFORMATION

**Alternative Farming Systems Information Center (AFSIC)**
National Agricultural Library
10301 Baltimore Avenue, Room 132
Beltsville, MD 20705
301.504.6559
www.nal.usda.gov/afsic

**American Farm Bureau Federation (AFBF)**
600 Maryland Avenue, SW, Suite 1000
Washington, DC 20024
202.406.3600
www.fb.org

**American Society of Agronomy (ASA)**
Career Development & Placement Services
5585 Guilford Road
Madison, WI 53711
608.273.8080
www.agronomy.org

**American Society of Farm Managers & Rural Appraisers (ASFMRA)**
720 South Colorado Boulevard, Suite 360-S
Glendale, CO 80246-2664
303.758.3513
info@asfmra.org
www.asfmra.org

**National Agri-Marketing Association (NAMA)**
11020 King Street, Suite 205
Overland Park, KS 66210
913.491.6500
agrimktg@nama.org
www.nama.org

**National FFA Organization**
P.O. Box 68960
6060 FFA Drive
Indianapolis, IN 46268-0960
317.802.6060
www.ffa.org

**National Sustainable Agriculture Information Service**
P.O. Box 3838
3040 Continental Drive
Butte, MT 59702
800.346.9140
askanag@ncat.org
attra.ncat.org

**Water Environment Federation (WEF)**
Public Education Manager-Career Information
601 Wythe Street
Alexandria, VA 22314
800.666.0206
csc@wef.org
www.wef.org

---

*Simone Isadora Flynn; updated by Stuart Paterson*

## *Conversation With...*
## COLLEEN HISTON

Co-owner/Operator
Shepherds Manor Creamery, LLC, New Windsor, MD
Sheep dairy farming, 12 years

**What was your individual career path in terms of education/training, entry-level job, or other significant opportunity?**

When our children were 7 and 8 years old, my husband Michael and I moved our family from the Washington, DC suburbs to a 2 1/2 acre farm in rural Maryland. The first thing we did was enroll them in the county 4-H. My daughter had a couple of market lambs, and the next year we bought a heifer, which my son preferred. They were very active for many years and were enriched by so many wonderful experiences. Then they went off to college, and we didn't have animals for awhile.

Michael and I have always had businesses along with our regular jobs, including a cleaning business early on, an embroidery business, and then a silk-screening business. I've done wine pairing dinners, and people urged me to become a chef. A few things came together to start us down the road to operating a sheep dairy.

We started missing the people we knew from 4-H fairs in the summer, so we bought a few breeding sheep, and my daughter showed me how to fit them, which is the process of getting them ready to show. Then we visited California a couple of times and got to know a cheese monger at a farmer's market. One percent of the sheep's cheese in the United States is produced here in this country. That spurred us to start doing research into sheep dairy farming. We joined the National Dairy Sheep Association and took cheesemaking classes, including a two-week course in Vermont. Finally, we bought 50 sheep.

After making do for a couple of years with the help of friends with acreage for our sheep, we bought this 22-acre farm. Over the years, I've learned to research grants and other funding sources. We had to build a building that cost $500,000; and if you'd told me in the beginning we would do that, I wouldn't have believed you. You have to be very aggressive to create what we've created here.

Sheep dairying is seasonal. We started milking for three months a year and now are up to seven. Michael handles the shepherding and milking side of the operation; I focus on the cheesemaking, marketing, and production side, except during lambing, when I am in the barn alongside Michael.

You have to be able to wear several hats because you can't afford to automatically hire a cheesemaker or a shepherd. We slowly brought in workers to help with things like milking; I was able to quit my accounting job after four years. I sell the cheese I make at farmer's markets and to upscale restaurants in the Washington, DC-Baltimore area.

Michael has always had another job with flexible hours; he works for an engineering company diagnosing water and drainage problems. My former employer asked me to come back to temporarily fill in when an accountant left at the beginning of 2020. Soon COVID-19 hit, and with the uncertainty I've stayed on. We've done OK during the first year of the pandemic because farmers' markets increased.

**What are the most important skills and/or qualities for someone in your profession?**
Flexibility, tenacity, endurance, and patience. You must have passion and drive. You must be able to adapt on a dime. You have to really want to make it work. Money helps, but it's not the key.

**What do you wish you had known going into this profession?**
We basically put the cart before the horse because that's what we thought was right. We should have purchased our property, set up the dairy, then bought the sheep. Instead, we bought the sheep first because we already knew how to care for them, and we didn't think the breeds we wanted were readily available. They became available once we made the right contacts. So, we lambed for two seasons before purchasing this farm.

We've given up a lot to do this. We can't go anywhere because caring for the animals comes first. You have to be willing to go outside in 20 degrees or pouring rain before you eat so the sheep eat. You'll also get dirty as heck. If you're not willing to do that, don't even think about it.

Things go wrong: the cheese recipe doesn't turn out right or a customer gets angry. You have to be level-headed and handle those things. Go have your tantrum by yourself, then come back refreshed.

**Are there many job opportunities in your profession? In what specific areas?**
There are only about 100 sheep dairies in the United States. There are cheesemaking opportunities that are possible—not necessarily with sheep—using all milks, but you have to have extensive training. Milking opportunities will likely require relocation. Starting your own dairy from scratch is super-challenging and many fail. Those that survive are usually the few really big ones and the very small ones that are willing to keep their passion alive. We are an unusual size because we are on the small end of the mid-sized dairies.

**How do you see your profession changing in the next 5 years? How will technology impact that change, and what skills will be required?**
Sheep's milk cheese is becoming more popular and that's helping. Greek feta is made with sheep's milk, for instance. As a product, it's becoming more recognizable.

**What do you enjoy most about your job, what do you enjoy least about your job?**
I enjoy sharing knowledge about our product, having people taste my cheese and liking it, and the success associated with having a worthy product. I love to cook, but if I were a chef I'd be

working hard in the kitchen and rarely experience the satisfaction that comes from a happy customer. I get that because I go out to markets; I deal directly with all my customers. I enjoy the fact that I have variety including outside work, inside work, spending time with the sheep, making a great product with my hands, [and] the results when it turns out the way I want it to. It's great.

The difficulty is long hours, seven days a week. I miss social events. I sometimes miss life events. But I am willing to do that for now because the rewards outweigh the sacrifices.

**Can you suggest a valuable "try this" for students considering a career in your profession?**

Find work on a farm with animals to see if you're up for it. Taking care of animals in all types of weather and conditions is a commitment. Learn how to milk and take care of the sheep, spend time with somebody like me in the cheese room. Sometimes you can volunteer, and some internships pay.

# Fashion Designer

## Snapshot

**Career Cluster(s):** Arts, A/V Technology & Communications; Business Management & Administration; Manufacturing

**Interests:** Art; creativity; design; fashion

**Earnings (Yearly Average):** $73,790

**Employment & Outlook:** Decline Expected

## OVERVIEW

### Sphere of Work

Fashion designers create original clothing, accessories, and footwear. They sketch designs, select fabrics and patterns, and give instructions on how to make the products they design. They may work for larger apparel companies, or own their own businesses, including e-commerce options to forego costly traditional brick-and-mortar stores.

### Work Environment

Fashion designers primarily work indoors, sketching designs and assembling prototypes. However, they may also travel internationally to attend fashion shows and conferences, meet suppliers and manufacturers, and simply for inspiration. Fashion designers occasionally work many hours to meet production deadlines or prepare for fashion shows. Generally, designers who freelance are under contract; these

A fashion designer at work in the studio. Photo via iStock.com/scyther5. [Used under license.]

designers often have long workdays that require them to adjust to their clients' schedules and deadlines.

**Profile**

**Interests:** Things, People, Data
**Working Conditions:** Both Inside and Outside
**Physical Strength:** Medium Work
**Education Needs:** Bachelor's Degree
**Licensure/Certification:** Usually Not Required
**Opportunities for Experience:** Internship, Apprenticeship
**Interest Score:** AER

## Occupation Interest

Fashion designers have a love for art, design, clothing and fashion, and the latest trends. Moreover, designers strive to be the next trend, and work hard to influence what people wear. Designers with an entrepreneurial spirit may want to be their own boss and sell their designs directly to customers, either in brick-and-mortar or online, or both.

## A Day in the Life—Duties and Responsibilities

Larger apparel companies typically employ a team of designers headed by a creative director. Some fashion designers specialize in clothing, footwear, or accessory design; others create designs in all three fashion categories.

For some fashion designers, the first step in creating a new design is researching current fashion and making predictions about future trends, such as by reading reports published by fashion industry trade groups. Other fashion designers create collections using a variety of inspirations, including art media, their surroundings, or cultures they have experienced and places they have visited.

**Duties and Responsibilities**

- Studying fashion trends and creating designs that will appeal to consumers
- Deciding on a theme for a collection
- Using computer-aided design (CAD) programs to create designs
- Visiting manufacturers or trade shows to get samples of fabric
- Selecting fabrics, embellishments, colors, or a style for each garment or accessory
- Working with other designers or team members to create prototype designs
- Presenting design ideas to creative directors or showcase ideas in fashion or trade shows
- Marketing designs to clothing retailers or to consumers
- Overseeing the final production of designs

After they have an initial idea, fashion designers try out various fabrics and produce a prototype, often with less expensive material than will be used in the final product. They work with models to see how the design will look and adjust the designs as needed.

Although most designers first sketch their designs by hand, many now also sketch their ideas digitally with Computer-aided Design (CAD) programs. CAD allows designers to see their work on virtual models. They can try different colors, designs, and shapes while making adjustments more easily than they can when working with real fabric on real people.

Designers produce samples with the actual materials that will be used in manufacturing. Samples that get good responses from fashion editors or trade and fashion shows are then manufactured and sold to consumers.

The design process may vary by specialty, but it generally takes 6 months, from initial design concept to final production, to release either the spring or fall collection. In addition to releasing designs during the spring and fall, some companies release new designs every month.

The Internet and e-commerce allow fashion designers to offer their products outside of traditional brick-and-mortar stores. These designers ship directly to the consumer, without having to invest in a physical shop to exhibit their product lines or collections.

## OCCUPATION SPECIALTIES

**Accessory Designer**
Accessory designers design and produce items such as handbags, suitcases, belts, scarves, hats, hosiery, and eyewear.

**Clothing Designer**
Clothing designers create and help produce men's, women's, and children's apparel, including casual wear, suits, sportswear, evening wear, outerwear, maternity clothing, and intimate apparel.

**Costume Designer**
Costume designers create costumes for the performing arts and for motion picture and television productions. They research the styles worn during the period in which the performance is set, or they work with directors to select and create appropriate attire. They also must stay within the production's costume budget.

**Footwear Designer**
Footwear designers create and help produce different styles of shoes and boots. As new materials, such as lightweight synthetic materials used in shoe soles, become available, footwear designers produce new designs that combine comfort, form, and function.

## WORK ENVIRONMENT

### Immediate Physical Environment

Many fashion designers work in-house for wholesalers or manufacturers. These wholesalers and manufacturers sell apparel and accessories to retailers or other marketers for distribution to individual stores, catalog companies, or online retailers.

Self-employed fashion designers typically create high-fashion garments and one-of-a-kind (custom) apparel. In some cases, a self-employed fashion designer may have a clothing line that bears his or her name.

### Human Environment

Fashion designers should expect to work with others when working for an apparel company, including superiors, while those who design and sell their own clothing may work independently, or with a small team. Most designers travel several times a year to trade and fashion shows to learn about the latest trends. Designers also sometimes travel to other countries to meet suppliers of materials and manufacturers who make the final products.

### Technological Environment

Fashion designers must be comfortable operating all equipment needed to outline and produce their creations, from sketch to prototype. The more adept they are, the more polished the prototype will look. Further, if the designer plans to sell his or her creations directly to the public, they must be prepared to create not just a prototype, but a final product ready for purchase. Computer-aided design programs and graphics editing software aid in this creation process. Entrepreneurial designers should also be familiar with e-commerce platforms and business management software to connect with customers and manage business operations.

## EDUCATION, TRAINING, AND ADVANCEMENT

### High School/Secondary

Although it is not essential for fashion designers to have a bachelor's degree to work in the field, high school students should be aware that it greatly increases the chances of being hired, and, therefore, should plan to attend postsecondary school. High school courses should be geared towards art, design, and business.

Students should also seek co-op or similar programs to gain real-world experience and make contacts in the industry.

**Suggested High School Subjects**

- Algebra
- Art/Design
- Biology
- Earth or Life or Physical Science
- Economics
- English
- Entrepreneurship
- Geometry
- History
- Physics
- Political Science
- Psychology
- Trigonometry

***Transferable Skills and Abilities***

**Artistic Ability**

- Expressing vision for design through illustration

**Communication Skills**

- Communicating effectively throughout the design process, such as instructing sewers about garment construction

**Computer Skills**

- Using CAD programs and graphics editing software

**Creativity**

- Working with a variety of fabrics, shapes, and colors to realize ideas that are unique, functional, and stylish

**Decision-making Skills**

- Deciding which ideas to incorporate into designs

**Detail-oriented**

- Having a good eye for small differences in color and other details that can make a design successful

**Related Career Pathways/Majors**

*Arts, A/V Technology & Communications Career Cluster*

- Visual Arts Career Pathway

*Business, Management & Administration Career Cluster*

- Business Information Management Pathway
- General Management Pathway
- Operations Management Pathway

*Manufacturing Career Cluster*

- Manufacturing Production Process Development Pathway
- Production Pathway
- Quality Assurance Pathway
- Logistics & Inventory Control Pathway

## Postsecondary

Many fashion designers have a bachelor's degree in a related field, such as fashion design or fashion merchandising. Employers usually seek applicants who are creative and who have technical knowledge of the production processes for clothing, accessories, or footwear. In these programs, students learn about textiles and fabrics and how to use CAD technology. They also work on projects they can add to their portfolio, which highlights their designs.

## Fast Fact

**The t-shirt is one of the world's most popular items of clothing, with about two billion sold annually.**
Source: thefactshop.com

Two billion t-shirts are sold annually around the world. Photo via iStock.com/PeopleImages. [Used under license.]

For many artists, including fashion designers, developing a portfolio—a collection of design ideas that demonstrates their styles and abilities—is essential. Students studying fashion design often have opportunities to develop their portfolios further by entering their designs in student or amateur contests. When making hiring decisions, employers rely on these portfolios to gauge talent and creativity.

The National Association of Schools of Art and Design (NASAD) accredits more than 360 postsecondary institutions with programs in art and design, and many of them award degrees in fashion design. These schools often require students to have completed basic art and design courses before entering a program. Applicants usually must submit sketches and other examples of their artistic ability.

**Related College Majors**

- Fashion Merchandising
- Industrial and Product Design
- Interior Design
- Marketing
- Studio Arts
- Theater Design and Stagecraft

### Adult Job Seekers

Adults seeking employment as fashion designers will have better opportunities for job prospects if they come from a related industry and especially if they have a portfolio to show prospective employers or clients, if freelancing.

### Additional Requirements

Fashion designers often gain experience in the fashion industry through internships or by working as an assistant designer. Internships introduce aspiring fashion designers to the design process, help to build their knowledge of textiles and colors, and provide real-life experience on how the industry works.

## EARNINGS AND ADVANCEMENT

Earnings depend on the industry in which fashion designers work—such as entertainment, management, or apparel—and whether they are employed by a company or work under contract as freelancers. Median annual earnings of fashion designers were $73,790 in 2019. The lowest 10 percent earned less than $37,260, and the highest 10 percent earned more than $149,010.

Fashion designers may receive paid vacations, holidays, and sick days; life and health insurance; and retirement benefits. These are usually paid by an employer. Self-employed fashion designers must pay for their own benefits.

## EMPLOYMENT AND OUTLOOK

Fashion designers held 28,300 jobs in 2019. As most apparel continues to be produced internationally, employment of fashion designers in the apparel manufacturing industry is expected to decline 4 percent through the year 2029.

Applicants who have formal education in fashion design; are proficient in technologies such as CAD; have excellent portfolios; and have industry experience will have the best job prospects. However, strong competition for jobs is expected because of the large number of people who seek employment as fashion designers and the relatively few positions available.

In addition, it may be necessary for some fashion designers to relocate, because employment opportunities for fashion designers are concentrated in New York and California.

### Related Occupations

- Art Director
- Floral Designer
- Graphic Designer
- Industrial Designer
- Jeweler/Precious Stone and Metal Worker
- Model
- Purchasing Manager/Buyer/Purchasing Agent

## MORE INFORMATION

**Accrediting Commission for Community and Precollegiate Arts Schools (ACCPAS)**
11250 Roger Bacon Drive, Suite 21
Reston, VA 20190-5248
703.437.0700
info@arts-accredit.org
accpas.arts-accredit.org

**American Apparel & Footwear Association (AAFA)**
740 6th Street NW, 3rd and 4th Floors
Washington, DC 20001
202.853.9080
www.aafaglobal.org

**Council of Arts Accrediting Associations (CAAA)**
11250 Roger Bacon Drive, Suite 21
Reston, VA 20190-5248
703.437.0700
info@arts-accredit.org
www.arts-accredit.org
National Office for Arts Accreditation (NOAA):
www.arts-accredit.org/national-office-for-arts-accreditation

**Council of Fashion Designers of America (CFDA)**
65 Bleecker Street, 11th Floor
New York, NY 10012
212.302.1821
info@cfda.com
cfda.com

**National Association of Schools of Art and Design (NASAD)**
11250 Roger Bacon Drive, Suite 21
Reston, VA 20190-5248
703.437.0700
info@arts-accredit.org
nasad.arts-accredit.org

**United States Fashion Industry Association (USFIA)**
1730 Rhode Island Avenue NW, Suite 312
Washington, DC 20036
202.419.0444
info@usfashionindustry.com
www.usfashionindustry.com

---

*Stuart Paterson*

## *Conversation With...*
## ALI VON PARIS

Founder & CEO
Route One Apparel, Towson, MD
Entrepreneur, apparel industry, 10 years

**What was your individual career path in terms of education/training, entry-level job, or other significant opportunity?**

I started Route One Apparel in my dorm room when I was an undergraduate at the University of Maryland, which has a huge campus along Route 1. I was a double major student and have a bachelor's degree in finance and another in supply chain. I realized early on that I would be dealing with global logistics, so I wanted to fully understand the process of forecasting inventory, negotiations, and import knowledge. Marketing and design come more naturally to me.

Throughout my education I worked minimum wage jobs: at a bagel shop, at restaurants. I really wasn't sure what I wanted to do in a career. I was told what I should do, that I should study finance. I got an internship with a financial company, and it wasn't what I wanted to do.

At the same time, there was a popular bar near campus that was closing, and I thought it would be great for people to have a memento of all the good times there. I was in my junior year, and I designed a t-shirt to pay homage to the bar. It took off on social media, and I started making and selling t-shirts in my dorm room. While I was considering my profession, I was seeing my enterprise grow. I built "street teams" who helped market the t-shirts on campus. I was running all over campus building my business when the University of Maryland Dingman Center for Entrepreneurship reached out to me. They corralled me and said, "You need to get yourself under control and have a 5-year plan." They sat me down and repositioned my thinking. They forced me to think about words and ideas, business and future planning, and they encouraged me to compete in Cupid's Cup, a competition for entrepreneurs who are students. The prize was $15,000 in startup money. I didn't win, but it was a business boot camp. I placed top five and losing actually fueled me even more to prove the judges wrong.

The financial company where I interned offered me a full-time job that would start after graduation. But I turned it down because I wanted to see my business grow. From that point on, I never had any other job other than working for myself.

I created Route One Apparel as an online fashion company that linked people with a sense of community by focusing on Maryland motifs including the state flag design and crabs. Then as our first customers got married and started families, we added baby clothes to our line. We continue to evolve. We have deep and growing relationships now with companies closely identified with Maryland and the region including Old Bay, Utz, and National Bohemian. And we've expanded beyond apparel and now sell some food and drink products. We are growing our custom product capabilities as well. For example, we've custom-made face masks and other items for over 250 businesses, organizations, and charities this year. We also are collaborating with other vendors on products. Most recently, we're working on a collaborative collection with the American Visionary Art Museum in Baltimore. We now have about 20 employees.

I'm not the first entrepreneur in my family. My great grandfather founded a moving company in Baltimore, and it's been in my family for 150-plus years. Business talk has always been a topic of conversation in my household and with extended family—that, and music. Both are deeply rooted in my family. Without even realizing it at the time, I felt very comfortable starting my business. I didn't tell my parents what I was doing until after I graduated. They were obviously worried I wouldn't be applying my studies to a "career" starting out of college, but they were willing to let me see how things went and were very supportive. My dad actually works for me now.

**What are the most important skills and/or qualities for someone in your profession?**
You have to be confident and know that you aren't going to know the answers to everything. You need resilience. If you don't succeed in a certain decision, don't give up. I've actually learned more from things that didn't go well. You need organization and structures because you're going to be wearing many hats. Celebrate the small wins and big ones. Don't be intimidated by other people's success. The reality is everyone is kind of navigating their own life story, everyone has a beginner story. Don't see progress as a leap. Focus on tasks and make small steps. Don't be upset if people don't take you seriously when you're starting out.

**What do you wish you had known going into this profession?**
I wish I'd known how government policy affects working for yourself. We're all so much more connected to how our government makes policy than we think. I was on financial aid in college; and when I graduated, I started paying off my student debt. At some point I realized my interest rate was the same as my monthly payment, and I paid off my loan early to avoid those interest payments. I paid off the loan, and I was taxed 30 percent. I didn't know I couldn't deduct the loan as a business expense.

**Are there many job opportunities in your profession? In what specific areas?**
I am 100 percent for starting a small business. I've gained understanding of my own self-worth, and it's empowered me.

Online e-commerce is the future. The cool thing about internet businesses is that a lot of people see things they are frustrated with, and they come up with solutions. You don't need to be the first to make something; you just need to have a good solution.

Design and marketing will never go awayand are becoming more digital.

**How do you see your profession changing in the next 5 years? How will technology impact that change, and what skills will be required?**

E-commerce is going to be huge. The barriers to entering will be a little tougher because e-commerce websites are getting more expensive.

Fulfillment is becoming more automated. In some areas, robots fulfill orders, or a third party is used to fulfill orders instead of a company stocking its inventory. Rules are changing in digital marketing in terms of what data is collected, how it is stored, and how it can be used.

**What do you enjoy most about your job? What do you enjoy least about your job?**

I started my business because I didn't want to dress up in a corporate world, and I wanted to make my own hours. But I feel like I work more. It's in my DNA, and I have this guilt when I'm not working.

I least like the mental strain. The business is your baby, and you put a lot of your personal life on hold to take care of it. I have a hard time separating myself from the business. When people ask me how I'm doing, I say, "Route One is great." Stepping away is probably the hardest thing.

**Can you suggest a valuable "try this" for students considering a career in your profession?**

Almost every college has an entrepreneurship center, and they welcome people to reach out to them. Don't expect pay in the beginning but volunteer to help in the entrepreneurship center. You'll get so much exposure to the different types of businesses and ideas and just be immersed with creative minds. Build a relationship with the career center and don't be afraid to ask questions.

# Food Service Manager

## Snapshot

**Career Cluster(s):** Business, Management & Administration; Hospitality & Tourism; Human Services

**Interests:** Food; hospitality; business; consumer services

**Earnings (Yearly Average):** $55,320

**Employment & Outlook:** Slower Than Average Growth Expected

## OVERVIEW

### Sphere of Work

Food service managers are responsible for the daily operation of restaurants or other establishments that prepare and serve food and beverages. They direct staff to ensure that customers are satisfied with their dining experience, and they manage the business to ensure that it is profitable. In an entrepreneurial context, food service managers may also own the restaurant or business in question, such as a food truck or food cart, possibly with other partners in the business.

### Work Environment

Full-service restaurants (those with table service) may have a management team that includes a general manager, one or more assistant managers, and an executive chef. Other food-related businesses, such as mobile food trucks, may have minimal staff, meaning the manager may also serve as executive chef. Many food service managers work long shifts, and the job is often hectic. Moreover, dealing with dissatisfied customers can sometimes be stressful.

A restaurant manager oversees her staff. Photo via iStock.com/stockstudioX. [Used under license.]

## Occupation Interest

Food service managers must thrive in a fast-paced and customer-oriented environment, and likely have a passion for food and hospitality, in general, as well as good business sense. They strive to give customers the best experience possible, thereby increasing their restaurant's stature and, hopefully, profits. Restaurants are often reviewed, both in established publications and by patrons on the Internet, so successful managers must be able to use these critiques to better their business, or risk losing customers. Manager owners are faced with increased risk, as their personal success and the success of their staff depend on the success of the restaurant in the public eye. Their role may also entail a strong sales and marketing component.

### *Profile*

**Interests:** Things, People, Data
**Working Conditions:** Both Inside and Outside
**Physical Strength:** Medium Work
**Education Needs:** On-the-Job Training, High School Diploma, Junior/Technical/Community College
**Licensure/Certification:** Optional
**Opportunities for Experience:** Part-Time Work, Internships
**Interest Score:** ECR

## A Day in the Life—Duties and Responsibilities

Managers coordinate activities of the kitchen and dining room staff to ensure that customers are served properly and in a timely manner. They oversee orders in the kitchen, and, if needed, they work with the chef to remedy any delays in service.

Food service managers are responsible for all functions of the business related to employees. For example, most managers interview, hire, train, oversee, appraise, discipline, and sometimes fire employees. Managers also schedule work hours, making sure that enough workers are present to cover each shift. During busy periods, they may expedite service by helping to serve customers, processing payments, or cleaning tables.

Managers also arrange for cleaning and maintenance services for the equipment and facility in order to comply with health and sanitary regulations. For example, they may arrange for trash removal, pest control, and heavy cleaning when the dining room and kitchen are not in use.

### *Duties and Responsibilities*

- Hiring, training, overseeing, and sometimes firing employees
- Ordering food and beverages, equipment, and supplies
- Overseeing food preparation, portion sizes, and the overall presentation of food
- Inspecting supplies, equipment, and work areas
- Ensuring that employees comply with health and food safety standards
- Addressing complaints regarding food quality or service
- Scheduling staff hours and assigning duties
- Managing budgets and payroll records
- Establishing standards for personnel performance and customer service

Most managers prepare the payroll and manage employee records. They also may review or complete paperwork related to licensing, taxes and wages, and unemployment compensation. Although they sometimes assign these tasks to an assistant manager or a bookkeeper, most managers are responsible for the accuracy of business records.

Some managers add up the cash and charge slips and secure them in a safe place. They also may check that ovens, grills, and other equipment are thoroughly cleaned and secured, and that the establishment is locked at the close of business.

## WORK ENVIRONMENT

### Immediate Physical Environment

Most food service managers work full-time. Managers at fine-dining and fast-food restaurants often work long shifts, and some work more than 40 hours per week. Managers of food service facilities or cafeterias in schools, factories, or office buildings usually work traditional business hours. Managers may be called in on short notice, including evenings, weekends, and holidays. Some managers may also manage multiple locations. Managers of alternative food businesses such as food trucks must go where their customers are, such as fairs, concerts, expos, and other public events. This often requires travel and uneven working hours and conditions.

Kitchens are usually crowded and filled with dangerous objects and areas, such as hot ovens and slippery floors. As a result, injuries are a risk for food service managers, who spend some of their time helping in the kitchen. Common hazards include slips, falls, and cuts that are seldom serious. To reduce these risks, managers often wear nonslip shoes when in the kitchen.

### Human Environment

Food service managers deal with people daily throughout their shifts. They oversee the actions of their employees and must be able to adequately discipline when needed. They also oversee shift schedules, which require organization and communication with a sometimes-large team of employees. Further, they deal with other key people in the restaurant, such as executive chefs, to keep operations flowing smoothly. In manager-owner situations, they may also deal with financial backers and others on a business level, which are crucial to the continued operation of the restaurant as a business. Managers also regularly deal with customers, both satisfied and unsatisfied. In the latter case, they must be able to oversee all manner of disputes to both satisfy the customer and protect the business.

### Technological Environment

From a business standpoint, food service managers must be adept at using accounting and inventory software, as well as other database systems, and any other programs or systems the restaurant utilizes in its day-to-day operations. Manager-owners may also benefit from experience utilizing social media and other digital avenues for promotion.

## EDUCATION, TRAINING, AND ADVANCEMENT

### High School/Secondary

Most applicants qualify with a high school diploma and several years of work experience in the food service industry as a cook, waiter or waitress, or counter attendant. Some applicants have received additional training at a community college, technical or vocational school, culinary school, or 4-year college. High school students thinking of a career in food service should start by getting a part-time job in a restaurant to gain experience in the industry and expanding education to include business or culinary courses in college.

**Suggested High School Subjects**

- Algebra
- Biology
- Chemistry
- Civics
- Earth or Life or Physical Sciences
- Economics
- English
- Entrepreneurship
- Finance/Accounting
- Geography
- Geometry
- History
- Psychology
- Statistics

**Related Career Pathways/Majors**

*Business, Management & Administration Career Cluster*

- Business Information Management Pathway
- General Management Pathway

- Human Resources Management Pathway
- Operations Management Pathway

*Hospitality & Tourism Administration Career Cluster*

- Restaurants & Food/Beverage Services Pathway

*Human Services Career Cluster*

- Consumer Services Pathway

## Transferable Skills and Abilities

**Business Skills**

- Understanding all aspects of the restaurant business
- Budgeting for supplies, setting prices, and managing workers to ensure that the restaurant is profitable

**Communication Skills**

- Giving clear orders to staff and being able to communicate effectively with employees and customers

**Customer-service Skills**

- Being courteous and attentive when dealing with patrons
- Satisfying customers' dining needs is critical to business success and ensuring customer loyalty

**Detail-oriented**

- Ensuring that there is enough food to serve to customers
- Maintaining financial records
- Ensuring that the food meets health and safety standards

**Leadership Skills**

- Establishing good working relationships to maintain a productive work environment
- Motivating workers and leading by example

**Organizational Skills**

- Keeping track of many different schedules, budgets, and staff; this becomes more complex as the size of the restaurant or food service facility increases

**Physical Stamina**

- Working long shifts and sometimes spending entire evenings on one's feet helping to serve customers

**Problem-solving Skills**

- Resolving personnel issues and customer-related problems.

### Postsecondary

Although a bachelor's degree is not required, some postsecondary education is increasingly preferred for many manager positions, especially at upscale restaurants and hotels. Some food service companies, hotels, and restaurant chains recruit management trainees from college hospitality or food service management programs. These programs may require the participants to work in internships and to have food-industry-related experiences to graduate.

Many colleges and universities offer bachelor's degree programs in restaurant and hospitality management or institutional food service management. In addition, numerous community colleges, technical institutes, and other institutions offer associate degree programs in the field. Some culinary schools offer programs in restaurant management with courses designed for those who want to start and run their own restaurant.

Most programs provide instruction in nutrition, sanitation, and food preparation, as well as courses in accounting, business law, and management. Some programs combine classroom and practical study with internships.

## Fast Fact

**Americans gobble one billion pounds of shrimp every year, and that's out of the five billion pounds produced. The world is home to 2,000 different shrimp species!** Source: southfloridareporter.com

Shrimp makes a delicious seafood treat. Photo via iStock.com/grandriver. [Used under license.]

**Related College Majors**

- Culinary Science
- Foodservice Systems Administration
- Hospitality Administration
- Hotel, Motel, & Restaurant Management
- Wine Steward/Sommelier

### Adult Job Seekers

Most food service managers start working in industry-related jobs, such as cooks, waiters and waitresses, or hosts and hostesses. They often spend years working under the direction of an experienced worker, learning the necessary skills before they are promoted to manager positions.

### Professional Certification and Licensure

Although certification is not required, managers may obtain the Food Protection Manager Certification (FPMC) by passing a food safety exam. The American National Standards Institute (ANSI) accredits institutions that offer the FPMC.

In addition, the National Restaurant Association Educational Foundation (NRAEF) awards the Foodservice Management Professional (FMP) designation, a voluntary certification to managers who typically meet the following criteria:

- Have supervisory experience in food service
- Have specialized training in food safety
- Pass a multiple-choice exam

The certification attests to professional competence, particularly for managers who learned their skills on the job.

### Additional Requirements

Managers who work for restaurant chains and food service management companies may be required to complete programs that combine classroom instruction and on-the-job training. Topics may include food preparation, sanitation, security, company policies, personnel management, and recordkeeping.

## EARNINGS AND ADVANCEMENT

Earnings depend on the size and caliber of the restaurant, whether the manager oversees more than one location, and whether the manager also owns all or part of the business. Median annual earnings of food service managers were $55,320 in 2019. The lowest 10 percent earned less than $33,210, and the highest 10 percent earned more than $93,040.

Food service managers may receive paid vacations, holidays, and sick days; life and health insurance; and retirement benefits. These are usually paid by the employer if the business is not self-owned.

## EMPLOYMENT AND OUTLOOK

Food service managers held 352,600 jobs in 2019. Thirty-two percent were self-employed. Employment is expected to grow slower than the average for all occupations through the year 2029, at a rate of 1 percent, due to more dining establishments relying on chefs and head cooks instead of hiring additional food service managers. Food service managers will still be needed to oversee food preparation and service as people continue to dine out, purchase takeout meals, and have food delivered to their homes or workplaces.

Although job opportunities should be good overall, they should be best for food service managers with several years of work experience in a restaurant or food service establishment. Most job openings will result from the need to replace managers who leave the occupation.

Jobseekers with a combination of work experience in food service and a bachelor's degree in hospitality, restaurant, or food service management should have an edge when competing for jobs at upscale hotels and restaurants.

### Related Occupations

- Bartender
- Chef/Head Cook
- Lodging Manager

- Sales Manager
- Waiter/Waitress

## MORE INFORMATION

**American Culinary Federation (ACF)**
180 Center Place Way
St. Augustine, FL 32095
904.824.4468
acf@acfchefs.net
www.acfchefs.org

**American National Standards Institute (ANSI)**
330 E. Kilbourn Avenue, Suite 925
Milwaukee, WI 53202
414.501.5494
anabpd.ansi.org

**Association of Nutrition & Foodservice Professionals (ANFP)**
406 Surrey Woods Drive
St. Charles, IL 60174
800.323.1908
info@ANFPonline.org
www.anfponline.org

**International Foodservice Distributors Association (IFDA)**
1660 International Drive, Suite 550
McLean, VA 22102
703.532.9400
www.ifdaonline.org

**International Foodservice Manufacturers Association (IFMA)**
Two Prudential Plaza
180 N. Stetson Ave., Suite 850
Chicago, IL 60601
312.540.4400
www.ifmaworld.com

**National Restaurant Association**
2055 L Street NW, Suite 700
Washington, DC 20036
202.331.5900
askus@restaurant.org
www.restaurant.org
National Restaurant Association Educational Foundation: chooserestaurants.org
Restaurant Law Center: restaurantlawcenter.org
ServSafe Accreditation: www.servsafe.com

**Society for Hospitality and Foodservice Management (SHFM)**
326 E. Main Street
Louisville, KY 40202
502.574.9931
shfm@hqtrs.com
www.shfm-online.org

---

*Stuart Paterson*

## *Conversation With...*

# DJENABA JOHNSON-JONES

Founder & CEO
Hudson Kitchen, Kearny, NJ
Entrepreneur, 6 years

**What was your individual career path in terms of education/training, entry-level job, or other significant opportunity?**
I stumbled upon a career in food by accident. Growing up in Arlington, Texas, I wanted to work in fashion and earned my degree in Fashion Merchandising at the University of North Texas. I minored in business and had various internships including at Ann Taylor in New York City. After I graduated, I worked in product development for County Seat stores in Dallas for three years—at the time, a competitor to the Gap—then went to graduate school at Clark Atlanta University for an MBA in marketing. I wanted to transition to magazine publishing, but an MBA doesn't translate well to publishing. I ended up getting on a plane and moving to New York City, where I found an apartment and started looking for work. Six months later, I started as Assistant Manager of Corporate Marketing at *Essence Magazine*. I moved on to Condé Nast to work at *Brides Magazine* and focused on digital marketing. At the time, the question was: how do you create websites for magazines and sell advertising to support them? After I had my second child, I freelanced for three or four years at various magazine publishers, then returned to Condé Nast for five years. I was Digital Brand Development Director for *W* magazine, which was the liaison between editorial and advertising, when I was laid off as often happens in the corporate world.

I'd always wanted to own my own business and at that point I decided I wanted to launch a company doing something that did not feel like work. I enjoyed exercising, particularly lifting weights. So, I pursued a personal training certification with plans to launch a high-end concierge business around helping executives get healthy through fitness and eating nutritious meals. I started working with a chef to create recipes for a meal delivery service and began searching for a commercial kitchen to rent in my area. I was surprised to find that most small food businesses rented church kitchens and restaurants after hours.

Over time, I abandoned my plans to open a personal training and meal delivery business and pivoted to helping aspiring and established food business owners through commercial kitchen and storage space and food business education.

My market research study showed an overwhelming need: there were only six 24-hour commercial kitchens in New Jersey. At first, I was thinking in terms of a small property but after attending conferences and talking to people, a shared kitchen owner from Virginia recommended that I lease a warehouse space. She was right; I rented an empty white box and was able to build it out for my specific business needs.

I spent five years in business development and opened in December 2019. I started with two businesses as clients and have grown to twenty. I sell kitchen memberships. Members sign a short-term contract and can use the facility 24 hours a day, seven days per week.

During the time I was looking for a location, I launched an education program. What started as continuing education at a community college—workshops such as "The First 10 Steps to Starting a Food Business"—turned into a course called the Food Business Bootcamp®, complete with an 80-page handbook. COVID-19 halted those courses for a year, but I am in the process of re-launching on a virtual platform.

My clients' businesses are growing. Most are consumer-packed goods that sell direct to consumer through their websites. I also work with meal prep companies and food trucks. Hudson Kitchen also creates the benefit of being part of a community. Members seek each other out for business advice and benefit from cooperative purchasing to secure lower prices for ingredients and packaging.

**What are the most important skills and/or qualities for someone in your profession?**

You need to be able to step out there and take a risk. I started cold emailing and asking people to teach at my Bootcamp course or sit on a panel for a networking event and they would say, "yes."

Also, when running a shared space, you encounter people from all walks of life so it's important to have the ability to deal with different personalities. And, you need the ability to switch tasks quickly—one minute you're giving a tour to a prospective client or being interviewed on a podcast and the next you are taking out the garbage.

**What do you wish you had known going into this profession?**

I think the fact that I did not have specific food experience or experience running a kitchen facility has helped me. I was not caught up in how things should be and focused on how I wanted them to be. Even in the financing process, I worked with small nonprofit organizations that read my business plan and made introductions, so I got offers from multiple banks. I didn't know how many small business resources were available, and there are many—a lot for free or nominal costs.

I also realized along the way that businesses need more than just a place to cook. They need support—coaching, access to tools and resources that aid in business growth and most importantly, a community. That's why I created a model, so my clients not only have access to a commercial kitchen, they also receive mentorship and training through our Food Business Bootcamp® course. Also, with the architect plans, city permitting process, and construction build-out, it took longer than I anticipated to get the kitchen open.

**Are there many job opportunities in your profession? In what specific areas?**
Yes! It takes a lot of manpower to run a commercial kitchen. Specifically, operations, facilities management, and marketing are areas of opportunity.

**What do you enjoy most about your job? What do you enjoy least about your job?**
My job is so much fun! I enjoy helping people start their own food ventures because their backstories are so interesting. Having a human connection to my clients is very important—their families; what are their goals; do they want to grow into a national business. As my business grows, I plan to delegate more of the day-to-day kitchen management duties to other employees so that I can focus on the thing that I love most, developing educational programming for members and the community at large.

**Can you suggest a valuable "try this" for students considering a career in your profession?**
In order to understand the ins and outs of running a shared kitchen business, I recommend that students shadow a kitchen manager for a day. Also, it's important to understand the different types of businesses that work out of a shared kitchen, so consider getting a job on a food truck or working the booth at a farmers' market.

## *Conversation With...*
## LUCAS MYERS

Owner & Director of Operations, SoPo Seafood
Owner & Operator, O' Oysters, South Portland, ME
Seafood industry, 20+ years

**What was your individual career path in terms of education/training, entry-level job, or other significant opportunity?**

My family moved to Auburn, Maine when I was four. I went to Skidmore College in Saratoga Springs, New York, because I am a baseball player, and they really wanted me to play for their baseball team. They gave me my best financial aid package, and I enjoyed the small liberal arts college atmosphere. But going into college, I didn't really know what I was going to do with my life—maybe be an educator. I found my way to the philosophy department and realized it was at the root of history and politics. Throwing any desire for financial security to the wind, I became a philosophy major and earned my BA in the subject.

I graduated, traveled, worked in restaurants, and applied for a job at a wholesale seafood company in Portland simply as a means to pay the bills. I scaled and gutted fish in the production room and very much enjoyed the camaraderie in the packing room. I quickly became fascinated with the product, which included seafood from Europe and Japan and, of course, domestic harvests. I left to teach for a year, then hit the Appalachian Trail. When I returned, I applied again at the seafood company, this time for a job in the sales department and stayed for 16 years. I rose through the ranks until I was pretty much running the show, directing production, purchasing, sales, and dealing with top accounts including chefs at white tablecloth restaurants. My last titles were Senior Account Manager and Wholesale Sales Manager.

About the time I returned to the seafood company, my now-wife and I partnered with a friend to buy a 4-unit apartment building in Portland. We lived in one apartment as we renovated, moving from one apartment to the next as work progressed. That was my first taste of entrepreneurship. Through our sweat equity we were able to pay our bills with the rents and provide housing for three other family units. It was a good feeling. It also led us to buy other units over the next 15 years, and now we operate Myers Property Management. It has created a capital stream, something we can fall back on if one of us loses our job. That has been a big part of me being able to dead focus on my entrepreneurial drive.

In the seafood industry, I saw a niche opportunity. I dealt with a lot of caterers who not only needed 500 oysters but by the way, do you sell oyster knives and know anybody who shucks oysters? The idea came to me that I could be that person. I could create a mobile oyster bar and subcontract to caterers, and they could deal with the clients and pay me directly. I could still have my foot in the seafood industry, maybe diversify, and eventually sell the carts as units to other people.

This was a low-cost entry into the market. I had the skill set to do it, and it was a wide-open door for me to walk through. At the same time, my children were little, my wife and I were both working, and we basically had a straight hand-off caring for the kids when I got home at 5 or 6 p.m. This situation was another reason pushing me to get out of a job that was demanding 60 or 70 hours a week and put that time toward something that was my own.

The O'Oyster cart is like a rickshaw. I also designed shucking tables that can get to a place the cart can't go, like the beach. I got licensed as a caterer and mobile food vendor—the cart goes in back of a trailer, I park anywhere and roll the cart to where it needs to be. The cart looks great. I set up at the ferry and cruise ship terminals or the farmer's market in Portland. I park it at a rural farm wedding. All the sudden, caterers were calling. People hired me for private parties.

COVID shut down those parties, and we backed off oysters. That gave me time to focus on the next stage of my long-term business goal, which was to start a wholesale seafood company. I could buy oysters direct from the harvester and supply my company, increase margins, and reduce costs. If I were to franchise my carts, I could supply the oysters. A colleague who wanted to sell seafood to restaurants joined forces with me, and we formed SoPo Seafood. We sell in our area, and we've also developed an online presence so people from all over the country can purchase from us. I can send oysters with an oyster glove and knife, and people can watch my tutorial on how to shuck an oyster.

We are focused on Maine harvest such as finfish like cod, monk, hake, and haddock. We get scallops through divers and dayboat fishermen. We bring in wild Alaskan sockeye salmon and have a caviar line from domestic farm-raised sturgeon.

Now we are aiming to open a brick-and-mortar retail shop in South Portland this spring. This is located on a critical side of a bridge into Portland that gets clogged with traffic in summer. The retail store will include a restaurant with a raw bar and dishes such as crab salads and lobster rolls that are simply presented so people get the confidence to do something similar at home.

**What are the most important skills and/or qualities for someone in your profession?**
A sense of calm under pressure, ability to multitask, determination, a commitment to professionalism, "people skills," and adept mathematics.

**What do you wish you had known going into this profession?**
I wish I had known a benevolent, wealthy, silent, angel investor.

Right now, I'm self-financed. I'm applying to a bank for a business loan this week and have made a connection to a seafood-focused lender. It's what I want to be doing but it's a little nerve-wracking.

**Are there many job opportunities in your profession? In what specific areas?**

Yes, in sales. People who can sell are the stars of our industry.

**How do you see your profession changing in the next 5 years? How will technology impact that change, and what skills will be required?**

There's a constant push in the seafood industry to remove the wholesaler from the supply chain. Technology may finally allow this to happen on a macro scale. Online markets will take the place of the wholesaler allowing harvesters to market themselves and direct-ship to end users. Not on the micro scale though, those who maintain a commitment to professionalism and are skilled learners will be able to flourish in niche boutique markets.

**What do you enjoy most about your job? What do you enjoy least about your job?**

I enjoy my product most. Oysters are my favorite. Eating an oyster that's really good is just the most satisfying gastronomical experience I can have.

I do not enjoy when variables outside of my control result in a customer's dissatisfaction.

**Can you suggest a valuable "try this" for students considering a career in your profession?**

Start small. My love for oysters resulted in this goal of having an oyster bar and starting with a cart was an entry into the field of oysters that was very feasible for me to do with little risk. Starting small forces you to think creatively.

# Funeral Home Manager

**Snapshot**

**Career Cluster(s):** Business, Management & Administration; Health Science; Human Services

**Interests:** Helping others; organization; business

**Earnings (Yearly Average):** $76,350

**Employment & Outlook:** Decline Expected

## OVERVIEW

### Sphere of Work

Funeral service workers organize and manage the details of a ceremony honoring a deceased person. Funeral home managers oversee the general operations of a funeral home business and may own the business themselves. They perform a variety of duties, such as planning and allocating the resources of the funeral home, managing staff, and handling marketing and public relations.

### Work Environment

Funeral services traditionally take place in a house of worship, in a funeral home, or at a gravesite or crematory. However, some families prefer to hold the service in their home or in a social center. Most funeral service workers are employed full-time, and some work more than 40 hours per week. They are often on call;

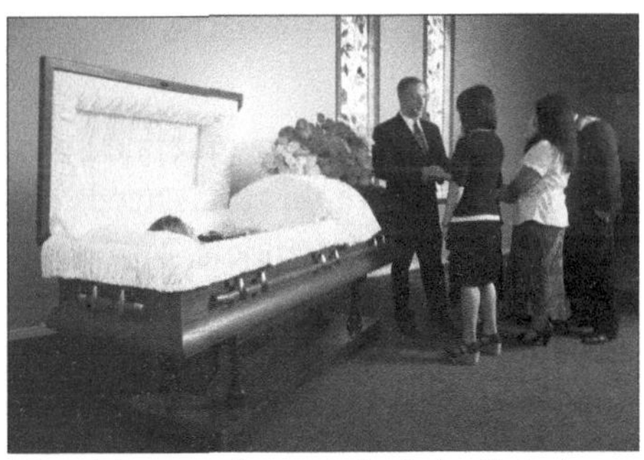

A funeral director receives guests at a viewing. Photo via iStock.com/RichLegg. [Used under license.]

irregular hours, including evenings and weekends are common.

## Occupation Interest

Individuals drawn to funeral service work strive to provide a respectful and tasteful service to the family members and loved ones of deceased persons. They must be willing to work irregular hours to meet their obligations and always be courteous and compassionate. They also have strong business skills and are able to offer their services profitably.

### Profile

**Interests:** People, Things, Data
**Working Conditions:** Both Inside and Outside
**Physical Strength:** Medium Work
**Education Needs:** Associate Degree, Bachelor's Degree
**Licensure/Certification:** Varies By State
**Opportunities for Experience:** Internship, Apprenticeship
**Interest Score:** ECS

## A Day in the Life—Duties and Responsibilities

Funeral service workers help to determine the locations, dates, and times of visitations (wakes), funerals or memorial services, burials, and cremations. They manage other details as well, such as helping the family decide whether the body should be buried, entombed, or cremated. This decision is critical because funeral practices vary among cultures and religions.

### Duties and Responsibilities

- Offering counsel and comfort to families and friends of the deceased
- Providing information on funeral service options
- Arranging for removal of the deceased's body
- Preparing the remains (the deceased's body) for the funeral
- Filing death certificates and other legal documents with appropriate authorities

Most funeral service workers attend to the administrative aspects of a person's death, including submitting papers to state officials to receive a death certificate. They also may help resolve insurance claims, apply for funeral benefits, or notify the Social Security Administration (SSA) or the US Department of Veterans Affairs (VA) of the death.

Many funeral service workers help clients who wish to plan their own funerals in advance to ensure that their needs are met and to ease the planning burden on surviving family members.

Funeral service workers also may provide information and resources, such as support groups, to help grieving friends and family.

## OCCUPATION SPECIALTIES

### Mortician and Funeral Arranger

Morticians and funeral arrangers (also known as funeral directors or, historically, undertakers) plan the details of a funeral. They often prepare obituaries and arrange for pallbearers and clergy services. If a burial is chosen, they schedule the opening and closing of a grave with a representative of the cemetery. If cremation is chosen, they coordinate the process with the crematory. They also prepare the sites of all services and provide transportation for the deceased and mourners. In addition, they arrange the shipment of bodies out of state or out of country for final disposition. Finally, these workers deal with administrative duties. For example, they often apply for the transfer of any pensions, insurance policies, or annuities on behalf of survivors.

Many morticians and funeral arrangers embalm bodies. Embalming is a cosmetic and temporary preservative process through which the body is prepared for a viewing by family and friends of the deceased.

## WORK ENVIRONMENT

### Immediate Physical Environment

Funeral service workers typically perform their duties in a funeral home. Workers also may operate a merchandise display room, crematory, or cemetery, which may be on the funeral home premises. The work is often stressful, because workers must arrange the various details of a funeral within 24 to 72 hours of a death. In addition, they may be responsible for managing multiple funerals on the same day.

Although workers may come into contact with bodies that have contagious diseases, the work is not dangerous if proper safety and health regulations are followed. Those working in crematories are exposed to high temperatures and must wear appropriate protective clothing.

### Human Environment

Funeral service workers deal directly with grieving families daily and must have the emotional fortitude and compassion to cope with that pressure routinely. Managers also direct funeral home staff and oversee maintenance of the funeral home.

### Technological Environment

Funeral home managers must be acquainted with standard business software such as accounting and payroll, as well as any A/V/ technology made available to clients during services and wakes. As they typically provide documentation services, they must also be familiar with the processes and platforms used to request a death certificate, resolve insurance claims, apply for funeral benefits, and notify the SSA or the VA of a death.

## EDUCATION, TRAINING, AND ADVANCEMENT

### High School/Secondary

High school students can prepare to become a funeral service worker by taking classes in biology, chemistry, business, and public speaking. Students may gain relevant experience working part-time or summer jobs in a funeral home.

**Suggested High School Subjects**

- Accounting
- Algebra
- Biology
- Chemistry
- Civics
- Earth or life or Physical Science
- Economics
- English
- Entrepreneurship
- Geometry
- History
- Personal Finance
- Physics
- Pre-Calculus
- Public Speaking
- Psychology
- Sociology
- Statistics

***Transferable Skills and Abilities***

**Business Skills**

- Processing financial statements and managing a funeral home efficiently and profitably

**Compassion**

- Treating clients with care and sympathy in their time of loss

**Interpersonal Skills**

- Explaining and discussing all matters about services provided, tactfully

**Time-management Skills**

- Handling numerous tasks for multiple customers, often over a short timeframe

**Related Career Pathways/Majors**

*Business, Management & Administration Career Cluster*

- General Management Pathway

*Health Science Career Cluster*

- Support Services Pathway

*Human Services Career Cluster*

- Consumer Services Pathway
- Family & Community Services Pathway
- Personal Care Services Pathway

## Postsecondary

An associate degree in a funeral service or mortuary science education program is typically required for all funeral service workers to enter the occupation. Courses usually cover topics such as ethics, grief counseling, funeral service, and business law. Accredited programs also include courses in embalming and restorative techniques.

The American Board of Funeral Service Education (ABFSE) accredits funeral service and mortuary science programs, most of which offer a 2-year associate degree at community colleges. Some programs offer a bachelor's degree.

Although an associate degree is typically required, some employers prefer applicants to have a bachelor's degree.

### Related College Majors

- Funeral & Mortuary Science

## Adult Job Seekers

Funeral home managers typically have multiple years of experience working as a funeral director or mortician before becoming managers.

## Professional Certification and Licensure

Most states and Washington, DC, require workers to be licensed. An exception is Colorado, which offers a voluntary certification program. Although licensing laws and examinations vary by state, most applicants must meet the following criteria:

- Be 21 years old
- Complete an ABFSE accredited funeral service or mortuary science education program
- Pass a state and/or national board exam
- Serve an internship lasting 1 to 3 years
- Working in multiple states requires multiple licenses. For specific requirements, contact each applicable state licensing board.

Most states require funeral directors to earn continuing education credits to keep their licenses.

The Cremation Association of North America (CANA), International Cemetery, Cremation and Funeral Association (ICCFA), and the National Funeral Directors Association (NFDA) offer crematory certification designations. Many states require certification for those who will perform cremations. For specific requirements, contact your state board or the relevant professional organizations.

### Additional Requirements

Those studying to be morticians and funeral arrangers must complete training, usually lasting 1 to 3 years, under the direction of a licensed funeral director or manager. The training, sometimes called an internship or an apprenticeship, may be completed before, during, or after graduating from a funeral service or mortuary science program and passing a national board exam.

## EARNINGS AND ADVANCEMENT

Earnings depend on the size and location of the funeral home, and the number of clients served. Median annual earnings of funeral home managers were $76,350 in 2019. The lowest 10 percent earned less than $44,120, and the highest 10 percent earned more than $161,870.

Funeral service workers may receive paid vacations, holidays, and sick days; life and health insurance; and retirement benefits. These are usually paid by an employer if the business is not self-owned.

## EMPLOYMENT AND OUTLOOK

Funeral home managers held 28,600 jobs in 2019. Sixty-seven percent were self-employed. Employment is expected to decline through the year 2029, at a rate of 4 percent, as consumers increasingly prefer cremation, which costs less and requires fewer workers than traditional funeral arrangements.

Despite projected employment declines, about 4,300 openings for funeral service workers are projected each year, on average, over the decade. All those openings are expected to result from the need to replace workers who transfer to different occupations or exit the labor force, such as to retire.

Opportunities remain favorable for those who are licensed as both a funeral arranger and an embalmer, for those willing to relocate, and for certified crematory operators.

### Related Occupations

- Administrative Services/Facilities Manager
- Advertising/Promotions/Marketing Manager
- Human Resources Manager
- Physician/Surgeon
- Psychologist
- Social Worker

## MORE INFORMATION

**American Board of Funeral Service Education (ABFSE)**
992 Mantua Pike, Suite 108
Woodbury Heights, NJ 08097
816.233.3747
exdir@abfse.org
www.abfse.org

**Cremation Association of North America (CANA)**
499 Northgate Parkway
Wheeling, IL 60090-2646
312.245.1077
info@cremationassociation.org
www.cremationassociation.org

**International Cemetery, Cremation & Funeral Association (ICCFA)**
107 Carpenter Drive, Suite 100
Sterling, VA 20164
800.645.7700
iccfa.com

**National Funeral Directors & Morticians Association (NFDMA)**
6290 Shannon Parkway
Union City, GA 30291
800.434.0958
nfdma.com

**National Funeral Directors Association (NFDA)**
13625 Bishop's Drive
Brookfield, WI 53005
800.228.6332
nfda@nfda.org
nfda.org

---

*Stuart Paterson*

# Interior Designer

## Snapshot

**Career Cluster(s):** Architecture & Construction; Arts, A/V Technology & Communications; Business, Management & Administration; Human Services

**Interests:** Art; design; architecture; working with people

**Earnings (Yearly Average):** $56,040

**Employment & Outlook:** Decline Expected

## OVERVIEW

### Sphere of Work

Interior designers make indoor spaces functional, safe, and beautiful by determining space requirements and selecting essential and decorative items, such as colors, lighting, and materials. They must be able to draw, read, and edit blueprints. They also must be aware of building codes, inspection regulations, and other considerations, such as accessibility standards.

### Work Environment

Most interior designers work in offices, but technology has changed the way many designers work. For example, interior designers now use software rather than drafting tables to create two- or three-dimensional images. Interior designers also travel to clients' design sites.

An interior designer at work, with tablet computer and material samples. Photo via iStock.com/Naphat_Jorjee. [Used under license.]

### Occupation Interest

Interior designers have an artistic eye for the design and layout of dwellings and businesses and are able to work with clients to bring their wants and needs to life in the most appealing and functional ways possible. Designers also have a sound technical knowledge of architecture, codes, and standards, which must be factored into all design choices.

## Profile

**Interests:** Things, Data, People
**Working Conditions:** Inside
**Physical Strength:** Medium Work
**Education Needs:** Varies—Associate, Bachelor's, and Master's Degree
**Licensure/Certification:** Varies by State
**Opportunities for Experience:** Internship
**Interest Score:** AE

## A Day in the Life—Duties and Responsibilities

Interior designers work closely with architects, civil engineers, mechanical engineers, and construction laborers and helpers to determine how interior spaces will function, look, and be furnished. Interior designers read blueprints and must be aware of building codes and inspection regulations.

Although some sketches may be freehand, most interior designers use computer-aided design (CAD) software for most of their drawings. Throughout the design process, interior designers often use building information modeling (BIM) software to create three-dimensional visualizations that include construction elements such as walls or roofs.

Many designers specialize in particular types of buildings, such as homes, hospitals, or hotels; specific rooms, such as bathrooms or kitchens; or a specific style. Some designers work for home furnishings stores, providing design services to help customers choose materials and furnishings.

Some interior designers produce designs, plans, and drawings for construction and installation. These products may include information for construction and demolition, electrical layouts, and building permits. Interior designers may draft the preliminary design into documents ranging from simple sketches to construction schedules and attachments.

## Duties and Responsibilities

- Searching for and bid on new projects
- Determining the client's goals and requirements for the project
- Considering how the space will be used and how people will move through the space
- Sketching preliminary design plans, including electrical and partition layouts
- Specifying materials and furnishings, such as lighting, furniture, wall finishes, flooring, and plumbing fixtures
- Creating a timeline for the interior design project and estimate project costs
- Placing orders for materials and overseeing the installation of the design elements
- Overseeing construction and coordinating with general building contractors to implement the plans and specifications for the project
- Visiting the site after the project is complete, to ensure that the client is satisfied

## OCCUPATION SPECIALTIES

**Corporate Designer**
Corporate designers create interior designs for professional workplaces in a variety of settings, from small offices to large buildings. They focus on creating spaces that are efficient, functional, and safe for employees. In their designs, they may incorporate elements of a company's brand.

**Healthcare Designer**
Healthcare designers plan and renovate healthcare centers, clinics, doctors' offices, hospitals, and residential care facilities. They specialize in evidence-based design, which uses data and research in design decision making to achieve positive results for patients, residents, and facilities.

**Kitchen and Bath Designer**
Kitchen and bath designers specialize in kitchens and bathrooms and have expert knowledge of cabinet, fixture, appliance, plumbing, and electrical solutions for these rooms.

**Sustainable Designer**
Sustainable designers suggest strategies to improve energy and water efficiencies and indoor air quality as well as environmentally sustainable products, such as bamboo and cork for floors. They may obtain certification in Leadership in Energy and Environmental Design (LEED) from the US Green Building Council (USGBC). Such certification indicates expertise in designing buildings and spaces with sustainable practices in mind.

**Universal Designer**
Universal designers renovate spaces to make them more accessible. Often, these designs are used to renovate spaces for elderly people and people with special needs; however, universal designs benefit everyone. For example, an entryway without steps may be necessary for someone in a wheelchair, but it is also helpful for someone pushing a baby stroller.

## WORK ENVIRONMENT

### Immediate Physical Environment

Interior designers split their time between their office, including a home office if the designer if self-employed, and travelling to meet clients at the design site. In this way, designers may be able to set their own working hours but may need to adjust their workday to suit their clients' schedules and deadlines, including meeting with clients in the evening and on weekends.

### Human Environment

Interior designers are client-focused professionals by their nature, so human interaction is part of daily routine. Meetings with clients are crucial to establishing a project and keeping it on track, as are meetings with ancillary professionals such as architects, civil engineers, mechanical engineers, and construction laborers and helpers. If the designer works for a firm or other direct employer, they may have to provide project reports. Designers also spend a significant amount of time soliciting new clients, so the ability to sell oneself is an important quality.

### Technological Environment

Interior designers are increasingly reliant on computer technology to plan and lay out the project space. CAD software is quite common, as is BIM software. A mastery of drafting tools and techniques is also important, as is being able to provide drawings and documentation to fit clients' needs. Designers must stay on top of current trends and emerging technologies such as green building and energy efficiency technologies.

## EDUCATION, TRAINING, AND ADVANCEMENT

### High School/Secondary

High school students interested in a career in interior design should focus equally on art and design courses as well as mathematics, and English to improve communication skills. Thought should be given to postsecondary goals: associate, bachelor's, or master's degrees in interior design. Colleges offering these degrees often require applicants to submit sketches, so high school students should begin to prepare a portfolio of ideas.

**Suggested High School Subjects**

- Algebra
- Art/Design
- Biology
- Chemistry
- Earth or Life or Physical Science
- Economics

- English
- Geometry
- History
- Physics
- Political Science
- Pre-Calculus
- Psychology
- Statistics
- Trigonometry

**Related Career Pathways/Majors**

*Architecture & Construction Career Cluster*
- Design/Pre-Construction Pathway

*Arts, A/V Technology & Communications Career Cluster*
- Visual Arts Career Pathway

*Business Management & Administration Career Cluster*
- General Management Pathway

*Human Services Career Cluster*
- Consumer Services Pathway

### Transferable Skills and Abilities

**Artistic Ability**
- Using sense of style to develop aesthetically pleasing designs

**Creativity**
- Imaginatively selecting furnishings and fabrics and creating functional spaces that serve the client's needs and fit the client's lifestyle

**Detail-oriented**
- Measuring interior spaces and creating drawings that can be used by workers such as engineers or other designers

**Interpersonal Skills**
- Communicating effectively with clients and others
- Soliciting new clients and new work and collaborating with other designers, engineers, and general building contractors on ongoing projects

**Problem-solving Skills**
- Addressing challenges, such as construction delays or unavailability of certain materials, while keeping the project on time and within budget

**Visualization**
- Possessing a strong sense of proportion and visual awareness in order to understand how the pieces of a design will fit together to create the intended environment

## Postsecondary

Interior designers entering the occupation usually need a bachelor's degree in any field. Coursework should include classes in interior design, drawing, and CAD.

Programs in interior design are available at the associate, bachelor's, and master's degree levels. Applicants to these programs may need to submit sketches and other examples of their artistic ability.

The National Association of Schools of Art and Design (NASAD) accredits more than 360 postsecondary colleges, universities, and independent institutes that have programs in art and design. The Council for Interior Design Accreditation (CIDA) accredits about 180 professional-level (bachelor's or master's degree) interior design programs.

Nearly 100 colleges and universities are affiliated with the National Kitchen & Bath Association (NKBA). These schools offer programs on kitchen and bath design at the certificate, associate degree, and bachelor's degree levels.

**Related College Majors**

- Commercial & Advertising Art
- Commercial Photography
- Fashion/Apparel Design
- Graphic Design
- Illustration
- Industrial & Product Design

## Adult Job Seekers

Adults seeking employment as interior designers should have a background in art, design, or technical fields such as architecture. Individuals working in real estate would have the advantage of a ready-made pool of potential clients. Since a degree in interior design is almost always required, adults should research the desired career path and plan accordingly to achieve the relevant academic goals.

## Professional Certification and Licensure

Licensure requirements vary by state. In some states, only licensed designers may do interior design work. In other states, both licensed and unlicensed designers may do such work; however, only licensed designers may use the title "interior designer." In still other states, both licensed and unlicensed designers may call themselves interior designers and do interior design work.

In states with laws restricting the use of the title "interior designer," only candidates who pass their state-approved exam, most commonly the National Council for Interior Design Qualification (NCIDQ) exam, may call themselves registered interior designers. Candidate eligibility for taking the NCIDQ exam includes having at least a bachelor's degree in interior design and 2 years of full-time work experience.

California requires a different exam, administered by the California Council for Interior Design Certification (CCIDC). To take this exam, eligible candidates must have a combination of education and experience.

Voluntary certification in an interior design specialty, such as environmental design, allows designers to demonstrate expertise in a particular area of the occupation. Interior designers often specialize to distinguish the type of design work they do and to promote their expertise. Certifications usually are available through professional and trade associations and are independent of the NCIDQ licensing examination.

## EARNINGS AND ADVANCEMENT

Earnings depend on whether an interior designer is self-employed or employed by a firm, whether they specialize in certain types of design, and the size and duration of projects. Median annual earnings of interior designers were $56,040 in 2019. The lowest 10 percent earned less than $31,970, and the highest 10 percent earned more than $96,470.

Interior designers may receive paid vacations, holidays, and sick days; life and health insurance; and retirement benefits. These are usually paid by an employer if the designer is not self-employed. Travel expenses may also be covered by an employer.

## EMPLOYMENT AND OUTLOOK

Interior designers held 77,900 jobs in 2019. Twenty-two percent were self-employed. Employment is expected to decline 5 percent through the year 2029. There may be some demand created by new construction, but opportunities for self-employed interior designers to renovate existing homes, commercial buildings, and other facilities should be limited. Relatively few interior designers are directly employed in the construction industry, but many of these workers depend heavily on that industry to generate new projects.

Job prospects should be best in high-income areas, because wealthy clients are more likely than others to engage in remodeling and renovating their spaces. Keeping up to date with the newest design tools, such as 3D CAD software, also will improve job prospects.

### Related Occupations

- Architect
- Art Director
- Craft/Fine Artist
- Fashion Designer
- Floral Designer

- Graphic Designer
- Industrial Designer
- Landscape Architect

## MORE INFORMATION

**American Academy of Healthcare Interior Designers (AAHID)**
8735 W. Higgins Road, Suite 300
Chicago, IL 60631
847.375.6870
info@aahid.org
aahid.org

**American Society of Interior Designers (ASID)**
1152 15th Street NW, Suite 910
Washington, DC 20005
202.546.3480
membership@asid.org
www.asid.org

**Council for Interior Design Accreditation (CIDA)**
206 Grandville Avenue, Suite 350
Grand Rapids, MI 49503-4014
248.875.6705
info@accredit-id.org
www.accredit-id.org

**Council for Interior Design Qualification (CIDQ)**
225 Reinekers Lane, Suite 210
Alexandria, VA 22314
202.721.0220
inquiries@cidq.org
www.cidq.org

**Fairchild Books Interior Design Library**
c/o Bloomsbury Publishing Inc.
1385 Broadway, 5th Floor
New York, NY 10018
212.419.5300
askacademic@bloomsbury.com
www.fairchildbooksinteriordesign.com

**Interior Design Educators Council (IDEC)**
111 West Jackson Boulevard, 14th Floor
Chicago, IL 60604
630.544.5057
info@idec.org
www.idec.org

**International Design Continuing Education Council (IDCEC)**
4576 Yonge Street, Suite 405
Toronto, ON M2N 6N4
Canada
888.890.5515
admin@idcec.org
www.idcec.org

**International Interior Design Association (IIDA)**
111 E. Wacker Drive, Suite 222
Chicago, IL 60601
888.799.4432
iidahq@iida.org
iida.org

**National Association of Schools of Art and Design (NASAD)**
11250 Roger Bacon Drive, Suite 21
Reston, VA 20190-5248
703.437.0700
info@arts-accredit.org
nasad.arts-accredit.org

**National Kitchen and Bath Association (NKBA)**
800.843.6522
info@nkba.org
nkba.org

---

*Stuart Paterson*

## *Conversation With...*
## PERILEE OLSON

Interior Designer
Cabbages & Kings Interiors, Sandwich, MA
Interior Design, 21 years

**What was your individual career path in terms of education/training, entry-level job, or other significant opportunity?**

I majored in fine arts, with a focus on graphic design, at the Rochester Institute of Technology in New York, graduating with a Bachelor of Fine Arts degree in 1991. After graduating from college, I worked in the graphic design field for a short time, and realized I didn't like it.

While working in graphic design I took a part-time job at The Limited clothing store, which at the time had a chain of retail stores. I was attracted to the visual merchandising aspect of the job—setting up window displays and display racks in the store—all of the pretty stuff. Pretty soon after starting work for The Limited, the chain hired me full-time to handle visual merchandising for all of their stores in Boston and Eastern Massachusetts.

Then I moved to the Pottery Barn chain of stores and went from fashion design to home design. My territory widened to include all of New England.

I realized that form of design was definitely my groove. The idea was to attract people to get them to buy products, so if I did a good job, my displays were torn apart immediately by customers buying up all the product.

Seeking a bit more permanent outlet for my creativity, I decided to make the transition to residential design. I could do the same kind of work, but it would last forever. I started helping out a friend in her interior design shop as a sideline and eventually ended up working with clients. Then I got married and moved with my husband to Cape Cod in Massachusetts. That's when I started my own firm.

One of the first things I did was join a business networking group and hold a drawing for four free one-day redesigns of the members' homes. During redesigns, I use what clients have to create a more beautiful, cohesive, and functional interior. The people who won my one-day services showed off their homes to families and friends and word of business started spreading through residential developments and golf course communities. At the end of the redesign, I left the clients with a wish list, and most of the time they called me to execute the design. I was in business.

Only the first four redesigns were free, but they were key. They got people to think of redesigning their homes—with my help. Eventually, redesign became more of a sideline in my business after I started working with a high-end home builder. He was the husband of a client for whom I had done a home redesign. The client really liked it, and her husband asked me to take a look at a foreclosed house he wanted to flip.

I went in and said, "Here's what you need to do to sell it." I suggested which walls to take down and chose the paint colors, lighting, and tile work. I found I loved the contractor's side of home design and adapted to it easily. The builder hired me to work for his company, and now I work up and down the East Coast. I've worked in New Hampshire, Boston, Nantucket, Manhattan, Florida, and Anguilla in the Caribbean.

I never planned a career in high-end home interior design. I just kept following the path of opportunity in front of me. When I built my business model, I wanted my design to be accessible, something normal people like me could afford.

I still do a very wide range of projects. When I work on these larger homes the projects tend to take a year or two, which leaves me time for smaller projects. That's why I picked the name "Cabbages and Kings" for my business—it speaks to all kinds of people.

**What are the most important skills and/or qualities for someone in your profession?**

You have to have an innate talent for interior design. You have to have a natural sense of color and proportion and an interest in different types of materials. Everybody wants to do interior design. It seems super glamorous and fun. But while you can learn the language and process used in construction, if you aren't naturally talented in design, you won't last long in the field.

**What do you wish you had known going into this profession?**

I wish I had known how much of interior design relies on innate talent. I would have taken a broader range of courses in college—studied computers or taken extra years of French. I would have spent less time on things that already came easily to me.

**Are there many job opportunities in your profession? In what specific areas?**

There aren't a ton of jobs doing what I do, which is design of 10,000-square-foot homes. But there are a lot of other opportunities in design from visual merchandising and one-day redesigns to more traditional scale interior design in the 1,500 to 3,000-square-foot market. There is also contract work for commercial businesses—boutiques, restaurants, and hotels. The key is just to be open-minded and try any opportunity that presents itself until you find the type of design that suits you.

**How do you see your profession changing in the next 5 years? How will technology impact that change, and what skills will be required?**

Green building is becoming huge. Traditional home designs are going out the window. Formal dining rooms are becoming family rooms. People want home design that reflects how they live their lives. Also, thanks to online companies like Wayfair and Overstock, there's good design out there at affordable prices. People have more access to great design.

Computer-aided design (CAD) is widely used in home design—but not by me. I don't have a head for computers. I don't like them, and I'm not interested in them. I like paper and pencil. I don't expect my clients to pay for the extra time it takes to draw by hand. But I prefer it. And it hasn't impacted my career.

**What do you enjoy most about your job? What do you enjoy least about your job?**
What I enjoy most is creating a setting for people's lives, for all of their moments, good and bad. What I like least is paperwork. Hate it. I can't even tell you how much I hate it.

**Can you suggest a valuable "try this" for students considering a career in your profession?**
You need to get out in front of other people. Volunteer to do visual merchandising at a local store. Offer to help friends redesign their rooms. When you go to college, take a few courses in design and see how it goes before committing to the field. I'm proof you don't need a degree in interior design to be successful in the field.

# Lawyer

## Snapshot

**Career Cluster(s):** Business, Management & Administration; Law, Public Safety, Corrections & Security

**Interests:** Law & justice; regulations

**Earnings (Yearly Average):** $122,960

**Employment & Outlook:** As Fast As Average Growth Expected

## OVERVIEW

### Sphere of Work

Lawyers advise and represent individuals, businesses, and government agencies on legal issues and disputes. Although some lawyers work for firms or corporations, others have a desire to open their own practices.

### Work Environment

Lawyers mainly work in offices and courtrooms, although many are required to travel in order to meet with clients. Being a lawyer can be a high-stress occupation, especially during trials or when facing deadlines.

### Occupation Interest

Lawyers are highly organized, analytical people who have a desire to uphold the law and either advocate for or advise clients on their legal rights. This can take many forms, from criminal prosecutions and defense to tax, labor, and corporate law. In business, lawyers are essential in order to legally conduct financial transac-

A lawyer questions a witness before the jury in a courtroom. Photo via iStock.com/RichLegg. [Used under license.]

tions, and for areas such as patents and copyrights.

### Profile

**Interests:** People, Data, Things
**Working Conditions:** Both Inside and Outside
**Physical Strength:** Medium Work
**Education Needs:** Bachelor's Degree, Law Degree
**Licensure/Certification:** Bar Exam
**Opportunities for Experience:** Internship, Part-Time Work
**Interest Score:** EI

## A Day in the Life—Duties and Responsibilities

Lawyers, also called attorneys, function as both advocates and advisors.

As advocates, they represent one of the parties in a criminal or civil trial by presenting evidence and arguing in support of their client.

As advisors, lawyers counsel their clients about their legal rights and obligations and suggest courses of action in business and personal matters. All attorneys research the intent of laws and judicial decisions and apply the laws to the specific circumstances that their clients face.

Lawyers often oversee the work of support staff, such as paralegals and legal assistants and legal secretaries.

Lawyers may have different titles and different duties, depending on where they work.

In law firms, lawyers, sometimes called associates, perform legal work for individuals or businesses. Those who represent and defend the accused may be called criminal law attorneys or defense attorneys.

### Duties and Responsibilities

- Advising and representing clients in courts, before government agencies, and in private legal matters
- Communicating with clients, colleagues, judges, and others involved in the case
- Conducting research and analysis of legal problems
- Interpreting laws, rulings, and regulations for individuals and businesses
- Presenting facts in writing and verbally to their clients or others, and argue on behalf of their clients
- Preparing and filing legal documents, such as lawsuits, appeals, wills, contracts, and deeds

Attorneys also work for federal, state, and local governments. Prosecutors typically work for the government to file a lawsuit, or charge, against an individual or corporation accused of violating the law. Some may also work as public defense attorneys, representing individuals who could not afford to hire their own private attorney.

Others may work as government counsels for administrative bodies and executive or legislative branches of government. They write and interpret laws and regulations and set up procedures to enforce them. Government counsels also write legal reviews of agency decisions. They argue civil and criminal cases on behalf of the government.

Corporate counsels, also called in-house counsels, are lawyers who work for corporations. They advise a corporation's executives about legal issues related to the corporation's business activities. These issues may involve patents, copyrights, government regulations, contracts with other companies, property interests, taxes, or collective-bargaining agreements with unions.

Public-interest lawyers work for private, nonprofit organizations that provide legal services to disadvantaged people or others who otherwise might not be able to afford legal representation. They generally deal with civil cases, such as those having to do with leases, job discrimination, and wage disputes, rather than criminal cases.

## OCCUPATION SPECIALTIES

**Environmental Lawyer**
Environmental lawyers deal with issues and regulations that are related to the environment. For example, they may work for advocacy groups, waste disposal companies, or government agencies to help ensure compliance with relevant laws.

**Family Lawyer**
Family lawyers deal with a variety of legal issues that pertain to the family. They may advise clients regarding divorce, child custody, and adoption proceedings.

**Intellectual Property Lawyer**
Intellectual property lawyers deal with the laws related to inventions, patents, trademarks, and creative works, such as music, books, and movies. For example, an intellectual property lawyer may advise a client about whether it is acceptable to use published material in the client's forthcoming book.

**Securities Lawyer**
Securities lawyers work on legal issues arising from the buying and selling of stocks, ensuring that all disclosure requirements are met. They may advise corporations that are interested in listing in the stock exchange through an initial public offering (IPO) or in buying shares in another corporation.

### Tax Lawyer

Tax lawyers process a variety of tax-related issues for individuals and corporations. They may help clients navigate complex tax regulations, so that clients pay the appropriate tax on items such as income, profits, and property. For example, tax lawyers may advise a corporation on how much tax it needs to pay from profits made in different states to comply with Internal Revenue Service (IRS) rules.

## WORK ENVIRONMENT

### Immediate Physical Environment

Lawyers work mostly in offices. However, some travel to attend meetings with clients at various locations, such as homes, hospitals, or prisons. Others travel to appear before courts.

Lawyers may face demanding pressure during work—for example, during trials or when trying to meet deadlines. Most lawyers work full-time and many work more than 40 hours per week. Lawyers who are in private practice and those who work in large firms often work additional hours, conducting research and preparing and reviewing documents.

### Human Environment

Lawyers interact with others daily, as part of their routine work. There may be solitary moments of research and paperwork, but a great deal of time is spent meeting with clients, appearing in court, arguing cases in front of mediators and arbitrators, meeting with opposing lawyers, and working with support staff. Lawyers must be comfortable dealing with people one-on-one—sometimes relating to extremely sensitive or emotional matters—and public speaking, such as during court appearances.

### Technological Environment

Technological requirements depend on the sphere of the lawyers' work, but all lawyers must be comfortable using computers, including word processing software, as well as specialized software and platforms such as accounting software, presentation software, databases, and information retrieval platforms.

## EDUCATION, TRAINING, AND ADVANCEMENT

### High School/Secondary

Since becoming a lawyer typically requires 7 years of postsecondary schooling, high school students considering a career in law should plan ahead for their postsecondary career by striving for high grades in all subjects, with an emphasis on courses such as sociology, political science, psychology, and history. Science and math courses can help sharpen analytical skills, while English and language courses are essential for building communication and written skills. In general, courses that require a great deal of reading, analysis, and writing will help prepare high school students for the intensity of law school.

**Suggested High School Subjects**

- Biology
- Chemistry
- Civics
- Earth or Life or Physical Science
- Economics
- English
- Forensic Science
- Law Foundations
- History
- Math
- Physics
- Psychology
- Statistics
- Technical Writing

**Related Career Pathways/Majors**

*Business, Management & Administration Career Cluster*

- General Management Pathway

*Law, Public Safety, Corrections & Security Career Cluster*

- Legal Services Pathway

### Transferable Skills and Abilities

**Analytical Skills**

- Analyzing large amounts of information
- Determining relevant facts, and propose viable solutions

**Interpersonal Skills**

- Building a trusting relationship so that clients feel comfortable enough to share personal information related to their case

**Problem-solving Skills**

- Separating emotions and prejudice from clients' problems and objectively evaluating the relevant applicable information
- Preparing the best defense and recommendations for clients

**Research Skills**

- Finding those laws and regulations that apply to a specific matter, in order to provide the appropriate legal advice for clients

**Speaking Skills**

- Presenting and explaining their case to arbitrators, mediators, opposing parties, judges, or juries in a clear manner
- Speaking on behalf of clients

**Writing Skills**

- Preparing documents, such as wills, trusts, and powers of attorney with attention to detail

## Postsecondary

Becoming a lawyer usually takes 7 years of full-time study after high school—4 years of undergraduate study, followed by 3 years of law school. Most states and jurisdictions require lawyers to complete a Juris Doctor (JD) degree from a law school accredited by the American Bar Association (ABA). ABA accreditation signifies that the law school—particularly its curricula and faculty—meets certain standards.

A bachelor's degree is required for entry into most law schools, and courses in English, public speaking, government, history, economics, and mathematics are useful.

Almost all law schools, particularly those approved by the ABA, require applicants to take the Law School Admission Test (LSAT). This test measures applicants' aptitude for the study of law.

The JD degree program includes courses such as constitutional law, contracts, property law, civil procedure, and legal writing. Law students may choose specialized courses in areas such as tax, labor, and corporate law.

**Related College Majors**

- Arts & Humanities
- Business
- Communications
- Criminal Justice
- Economics
- English
- History
- Math
- Philosophy
- Political Science
- Psychology
- Science
- Sociology

## Adult Job Seekers

Adults seeking to become lawyers must be prepared to do the legwork required to reach that goal, including attending law school. Coming from a related field, such as criminal justice, business, and communications, is an asset, as is having worked in a position such as a paralegal or legal assistant.

## Professional Certification and Licensure

Prospective lawyers take licensing exams called "bar exams." Lawyers who receive a license to practice law are "admitted to the bar."

To practice law in any state, a person must be admitted to the state's bar under rules established by the jurisdiction's highest court. The requirements vary by state and jurisdiction. For more details on individual state and jurisdiction requirements, visit the National Conference of Bar Examiners (NCBE).

Most states require that applicants graduate from an ABA-accredited law school, pass one or more written bar exams, and be found by an admitting board to have the character to represent and advise others. Prior felony convictions, academic misconduct, and a history of substance abuse are just some factors that may disqualify an applicant from being admitted to the bar.

Lawyers who want to practice in more than one state often must take the bar exam in each state.

After graduation, lawyers must keep informed about legal developments that affect their practices. Almost all states require lawyers to participate in continuing legal education either every year or every 3 years.

Many law schools and state and local bar associations provide continuing legal education courses that help lawyers stay current with recent developments. Courses vary by state and generally cover a subject within the practice of law, such as legal ethics, taxes and tax fraud, and healthcare. Some states allow lawyers to take continuing education credits through online courses.

## Additional Requirements

Part-time jobs or summer internships in law firms, government agencies, and corporate legal departments provide valuable experience. Some smaller firms, government agencies, and public-interest organizations may hire students as summer associates after they have completed their first year at law school. Many larger firms' summer associate programs are eligible only to law students who have completed their second year. All these experiences can help law students decide what kind of legal work they want to focus on in their careers and may lead directly to a job after graduation.

## EARNINGS AND ADVANCEMENT

Many factors affect earnings, including the type of law practiced, a lawyer's position within a firm, the size of the firm or corporation, whether the lawyer is a public defender, or if he or she runs or is a partner in their own firm. Lawyers who own their own practices usually earn less than those who work in law firms or other business establishments. Median annual earnings of lawyers were $122,960 in 2019. The lowest 10 percent earned less than $59,670, and the highest 10 percent earned more than $208,000.

Lawyers may receive paid vacations, holidays, and sick days; life and health insurance; and retirement benefits. These are usually paid by an employer. Travel expenses may also be covered by an employer.

Newly hired attorneys usually start as associates and work on teams with more experienced lawyers. After several years, some lawyers may advance to partnership in their firm, meaning that they become partial owners of the firm. Those who do not advance within their firm may be forced to leave, a practice commonly known as "up or out."

After gaining a few years of work experience, some lawyers go into practice for themselves or move to the legal department of a large corporation. Very few in-house attorneys are hired directly out of law school.

## EMPLOYMENT AND OUTLOOK

Lawyers held 813,900 jobs in 2019. Seventeen percent were self-employed. Employment is expected to grow as fast as average through the year 2029, at a rate of 4 percent. Demand for legal work is expected to continue as individuals, businesses, and all levels of government require legal services in many areas.

Despite this need for legal services, more price competition over the next decade may lead law firms to rethink their project staffing to reduce costs to clients. Clients are expected to cut back on legal expenses by demanding less expensive rates and scrutinizing invoices. Work that was previously assigned to lawyers, such as document review, may now be given to paralegals and legal assistants. Also, some routine legal work may be outsourced to other, lower cost legal providers located overseas.

Although law firms will continue to be among the largest employers of lawyers, many large corporations are increasing their in-house legal departments to cut costs. For many companies, the high cost of hiring outside counsel lawyers and their support staffs makes it more economical to shift work to their in-house legal department. This shift will lead to an increase in the demand for lawyers in a variety of settings, such as financial and insurance firms, consulting firms, and healthcare providers.

The federal government is likely to continue to need lawyers to prosecute or defend civil cases on behalf of the United States, prosecute criminal cases brought by the federal government, and collect money owed to the federal government. However, budgetary constraints at all levels of government, especially the federal level, will likely moderate employment growth.

Despite the projected growth in new jobs for lawyers, competition for jobs should continue to be strong because more students are graduating from law school each year than there are jobs available. Some law school graduates who have been unable to find permanent positions turn to temporary staffing firms that place attorneys in short-term jobs. These firms allow companies to hire lawyers as needed and permit beginning lawyers to develop practical experience. Many other law school graduates and licensed lawyers end up finding work in other occupations or industries due to the difficulty in finding jobs with traditional legal employers.

Because of the strong competition, a law school graduate's willingness to relocate and his or her practical experiences are becoming more important. However, to be licensed in another state, a lawyer may have to take an additional state bar examination.

## Related Occupations

- Arbitrator/Mediator/Conciliator
- Judge/Hearing Officer
- Paralegal/Legal Assistant
- Postsecondary Teacher

## MORE INFORMATION

**American Bar Association (ABA)**
1050 Connecticut Avenue NW, Suite 400
Washington, DC 20036
202.662.1000
www.americanbar.org

**American Intellectual Property Law Association (AIPLA)**
1400 Crystal Drive, Suite 600
Arlington, VA 22202
703.415.0780
aipla@aipla.org
www.aipla.org

**Association of American Law Schools (AALS)**
1614 20th Street NW
Washington, DC 20009-1001
202.296.8851
info@aals.org
www.aals.org

**Federal Bar Association (FBA)**
1220 North Fillmore Street, Suite 444
Arlington, VA 22201
571.481.9100
fba@fedbar.org
www.fedbar.org

**Intellectual Property Owners Association (IPOA)**
1501 M Street NW, Suite 1150
Washington, DC 20005
202.507.4500
info@ipo.org
ipo.org

**Law School Admission Council (LSAC)**
62 Penn Street
Newtown, PA 18940
215.968.1001
LSACinfo@LSAC.org
www.lsac.org

**National Association for Law Placement (NALP)**
1220 19th Street NW, Suite 401
Washington, DC 20036-2405
202.835.1001
info@nalp.org
www.nalp.org

**National Association of Patent Practitioners (NAPP)**
701 Exposition Place, Suite 206
Raleigh, NC 27615
919.230.9635
napp@napp.org
www.napp.org

**National Conference of Bar Examiners (NCBE)**
302 South Bedford Street
Madison, WI 53703-3622
www.ncbex.org

**United States Patent and Trademark Office (USPTO)**
USPTO Madison Building
600 Dulany Street
Alexandria, VA 22314
800.786.9199
www.uspto.gov

---

*Stuart Paterson*

# *Conversation With...*

# GRANT BREWER

Executive Director
LICENSE: Center for Technology Commercialization
Virginia Tech, Blacksburg, VA
Entrepreneurial mentorship in academia, 22 years

**What was your individual career path in terms of education/training, entry-level job, or other significant opportunity?**

My grandfather lived a relatively long life, but life was hard on his body. He was injured during World War II, smoked, and worked in coal mines. He also taught me how to fish, hunt, and play baseball. One day he was that guy and the next day he couldn't get off the couch because he lost a leg due to old injuries. We lived in Alabama, and the VA there gave him a prosthetic leg like something you'd see on Captain Hook. He just kind of withered away from that point on. I thought they should be able to do more for their patients. So, I left for college actually wanting to make prosthetic legs for people who had had leg amputations.

I went into the bioengineering program at the University of Georgia, which was brand new at the time, and earned my BS in bioengineering.

My first job was at a company called CryoLife, Inc. in Atlanta, where I made $10/hour in a lab making a glue used for sealing wounds after surgery. I got a lot of exposure to US Food & Drug Administration (FDA) regulations and how big a deal quality control is in the biotech space. After a short tenure, I moved to a company called Serologicals in Charleston, South Carolina, that made highly concentrated antibody treatments to help people recover from exposure to rabies, hepatitis, that sort of thing. I was Director of Operations when the company was sold 4 years later.

At that point I moved into academia and worked in the tech transfer office at the Medical University of South Carolina. My original work involved surveying and assessing the research going on at the university for technologies of potential patentability and commercial interest. If an inventor was in his lab working on a widget, and Company X wanted to produce and market it, I'd hire a patent attorney to protect the rights to the widget, license it, and establish royalties on sales. I later transferred to running the university's incubator. An incubator looks at helping emerging companies understand what they need to do to make their company successful.

During this time, I also earned an MBA in Entrepreneurship from The Citadel. I've been part of a few startup companies with varying levels of success, from being purchased to completely flaming out. That's a typical entrepreneurial experience, and I have had a lot of experience picking ideas that have financial potential.

Here at Virginia Tech, I'm in charge of running an office of people who are handling patents and licensing. I spend a lot of time working on relationships between the university and outside entities—corporations and startups—who want to do business with the university.

For example, we have a professor who works on making devices to treat malignant tumors, a really interesting science. We patented that and licensed it to a pharmaceutical company who now has gotten the technology approved for use by the FDA, and it's being used to treat cancer patients and save lives. The goal is to get the technology out of the halls of academia and pages of journal articles and into the hands of people who can use it.

**What are the most important skills and/or qualities for someone in your profession?**
An ability to communicate well and get along with different types of people. You also need to understand the synergies and relationships between science and business because not everybody understands when good science is good business.

**What do you wish you had known going into this profession?**
That no one has a crystal ball into the future. You can only make the best decision you can make with the information at hand. I'm in a position where I'm being asked to pick winners to some extent, and our technologies are at a super early stage. Early on, it would have been helpful if I'd known that I just needed to take an objective and fair approach to my job as opposed to wondering which idea was going to be the next big commercial success.

**Are there many job opportunities in your profession? In what specific areas?**
Yes. Universities are becoming much more involved in the economic development of their communities, and there is more synergy between the university and nonacademic professionals. To the extent you can marry good analytic science skills with good business, there will be more opportunities. Most universities have a tech transfer office, and the best way to get involved is through the Association for University Tech Managers (https://autm.net).

**How do you see your profession changing in the next 5 years? How will technology impact that change, and what skills will be required?**
I think we're going to see a lot more focus on quantum technology and artificial intelligence and cyber security, and those will require a very different skill set from traditional science focused on life sciences. Biosciences will continue to grow, but we will see an explosion in these other fields. Among other impacts, it will affect healthcare by changing how we make medical treatment and diagnostic decisions.

**What do you enjoy most about your job? What do you enjoy least about your job?**
I most like using my skill set and the exercise of developing business opportunities from science opportunities. I least like the conflict that can arise; when you do a job with tough decisions, that's part of the job.

**Can you suggest a valuable "try this" for students considering a career in your profession?**

Listen to technology podcasts to keep abreast of technological innovations and where the energy and forward momentum is occurring.

# Loan Officer

## Snapshot

**Career Cluster(s):** Business, Management & Administration; Finance

**Interests:** Business; finance

**Earnings (Yearly Average):** $63,270

**Employment & Outlook:** As Fast As Average Growth Expected

## OVERVIEW

### Sphere of Work

Loan officers evaluate, authorize, or recommend approval of loan applications for people and businesses using a process called underwriting to assess whether applicants qualify for loans. Consumer loan officers specialize in loans to people, whereas commercial loan officers specialize in loans to businesses. Business loans are often essential to the instigation of, or continuance of, a business' operations. Further, mortgage loan officers specialize in loans used to buy real estate.

### Work Environment

Loan officers who specialize in consumer loans usually work in offices. Mortgage and commercial loan officers often work outside the office and meet with clients at their homes or businesses, as a means of assessing the client and viability of the property or business.

Loan officers, among other things, meet with loan applicants to gather personal information and answer questions. Photo via iStock.com/Drazen Zigic. [Used under license.]

### Occupation Interest

Loan officers have an interest in finance, math, and statistics, as well as a desire to help members of the public achieve financial and personal goals, while ensuring that the company for which the loan officer works is well-served. Loan officers make decisions that greatly affect peoples' lives—be it when securing a first mortgage, or a startup loan for an entrepreneurial endeavor.

### Profile

**Interests:** Data, People, Things
**Working Conditions:** Inside
**Education Needs:** On-the-Job Training, Bachelor's Degree
**Licensure/Certification:** Required, Varies
**Opportunities for Experience:** Internship
**Interest Score:** CES

## A Day in the Life—Duties and Responsibilities

Loan officers use a process called underwriting to assess whether applicants qualify for loans. After collecting and verifying all the required financial documents, the loan officer evaluates the information they obtain to determine the applicant's need for a loan and ability to pay back the loan. Most firms use underwriting software, which produces a recommendation for the loan based on the applicant's financial status. After the underwriting software produces a recommendation, loan officers review the output of the software and consider any additional information to make a final decision.

The work of loan officers has sizable customer-service and sales components. Loan officers often answer questions and guide customers through the application process. In addition, many loan officers must market the products and services of their lending institution and actively solicit new business.

Consumer loan officers specialize in loans to people. Consumers take out loans for many reasons, such as buying a car or paying college tuition. For some simple consumer loans, the underwriting process is fully automated. However, the loan officer is still needed to guide applicants through the process and to deal with cases with unusual circumstances. Some institutions—generally small banks and credit unions—do not use underwriting software and instead rely on loan officers to complete the underwriting process manually.

### Duties and Responsibilities

- Contacting companies or people to ask if they need a loan
- Meeting with loan applicants to gather personal information and answer questions
- Explaining different types of loans and the terms of each type to applicants
- Obtaining, verifying, and analyzing the applicant's financial information, such as credit rating and income level
- Reviewing loan agreements to ensure that they comply with federal and state regulations
- Approving loan applications or referring them to management for a decision

Commercial loan officers specialize in loans to businesses, which often use the loans to begin operations, buy supplies, and upgrade or expand existing operations. Commercial loans often are larger and more complicated than other types of loans. Because companies have such complex financial situations and statements, commercial loans typically require human judgment in addition to the analysis by underwriting software. Furthermore, some commercial loans are so large that no single bank will provide the entire amount requested. In such cases, loan officers may have to work with multiple banks to put together a package of loans.

Mortgage loan officers specialize in loans used to buy real estate (property and buildings), which are called mortgage loans. Mortgage loan officers work on loans for both residential and commercial properties. Often, mortgage loan officers must seek out clients, which requires developing relationships with real estate companies and other sources that can refer prospective applicants.

## OCCUPATION SPECIALTIES

**Loan Collection Officer**
Loan collection officers contact borrowers who fail to make their loan payments on time. They work with borrowers to help them find a way to keep paying off the loan. If the borrower continues to miss payments, loan officers start the process of taking away what the borrower used to secure the loan (called "collateral")—often a home or car—and selling it to repay the loan.

**Loan Underwriter**
Loan underwriters specialize in evaluating whether a client is creditworthy. They collect, verify, and evaluate the client's financial information provided on their loan application and then use loan underwriting software to produce recommendations.

## WORK ENVIRONMENT

### Immediate Physical Environment

Loan officers working on the consumer side spend most of their time in offices. Commercial loan officers, however, may spend quite a bit of time out of the office, traveling to meet applicants and assess properties and businesses in person. Most loan officers work full-time and some work extensive hours.

### Human Environment

While some loan officers may spend most of their time in an office working with software to generate recommendations, others require a person-to-person approach in order to assess and prepare the loan. Loan officers must exhibit good judgment and business sense, while also understanding that the decisions they make directly impact the lives of their clients. They are the gateway to funds that will help their clients to grow and succeed in life and in business, but the loans must also be profitable. In many cases loan officers need to "sell" themselves to attract business, whether by directly interacting with prospective clients, or networking with real estate agents or other firms.

### Technological Environment

Computer and software usage is common, including specialized underwriting software, as well as database software, accounting software, and platforms that allow the loan officer to access credit ratings. The officer must be extremely familiar with these programs to carry out day-to-day functions without error.

## EDUCATION, TRAINING, AND ADVANCEMENT

### High School/Secondary

High school students with an interest in entering the world of banking and finance should focus on math, economics, and statistics courses, while ensuring good grades in English to improve communication skills. Students should think ahead to postsecondary, in terms of what pathways and schools will help meet their career goals.

**Suggested High School Subjects**

- Algebra
- Biology
- Calculus
- Chemistry
- Earth or Life or Physical Science
- Economics
- English
- Geometry
- History
- Physics
- Psychology
- Statistics
- Trigonometry

**Transferable Skills and Abilities**

**Decision-making Skills**
- Assess an applicant's financial information and deciding whether to award the applicant a loan

**Detail-oriented**
- Paying attention to detail, as each piece of information on an application can have a major effect on the profitability of a loan

**Initiative**
- Seeking out new clients
- Promoting their lending institution and contacting people and firms to determine their need for a loan

**Interpersonal Skills**
- Guiding customers through the application process and answer their questions

**Related Career Pathways/Majors**

*Business, Management & Administration Career Cluster*

- Business Information Management Pathway

*Finance Career Cluster*

- Accounting Pathway
- Banking Services Pathway
- Business Finance Pathway

## Postsecondary

Loan officers typically need a bachelor's degree, usually in a field such as business or finance. Because commercial loan officers analyze the finances of businesses applying for credit, they need to understand general business accounting, including how to read financial statements.

**Related College Majors**

- Business
- Economics
- Finance

## Adult Job Seekers

Some jobseekers may be able to enter the occupation without a bachelor's degree if they have related work experience, such as experience in sales, customer service, or banking.

## Professional Certification and Licensure

Mortgage loan officers must have a Mortgage Loan Originator (MLO) license. To become licensed, they must complete at least 20 hours of coursework, pass an exam, and submit to background and credit checks. Licenses must be renewed annually, and individual states may have additional requirements.

Several banking associations, including the American Bankers Association (ABA) and the Mortgage Bankers Association (MBA), as well as a number of schools, offer courses, training programs, or certifications for loan officers. Although not required, certification shows dedication and expertise and, thus, may enhance a candidate's employment opportunities.

## Additional Requirements

Once hired, loan officers usually receive some on-the-job training. This may be a combination of formal, company-sponsored training and informal training during the first few months on the job.

## EARNINGS AND ADVANCEMENT

Earnings depend on the experience of the loan officer, the size of the firm for which they work, and their area of specialty. Median annual earnings of loan officers were $63,270 in 2019. The lowest 10 percent earned less than $32,560, and the highest 10 percent earned more than $132,680.

The form of compensation varies widely by employer. Some loan officers are paid a flat salary; others are paid on commission. Those on commission usually are paid a base salary plus a commission for the loans they originate. Loan officers also may receive extra commission or bonuses based on the number of loans they originate or how well the loans perform.

Loan officers may receive paid vacations, holidays, and sick days; life and health insurance; and retirement benefits. These are usually paid by the employer.

## EMPLOYMENT AND OUTLOOK

Loan officers held 316,900 jobs in 2019. Employment is expected to grow by 3 percent through the year 2029, about as fast as the average for all occupations. Increased demand for loan officers is expected as both businesses and individuals seek credit to finance commercial investments and personal spending. Loan officers will be needed to evaluate the creditworthiness of applicants and to determine the likelihood that loans will be paid back in full and on time.

However, the decline of bank branches and the increased use of productivity-enhancing technology in loan processing are expected to slow employment growth.

Job opportunities should be good for people with lending, banking, or sales experience. In addition, some firms require loan officers to find their own clients, so candidates with established contacts and a referral network should have the best job opportunities.

### Related Occupations

- Financial Analyst
- Financial Examiner
- Financial Manager
- Insurance Sales Agent
- Personal Financial Advisor
- Real Estate Broker/Sales Agent

- Securities/Commodities/Financial Services Sales Agent
- Tax Examiners/Collectors/Revenue Agent
- Teller

## MORE INFORMATION

**American Bankers Association (ABA)**
1120 Connecticut Avenue NW
Washington, DC 20036
800.226.5377
www.aba.com

**Mortgage Bankers Association (MBA)**
1919 M Street NW, 5th floor
Washington, DC 20036
202.557.2700
membership@mba.org
www.mba.org

**National Association of Mortgage Brokers (NAMB)**
601 Pennsylvania Avenue NW, South Building
Washington, DC 20004
202.434.8250
membership@namb.org
namb.org

**National Association of Mortgage Underwriters (NAMU)**
Presidential Circle
4000 Hollywood Boulevard, Suite 555-South
Hollywood, FL 33021
800.865.8550
contact@mortgage-underwriters.org
www.Mortgage-Underwriters.org

**National Association of Mortgage Processors (NAMP):**
www.mortgageprocessor.org
Nationwide Multistate Licensing System & Registry (NMLS) Resource Center
855.665.7123
mortgage.nationwidelicensingsystem.org

*Stuart Paterson*

# Machinist/Tool and Die Maker

**Snapshot**

**Career Cluster(s):** Business, Management & Administration; Manufacturing; Science, Technology, Engineering & Mathematics

**Interests:** Creativity; machines; tools; manual work; technical work; mathematics

**Earnings (Yearly Average):** $71,160

**Employment & Outlook:** As Fast As Average Growth Expected

## OVERVIEW

### Sphere of Work

Machinists and tool and die makers set up and operate a variety of computer-controlled and mechanically controlled machine tools to produce precision metal parts, instruments, and tools for a variety of industries. They may also own their own shops.

A machinist at a lathe. Photo by U.S. Air Force via Wikimedia Commons. [Public Domain.]

### Work Environment

Machinists and tool and die makers work in industrial settings with computer-controlled machine tools. Adhering to workplace health and safety protocols is important to avoid injury. Although many machinists and tool and die makers work full-time during regular business hours, some work evenings and weekends because facilities may operate around the clock. Some work more than 40 hours a week.

## Profile

**Interests:** Things, Data, People
**Working Conditions:** Both Inside and Outside
**Physical Strength:** Medium Work, Heavy Work
**Education Needs:** On-the-Job Training, High School Diploma with Technical Education, Junior/Technical/Community College, Apprenticeship
**Licensure/Certification:** Optional
**Opportunities for Experience:** Internship, Apprenticeship, Part-Time Work
**Interest Score:** RIC

### Occupation Interest

Machinists and tool and die makers are good with their hands, have strong math skills, and have an interest in creating specialized parts used in an array of industries, including metalworking, automotive, aerospace, and more. They take satisfaction in knowing that their precision-cut parts play a vital role in the functioning of everything from bicycles to space shuttles. Those who own their own shops have strong business skills as well.

## Duties and Responsibilities

**Machinists**

- Reading blueprints, sketches, or CAD and CAM files
- Setting up, operating, and disassembling manual, automatic, and CNC machine tools
- Aligning, securing, and adjusting cutting tools and workpieces
- Turning, milling, drilling, shaping, and grinding machine parts to specifications
- Measuring, examining, and testing completed products for defects
- Smoothing the surfaces of parts or products
- Presenting finished workpieces to customers and making modifications if needed

**Tool and Die Maker**

- Reading blueprints, sketches, specifications, or CAD and CAM files for making tools and dies
- Computing and verifying dimensions, sizes, shapes, and tolerances of workpieces
- Setting up, operating, and disassembling conventional, manual, and CNC machine tools
- Filing, grinding, and adjusting parts so that they fit together properly
- Testing completed tools and dies to ensure that they meet specifications
- Smoothing and polishing the surfaces of tools and dies

### A Day in the Life—Duties and Responsibilities

Machinists use machine tools, such as lathes, milling machines, and grinders, to produce precision metal parts. Many machinists must be able to use both manual and computer numerically controlled (CNC) machinery. CNC machines control the cutting tool speed and do all necessary cuts to create a part. The machinist determines the cutting path, the speed of the cut, and the feed rate by programming instructions into the CNC machine.

Although workers may produce large quantities of one part, precision machinists often fabricate small batches or one-of-a-kind items. The parts that machinists make range from simple steel bolts to titanium bone screws for orthopedic implants. Hydraulic parts, antilock brakes, and automobile pistons are other widely known products that machinists make.

Some machinists repair or make new parts for existing machinery. After an industrial machinery mechanic discovers a broken part in a machine, a machinist remanufactures the part. The machinist refers to blueprints and performs the same machining operations that were used to create the original part in order to create the replacement.

Some manufacturing processes use lasers, water jets, and electrified wires to cut the workpiece. As engineers design and build new types of machine tools, machinists must learn new machining properties and techniques.

On the other hand, tool and die makers construct precision tools or metal forms, called dies, that are used to cut, shape, and form metal and other materials. They produce jigs and fixtures—devices that hold metal while it is bored, stamped, or drilled—and gauges and other measuring devices.

Dies are used to shape metal in stamping and forging operations. They also make metal molds for die casting and for molding plastics, ceramics, and composite materials.

Tool and die makers use computer-aided design (CAD) programs to develop products and parts. They enter designs into computer programs that produce blueprints for the required tools and dies. Computer numeric control programmers, described in the metal and plastic machine workers profile, convert CAD designs into computer-aided manufacturing (CAM) programs that contain instructions for a sequence of cutting-tool operations. Once these programs are developed, CNC machines follow the set of instructions contained in the program to produce the part. Machinists normally operate CNC machines, but tool and die makers often are trained to both operate CNC machines and write CNC programs and, thus, may do either task.

## WORK ENVIRONMENT

### Immediate Physical Environment

Because machinists and tool and die makers work around machine tools that may present hazards, these workers must follow precautions to avoid injuries. For example, workers must wear protective equipment, such as safety glasses, to shield against bits of flying metal, earplugs to dampen the noise produced by machinery, and masks to limit their exposure to fumes.

### Human Environment

Human interaction depends on the size of the shop and the nature of the machinist's or tool and die maker's job. A shop with numerous employees might work on larger-scale projects requiring regular collaboration and teamwork, while a smaller shop might do more solitary, small-batch jobs. In all cases, employees must interact with their employer on assignments, and vice versa. Shop owners have the added responsibility of managing staffing and employment matters, as well as meeting with clients, including resolving disputes. Some machinists may also test their products in the field.

### Technological Environment

Machinists and tool and die makers must be extremely familiar with all the necessary tools of their trade, including manual and CNC machinery. They must be able to create and read blueprints, commonly using CAD and CAM software. As engineers design and build new types of machine tools, machinists must learn new machining properties and techniques.

## EDUCATION, TRAINING, AND ADVANCEMENT

### High School/Secondary

Machinists typically have a high school diploma or equivalent, whereas tool and die makers may need to complete courses beyond high school. High school courses in math, blueprint reading, metalworking, and drafting are considered useful.

**Suggested High School Subjects**

- Algebra
- Biology
- Chemistry
- Civics
- Earth or Life or Physical Science
- Economics
- English
- Entrepreneurship
- Geometry
- History
- Physics
- Pre-Calculus

- Psychology
- Statistics
- Trigonometry

**Related Career Pathways/Majors**

*Business, Management & Administration Career Cluster*

- General Management Pathway

*Manufacturing Career Cluster*

- Manufacturing Production Process Development Pathway
- Production Pathway

*Science, Technology, Engineering & Mathematics Career Cluster*

- Engineering & Technology Pathway
- Science & Mathematics Pathway

## Transferable Skills and Abilities

**Analytical Skills**

- Understanding technical blueprints, models, and specifications in order to craft precision tools and metal parts

**Manual Dexterity**

- Machining parts may demand accuracy to within .0001 of an inch, a level of accuracy that requires workers' concentration and dexterity

**Math Skills and Computer Application Experience**

- Using computers to work with CAD/CAM technology, CNC machine tools, and computerized measuring machines

**Mechanical Skills**

- Operating milling machines, lathes, grinders, laser and water cutting machines, wire electrical discharge machines, and other machine tools

**Physical Stamina**

- Standing for extended periods and performing repetitious movements

**Technical Skills**

- Understanding computerized measuring machines and metalworking processes, such as stock removal, chip control, and heat treating and plating

## Postsecondary

Some community colleges and technical schools have 2-year programs that train students to become machinists or tool and die makers. These programs usually teach design and blueprint reading, the use of a variety of welding and cutting tools, and the programming and function of CNC machines.

**Related College Majors**

- Machine Shop Technology/Assistant
- Machine Tool Technology/Machinist
- Tool & Die Technology

## Adult Job Seekers

Adults with a high school diploma and who have related work experience, such as sheet metal workers, mechanics, and machinery maintenance workers, stand a good chance of becoming machinists or tool and die makers if they undergo the required training.

### Professional Certification and Licensure

A number of organizations and colleges offer certification programs. The Skills Certification System, for example, is an industry-driven program that aims to align education pathways with career pathways. In addition, journey-level certification is available from state apprenticeship boards after the completion of an apprenticeship.

Completing a certification program provides machinists and tool and die makers with better job opportunities and helps employers judge the abilities of new hires.

### Additional Requirements

There are multiple ways for workers to gain competency in the job as a machinist or tool or die maker. One common way is through long-term on-the-job training, which lasts 1 year or longer.

Trainees usually work 40 hours per week and take additional technical instruction during evenings. Trainees often begin as machine operators and gradually take on more difficult assignments. Machinists and tool and die makers must be experienced in using computers to work with CAD/CAM technology, CNC machine tools, and computerized measuring machines. Some machinists become tool and die makers.

Some new workers may enter apprenticeship programs, which are typically sponsored by a manufacturer. Apprenticeship programs often consist of paid shop training and related technical instruction lasting several years. The technical instruction usually is provided in cooperation with local community colleges and vocational-technical schools. Workers typically enter apprenticeships with a high school diploma or equivalent.

## EARNINGS AND ADVANCEMENT

Earnings depend on the size of the machine shop, the scale of projects, industries served, and whether the machinist or tool and die maker owns the business.

Median annual earnings of machinists were $44,420 in 2019. The lowest 10 percent earned less than $27,940, and the highest 10 percent earned more than $66,610.

Median annual earnings of tool and die makers were $53,920 in 2019. The lowest 10 percent earned less than $33,820, and the highest 10 percent earned more than $77,940.

Machinists and tool and die makers may receive paid vacations, holidays, and sick days; life and health insurance; and retirement benefits. These are usually paid by an employer if the business is not self-owned.

## EMPLOYMENT AND OUTLOOK

Machinists and tool and die makers held 460,600 jobs in 2019. Employment is expected to grow as fast as average for all occupations through the year 2029, at a rate of 3 percent, with employment growth varying by specialty.

Employment of machinists is projected to grow 4 percent through the year 2029. With improvements in technologies, such as CNC machine tools, autoloaders, high-speed machining, and lights-out manufacturing, machinists will still be required to set up, monitor, and maintain these systems.

Employment of tool and die makers is projected to decline 5 percent through the year 2029. Advances in automation, including CNC machine tools, should reduce demand for tool and die makers to perform tasks, such as programming how parts fit together that computer software can perform.

Many job openings for machinists and tool and die makers are expected to arise each year from the need to replace workers who transfer to other occupations or leave the labor force, such as to retire.

### Related Occupations

- Boilermaker
- Industrial Machinery Mechanic/Machinery Maintenance Worker/Millwright
- Metal/Plastic Machine Worker
- Sheet Metal Worker
- Welder/Cutter/Solderer/Brazer

## MORE INFORMATION

**American Mold Builders Association (AMBA)**
7321 Shadeland Station Way, #285
Indianapolis, IN 46256
317.436.3102
info@amba.org
amba.org

**Association for Manufacturing Technology (AMT)**
7901 Jones Branch Drive, Suite 900
McLean, VA 22102-4206
800.524.0475
AMT@AMTonline.org
www.amtonline.org

**Fabricators and Manufacturers Association (FMA)**
2135 Point Boulevard
Elgin, IL 60123
888.394.4362
info@fmanet.org
www.fmamfg.org

**Manufacturing Institute (MI)**
733 10th Street NW, Suite 700
Washington, DC 20001
202.637.3426
Institute@nam.org
www.themanufacturinginstitute.org

**National Institute for Metalworking Skills (NIMS)**
10565 Fairfax Boulevard, Suite 10
Fairfax, VA 22030
844.839.6467
www.nims-skills.org

**National Tooling & Machining Association (NTMA)**
1357 Rockside Road
Cleveland OH 44134
800.248.6862
ntma.org

**Precision Machined Products Association (PMPA)**
6880 W Snowville Road
Brecksville, OH 44141
440.526.0300
gro.apmp@ofni
www.pmpa-national.com

**Precision Metalforming Association (PMA)**
6363 Oak Tree Boulevard
Independence, OH 44131-2500
216.901.8800
www.pma.org

---

*Stuart Paterson*

# Private Detective/Investigator

### Snapshot

**Career Cluster(s):** Business, Management & Administration; Law, Public Safety, Corrections & Security

**Interests:** Law & justice; investigation; surveillance

**Earnings (Yearly Average):** $50,510

**Employment & Outlook:** Much Faster Than Average Growth Expected

## OVERVIEW

### Sphere of Work

Private detectives and investigators search for information about legal, financial, and personal matters. They offer many services, such as verifying people's backgrounds and statements, finding missing persons, and investigating computer crimes.

### Work Environment

The work environment for private detectives and investigators ranges from office work, such as computer research and phone calls, to field work such as interviewing and surveillance. Private detectives and investigators often work irregular hours because they conduct surveillance and contact people outside

A private detective may conduct surveilance as part of the job, often from a hidden position. Photo via iStock.com/Andrey Popov. [Used under license.]

of normal work hours. They may work early mornings, evenings, weekends, and holidays.

### Profile

**Interests:** People, Data, Things
**Working Conditions:** Both Inside and Outside
**Physical Strength:** Medium Work
**Education Needs:** On-the-Job Training, High School Diploma with Work Experience
**Licensure/Certification:** Varies By State
**Opportunities for Experience:** On-The-Job Training
**Interest Score:** EC

### Occupation Interest

Private detectives and investigators are inquisitive, highly analytical individuals who enjoy taking on challenging cases and solving real-world mysteries, at the behest of clients. They typically come from related fields such as law enforcement, the military, or intelligence, where the required skill set is honed through years of work experience.

### A Day in the Life—Duties and Responsibilities

Private detectives and investigators offer many services for individuals, attorneys, and businesses. Examples include performing background checks, investigating employees for possible theft from a company, proving or disproving infidelity in a divorce case, and helping to locate a missing person.

Private detectives and investigators use a variety of tools when researching the facts in a case. Much of their work is done with a computer, allowing them to obtain information such as telephone numbers, details about social networks, descriptions of online activities, and records of a person's prior arrests. They make phone calls to verify facts and interview people when conducting a background investigation.

Detectives also conduct surveillance when investigating a case. They may watch locations, such as a person's home or office, often from a hidden position. Using cameras and binoculars, detectives gather information on people of interest.

Detectives and investigators must be mindful of the law when conducting investigations. Because they lack police authority, their work must be done with the same authority as a private citizen. As a result, detectives and investigators must have a good understanding of federal, state, and local laws, such as privacy laws, and other legal issues affecting their work. Otherwise, evidence they collect may not be useable in court, and they could face prosecution.

### Duties and Responsibilities

- Interviewing people to gather information
- Searching online, public, and court records to uncover clues
- Conducting surveillance
- Collecting evidence for clients
- Checking for civil judgments and criminal history

## OCCUPATION SPECIALTIES

**Skip Tracer**

Skip tracers specialize in locating people whose whereabouts are unknown. For example, debt collectors may employ them to locate people who have unpaid bills.

## WORK ENVIRONMENT

### Immediate Physical Environment

Private detectives and investigators work in many environments, depending on the case. Some spend more time in offices, researching cases on computers and making phone calls. Others spend more time in the field, conducting interviews or performing surveillance. In addition, private detectives and investigators may have to work outdoors or from a vehicle, in all kinds of weather, to obtain the information their client needs.

### Human Environment

Although investigators often work alone, some work with others while conducting surveillance or executing large, complicated assignments. Some may also choose to employ a team of investigators. Investigators must be comfortable dealing with clients and members of the public, sometimes in highly stressful situations. They may also need to deal professionally with the police and give evidence in court.

### Technological Environment

Private detectives and investigators must be able to use all tools at their disposal for solving cases, including standard computer software, databases, and a familiarity with social media and the Internet. Sophisticated camera equipment may also be required, as well as standard field tools such as binoculars. Private detectives and investigators should ideally have their own mode of transportation because travel is often required. On the business end, investigators who run their own firms must be familiar with standard software such as accounting and payroll.

## EDUCATION, TRAINING, AND ADVANCEMENT

### High School/Secondary

Education requirements vary greatly with the job, but most jobs require a high school diploma. Students with an interest in this line of work should prepare as though for a career in law enforcement, with courses such as English, civics, history, psychology, and sociology.

**Suggested High School Subjects**

- Algebra
- Biology
- Chemistry
- Civics
- Earth or Life or Physical Science
- Economics
- English
- Forensic Science
- Geometry
- History
- Physics
- Psychology
- Sociology
- Statistics

**Related Career Pathways/Majors**

*Business, Management & Administration Career Cluster*

- General Management Pathway

*Law, Public Safety, Corrections & Security Career Cluster*

- Law Enforcement Services Pathway
- Security & Protective Services Pathway

***Transferable Skills and Abilities***

**Communication Skills**

- Listening carefully and asking appropriate questions when interviewing a person of interest

**Decision-making Skills**

- Thinking on one's feet and making quick decisions, based on the limited information that they have at a given time

**Inquisitiveness**

- Wanting to ask questions and search for the truth

**Patience**

- Spending long periods conducting surveillance while waiting for an event to occur
- Investigating cases may take a long time, and they may not provide a resolution quickly—or at all

**Resourcefulness**

- Working persistently with whatever leads are available, no matter how limited, to determine the next step toward their goal
- Anticipating what a person of interest will do next

### Postsecondary

Some jobs may require a 2- or 4-year degree in a field such as criminal justice.

Private detectives and investigators must typically have previous work experience, usually in law enforcement, the military, or federal intelligence, each with its own educational requirements. Those in such related jobs, who retire after 20 or 25 years of service, may become private detectives or investigators in a second career.

Other private detectives and investigators may have previously worked as bill and account collectors, claims adjusters, paralegals, or process servers.

**Related College Majors**

- Criminal Justice/Police Science
- Cultural/Archaeological Resources Protection
- Cyber/Computer Forensics and Counterterrorism
- Financial Forensics & Fraud Investigation
- Law Enforcement Recordkeeping and Evidence Management
- Maritime Law Enforcement
- Protective Services Operations

## Professional Certification and Licensure

Most states require private detectives and investigators to have a license. Check with your state for more information; Professional Investigator Magazine has links to most states' licensing requirements. Because laws often change, jobseekers should verify the licensing laws related to private investigators with the state and locality in which they want to work.

Candidates may also obtain certification, although it is not required for employment. Still, becoming certified through professional organizations can demonstrate competence and may help candidates advance in their careers.

For investigators who specialize in negligence or criminal defense investigation, the National Association of Legal Investigators (NALI) offers the Certified Legal Investigator (CLI) certification. For other investigators, the American Society for Industrial Security (ASIS) International offers the Professional Certified Investigator certification.

## Additional Requirements

Most private detectives and investigators learn through on-the-job training, typically lasting between several months and a year.

Although new investigators must learn how to gather information, additional training depends on the type of firm that hires them. For example, investigators may learn to conduct remote surveillance, reconstruct accident scenes, or investigate insurance fraud. Corporate investigators hired by large companies may receive formal training in business practices, management structure, and various finance-related topics.

## EARNINGS AND ADVANCEMENT

Earnings depend on the experience of the investigator, the nature of the cases they work, and the clients for whom they work. Median annual earnings of private detectives and investigators were $50,510 in 2019. The lowest 10 percent earned less than $30,390, and the highest 10 percent earned more than $89,760.

Private detectives and investigators may receive paid vacations, holidays, and sick days; life and health insurance; and retirement benefits. These are usually paid by an employer if the investigator works for a firm. Travel expenses may also be covered.

## EMPLOYMENT AND OUTLOOK

Private detectives and investigators held 36,200 jobs in 2019. Three percent were self-employed. Employment is expected to grow much faster than all occupations through the year 2029, at a rate of 8 percent. However, because it is a small occupation, the fast growth will result in only about 3,000 new jobs over the 10-year period.

Continued lawsuits, fraud and other crimes, and interpersonal mistrust create demand for investigative services in industries such as legal services.

Background checks will continue to be a source of work for some investigators, as online investigations are not always sufficient.

Strong competition for jobs can be expected because private detective and investigator careers attract many qualified people, including relatively young retirees from law enforcement and the military.

Candidates with related work experience, as well as those with strong interviewing skills and familiarity with computers, may find more job opportunities than others.

### Related Occupations

- Accountant/Auditor
- Bill/Account Collector
- Claims Adjuster/Appraiser/Examiner/Investigator
- Financial Examiner

- Fire Inspector
- Forensic Science Technician
- Paralegal/Legal Assistant
- Police Officer/Detective
- Security Guard/Gambling Surveillance Officer

## MORE INFORMATION

**ASIS International**
1625 Prince Street
Alexandria, VA 22314-2882
703.519.6200
asis@asisonline.org
www.asisonline.org

**Council of International Investigators (CII)**
P.O. Box 1015
St. Helena, SC 29920
917.292.0613
lec@cii2.org
www.cii2.org

**International Intelligence Network (INTELLENET)**
P.O. Box 350
Gladwyne, PA 19035
734.320.9240
Intellenet@intellenet.org
www.intellenet.org

**National Association of Legal Investigators (NALI)**
P.O. Box 278
Bath, MI 48808
517.702.9835
www.nalionline.org

**National Association of Professional Process Servers (NAPPS)**
P.O. Box 4547
Portland, OR 97208-4547
503.222.4180
napps.org

**National Council of Investigation and Security Services (NCISS)**
P.O. Box 200615
Evans, CO 80620
800.445.8408
www.nciss.org

**National Defender Investigator Association (NDIA)**
P.O. Box 1900
San Marcos, CA 92079-1900
760.290.3909
nationaldefender@gmail.com
www.ndia.net

**Professional Background Screening Association (PBSA)**
110 Horizon Drive, Suite 210
Raleigh, NC 27615
919.459.2082
info@thepbsa.org
thepbsa.org

**World Association of Detectives (WAD)**
P.O. Box 20030
Evans, CO 80620
443.982.4586
Wad@Wad.net
www.wad.net

---

*Stuart Paterson*

# Property/Real Estate/Community Association Manager

**Snapshot**

**Career Cluster(s):** Architecture & Construction; Business, Management & Administration; Human Services

**Interests:** Real estate

**Earnings (Yearly Average):** $58,760

**Employment & Outlook:** Little or No Change Expected

## OVERVIEW

### Sphere of Work

Property, real estate, and community association managers take care of the many aspects of residential, commercial, or industrial properties. They make sure the property is well maintained, has a nice appearance, operates smoothly, and preserves its resale value. The manager may work for an employer or own the property they manage. Experienced managers may also open their own property management firms. Managerial duties such as these may also be part of those of a franchisee, who owns one or more properties operating under the banner of an established franchise.

Real estate officer showing property to prospective clients. Photo via iStock.com/kzenon. [Used under license.]

### Work Environment

Most property, real estate, and community association managers work out of a central office, but often visit the properties they manage to meet with tenants and employees. Most property, real estate, and community association managers work full-time, and some may work long hours, such as if they own the property themselves.

## Profile

**Interests:** People, Things, Data
**Working Conditions:** Both Inside and Outside
**Physical Strength:** Medium Work
**Education Needs:** On-the-Job Training, High School Diploma, Bachelor's Degree Optional
**Licensure/Certification:** Usually Not Required
**Opportunities for Experience:** Varies by State
**Interest Score:** EC

### Occupation Interest

Property, real estate, and community association managers have an interest in overseeing the operations of an entire building, be it a residential apartment, commercial business, or industrial location. Each type of property comes with unique challenges and requirements, so managers usually have a sound knowledge of building systems and the varying needs of tenants. Some entrepreneurs may solely invest in and manage locations on a broad level, while franchisees may also manage day-to-day business operations, such as with a fast-food restaurant.

## Duties and Responsibilities

- Meeting with prospective renters and showing them properties
- Discussing the lease and explaining the terms of occupancy or ownership
- Collecting monthly fees from tenants or individual owners
- Inspecting all building facilities, including the grounds and equipment
- Arranging for new equipment or repairs as needed
- Paying bills or delegating bill payment for such expenditures as taxes, insurance, payroll, and maintenance
- Contracting for trash removal, maintenance, landscaping, security, and other services
- Investigating and settling complaints, disturbances, and violations
- Keeping records of rental activity and owner requests
- Preparing budgets and financial reports
- Complying with anti-discrimination laws when renting or advertising, such as the Americans with Disabilities Act, the Federal Fair Housing Amendment Act, and local fair housing laws

### A Day in the Life—Duties and Responsibilities

When owners of homes, apartments, office buildings, or retail or industrial properties lack the time or expertise needed for the day-to-day management of their real estate properties, they often hire a property or real estate manager or a community association manager. Managers are employed either directly by the owner or indirectly through a contract with a property management firm.

Property and real estate managers oversee the operation of income-producing commercial or residential properties and ensure that real estate investments achieve their expected revenues. They oversee the financial operations of the property, making certain that rent is collected and that mortgages, taxes, insurance premiums, payroll, and maintenance bills are paid on time. They may review financial statements, and periodically report to the owners on the status of the property, occupancy rates, expiration dates of leases, and other matters. When vacancies occur, property managers may advertise the property or hire a leasing agent to find a tenant. They may also suggest to the owners the amount rent to charge.

Community association managers work on behalf of homeowner or community associations to manage the communal property and services of condominiums, cooperatives, and planned communities. Usually hired by a volunteer board of directors of the association, they oversee the daily affairs and supervise the maintenance of property and facilities that the homeowners use jointly through the association. Like property managers, community association managers collect monthly fees, prepare financial statements and budgets, negotiate with contractors, and help to resolve complaints. Community association managers also help homeowners and nonowner residents comply with association rules and regulations.

On-site property managers are responsible for the day-to-day operation of a single property, such as an apartment complex, an office building, or a shopping center. To ensure that the property is well maintained, on-site managers routinely inspect the grounds, facilities, and equipment to determine whether maintenance or repairs are needed. They meet with current tenants to see to requests for repairs or to resolve complaints. They also meet with prospective tenants to show vacant apartments or office space. In addition, on-site managers enforce the terms of rental or lease contracts along with an association's governing rules. They make sure that tenants pay their rent on time, follow restrictions on parking or pets, and follow the correct procedures when the lease is due to expire. Other important duties of on-site managers include keeping accurate, up-to-date records of income and expenditures from property operations and submitting regular expense reports to the senior-level property manager or the owner(s), if they do not themselves own the property.

Real estate asset managers plan and direct the purchase, sale, and development of real estate properties on behalf of businesses and investors. They focus on long-term strategic financial planning, rather than on the day-to-day operations of the property. In deciding to acquire property, real estate asset managers consider several factors, such as property values, taxes, zoning, population growth, transportation, and traffic volume and patterns. Once a site is selected, they negotiate contracts to buy or lease the property on the most favorable terms. Real estate asset managers review their company's real estate holdings periodically and identify properties that are no longer financially profitable. They then negotiate the sale of the properties or arrange for the end of leases.

## WORK ENVIRONMENT

### Immediate Physical Environment

Most property, real estate, and community association managers work in an office environment. However, many managers spend much of their time away from their desks. On-site managers, in particular, may spend a large part of their workday visiting the building engineer, showing apartments, dealing with owners and board members, checking on the janitorial and maintenance staff, or investigating problems reported by residents. Real estate asset managers may spend time away from home while traveling to company real estate holdings or searching for properties to buy.

Managing properties or community associations, or selling and leasing real estate, can sometimes be stressful. Property, real estate, and community association managers often attend evening meetings with residents, property owners, community association board members, or civic groups. As a result, long workdays are common. Some apartment managers are required to live in the apartment complexes where they work, so that they are available to respond to emergencies even when they are off duty.

### Human Environment

Managers must interact with people daily in order to perform their duties. This could involve meeting with tenants, employees such as janitorial staff, or customers if the manager is involved in day-to-day business operations carried out on the property. Managers may also interact with contractors to repair, modify, or enhance the property. Managers who do not own the property themselves will report to owner(s) of the property.

### Technological Environment

Property, real estate, and community association managers should be comfortable using recordkeeping, accounting, and database software, as well as general applications such as Microsoft Word. They should also have at least an understanding of how building systems work, in order to better coordinate with janitorial staff, engineers, and contractors. It is important for managers to maintain their skills through continuing education programs, and to learn about and implement new technologies, such as those relating to energy efficiency.

## EDUCATION, TRAINING, AND ADVANCEMENT

### High School/Secondary

Although many employers prefer to hire college graduates, a high school diploma combined with several years of related work experience is typically required for entry-level positions. Experience and knowledge of not only the properties themselves, but the business side, can be gained over time. In high school, students should take courses such as English for communication skills, as well as practical mathematics and business. Students can also reach out to nearby real estate agents or building managers to gain insight into the industry.

**Suggested High School Subjects**

- Accounting
- Algebra
- Biology
- Chemistry
- Civics
- Construction Math
- Earth or Life or Physical Sciences
- Economics
- English
- Entrepreneurship
- Forestry
- Geometry
- History
- Physics
- Psychology
- Statistics

**Related Career Pathways/Majors**

*Architecture & Construction Career Cluster*

- Maintenance/Operations Pathway

*Business Management & Administration Career Cluster*

- General Management Pathway

***Transferable Skills and Abilities***

**Communication Skills**

- Understand leasing or rental contracts
- Clearly explaining materials and answering questions raised by a resident or group of board members

**Customer-service Skills**

- Providing excellent customer service to keep existing clients and expand their business with new ones

**Interpersonal Skills**

- Interacting with people every day

**Listening Skills**

- Listening to and understanding residents and property owners in order to meet their needs

**Organizational Skills**

- Planning, coordinating, and directing multiple contractors at the same time, often for multiple properties

**Problem-solving Skills**

- Mediating disputes or legal issues between residents, homeowners, or board members

## Famous First

**The first modern-day franchiser is thought to be Martha Matilda Harper. Her hair care salons, called Harper Method Shops, were headquartered in Rochester, NY, and in 1891 she launched a franchising effort that peaked at more than 500 salons and training schools—replete with such benefits as training and branded products. The last salon closed in 1972.** Source: franchise.org.

Martha Matilda Harper. Photo via Wikimedia Commons. [Public Domain.]

- Operations Management Pathway

*Human Services Career Cluster*

- Consumer Services Pathway

### Postsecondary

Many employers prefer to hire college graduates for commercial management positions and offsite positions dealing with a property's finances or contract management. A bachelor's or master's degree in business administration, accounting, finance, real estate, or public administration is preferred for these types of positions.

#### Related College Majors

- Accounting
- Business Administration
- Finance
- Public Administration
- Real Estate

### Adult Job Seekers

Property, real estate, and community association managers typically have several years of prior work experience. Experience in real estate sales is a good background for on-site managers because real estate salespeople also show commercial properties to prospective tenants or buyers.

### Professional Certification and Licensure

Real estate managers who buy or sell property must have a real estate license in the state in which they practice. In a few states, property and community association managers also must have a real estate license. Managers of public housing subsidized by the federal government must hold certifications.

Property, real estate, and community association managers working in Alaska, Delaware, Florida, Georgia, Hawaii, Illinois, Nevada, Virginia, and the District of Columbia are required to obtain professional credentials or licensure. Requirements vary by state, but many managers working in states without requirements still obtain designations to show competence and professionalism. BOMI International, the Community Associations Institute (CAI), the Institute of Real Estate Management (IREM), the National Association of Residential Property Managers (NARPM), and the Community Association Managers International Certification Board (CAMICB) all offer various designations, certifications, and professional development courses. Most states require recertification every 2 years.

In addition, employers may require managers to attend formal training programs from various professional and trade real estate associations. Employers send managers to these programs to develop their management skills and expand their knowledge of specialized fields, such as how to operate and maintain mechanical systems in buildings, how to improve property values, insurance and risk management, personnel management, business and real estate law, community association risks and liabilities, tenant relations, communications, accounting and financial concepts, and reserve funding. Managers also participate in these programs to prepare themselves for positions of greater responsibility in property management. With related job experience, completing these programs and receiving a satisfactory score on a written exam can lead to certification or the formal award of a professional designation by the sponsoring association.

## EARNINGS AND ADVANCEMENT

Earnings depend on the size and type of the managed property (or properties), and whether the manager works for an employer or owns the property themselves. Median annual earnings of property, real estate, and community association managers were $58,760 in 2019. The lowest 10 percent earned less than $31,030, and the highest 10 percent earned more than $129,160.

Property, real estate, and community association managers may receive paid vacations, holidays, and sick days; life and health insurance; and retirement benefits. These are usually paid by an employer if the manager is not self-employed.

**Fast Fact**

**Colonel Sanders, who founded Kentucky Fried Chicken (KFC) was rejected 1,009 times before he found a restaurant willing to franchise. Plus, he was over 65.**
Source: lifehack.org

Col. Sanders. Photo by Edgy01, CC BY-SA 3.0 <https://creativecommons.org/licenses/by-sa/3.0>, via Wikimedia Commons.

Many people begin property management careers as assistant managers, working closely with a property manager. In time, many assistants advance to property manager positions.

Some people start as on-site managers of apartment buildings, office complexes, or community associations. As they gain experience, they may advance to positions of greater responsibility. Those who excel as on-site managers often transfer to assistant offsite property manager positions, in which they gain experience dealing with a broad range of property management responsibilities.

The responsibilities and compensation of property, real estate, and community association managers increase as these workers manage more and larger properties. Property managers are often responsible for several properties at a time. Some experienced managers open their own property management firms.

## EMPLOYMENT AND OUTLOOK

Property, real estate, and community association managers held 367,900 jobs in 2019. Thirty-eight percent were self-employed. Employment is projected to show little or no change through the year 2029. Employment demand will be driven by the number people living in buildings that property management companies operate, such as apartment buildings, condominiums, cooperatives, planned communities, and senior housing.

Growth in the single-family housing market may have a positive influence on demand, as some new housing developments will require property managers to oversee jointly owned common areas, such as pools, gyms, and business centers and to enforce homeowner association laws. However, the automation of some property management tasks, such as posting vacancies and assigning maintenance requests, may slow employment growth.

Job opportunities should be best for those with a bachelor's degree in business administration, real estate, or a related field and for those with professional certification.

Because of the projected increase in the elderly population, particularly good job opportunities are expected for those with experience managing retirement centers, age-restricted communities, and healthcare facilities.

### Related Occupations

- Administrative Services Manager
- Food Service Manager
- Lodging Manager
- Real Estate Broker/Sales Agent

## MORE INFORMATION

**BOMI International**
900 Bestgate Road, Suite 206
Annapolis, MD 21401
410.974.1410
service@bomi.org
www.bomi.org

**Community Association Managers International Certification Board (CAMICB)**
6402 Arlington Blvd., Suite 510
Falls Church, VA 22042
703.970.9300
info@camicb.org
camicb.org

**Community Associations Institute (CAI)**
6402 Arlington Blvd., Suite 500
Falls Church, VA 22042
703.970.9220
cai-info@caionline.org
www.caionline.org

**Institute of Real Estate Management (IREM)**
430 North Michigan Avenue
Chicago, IL 60611
800.837.0706
getinfo@irem.org
www.irem.org

**NAIOP Commercial Real Estate Development Association**
2355 Dulles Corner Boulevard, Suite 750
Herndon, VA 20171
703.904.7100
www.naiop.org

**National Association of Realtors (NAR)**
430 N. Michigan Avenue
Chicago, IL 60611-4087
800.874.6500
www.nar.realtor

**National Association of Residential Property Managers (NARPM)**
1403 Greenbrier Parkway, Suite 150
Chesapeake, VA 23320
800.782.3452
info@narpm.org
www.narpm.org

**National Property Management Association (NPMA)**
3525 Piedmont Road
Building 5, Suite 300
Atlanta, GA 30305
404.477.5811
www.npma.org

---

*Stuart Paterson*

# *Conversation With...*

# BRIAN J. WHICHER

President
Real Property Management Associates, Weymouth, MA
Property Management, 4 years

**What was your individual career path in terms of education/training, entry-level job, or other significant opportunity?**

I went to the University of Maine to study engineering but left to pursue a career in culinary arts, taking courses at Northeastern University in Boston, Massachusetts, Bunker Hill Community College in Boston, and Johnson and Wales University in Providence, Rhode Island.

I enjoyed culinary arts a lot. I probably read as many cookbooks as another student reads textbooks. My culinary career lasted 40 years.

I started out as a chef and then developed food products for restaurant groups, including Uno's. I developed menu items for Uno's restaurants, opened Uno's restaurants in the United States and abroad and finally ended up developing and running manufacturing at the Uno's pizza plant in Brockton,Massachusetts. After retiring from food services, I decided to open my own residential property management company.

My careers may seem very different, but food manufacturing requires some of the same skill sets, such as managing facility upkeep and safety and managing people.

Real Property Management is a franchise service. Franchise owners like myself buy in, and I pay part of my sales earnings back to the franchiser in royalties. The franchiser is a support structure for my company. Its employees continually search for ways to help franchisees improve our business and be successful.

**What are the most important skills and/or qualities for someone in your profession?**

Being good with people is important because you manage both residents and landlords.

You also develop relationships with vendors including plumbers and electricians. I look for people who are responsive to what I need and price themselves fairly. Quality vendors make your life much easier. They tend to be small independent contractors, and I make a point of paying them promptly, within 10 days.

Accounting skills are a necessity, as is an eye for detail and good work ethic. A typical day starts with my reviewing the books and making sure the different bank accounts—for rent checks, security deposits, and operating expense—are in balance. I do have a bookkeeper, but it's important to check and make sure things are being recorded correctly and to identify any errors that may occur.

You also have to have the skills it takes to develop a business plan and project sales revenues and costs. With any new business, you're not going to be making money upfront. You have to develop a survivor's plan and figure out what you need to live on in the first two years before the business starts to make money.

Continuing your education also is important. You need to stay on top of real estate laws and laws and regulations around fair housing and environmental toxins including lead, mold, and asbestos. I'm always taking continuing education courses. I have my real estate license and got certified in lead abatement.

Self-promotion is also critical. Solicit reviews from residents and landlords. That's important. When they go into your website, people want to read your good reviews.

**What do you wish you had known going into this profession?**
I wish I had known about the importance of maintaining a presence on the Internet and continually updating my website and social media accounting. I pay a monthly rate for people to work on my website and social media. I also get charged when someone clicks on my ad on Google. Marketing a company in this day and age is completely different than it was 15 years ago.

**Are there many job opportunities in your profession? In what specific areas?**
Over the past couple of years, small independent property management companies have become much more competitive. There were a few of these companies—now there are a lot. There is still definitely a future for small independents like myself.

There are also career opportunities with larger organizations that manage 300-plus unit apartment buildings or large condominium developments. State and federal housing agencies also need people trained in property management.

**How do you see your profession changing in the next 5 years? How will technology impact that change, and what skills will be required?**
The way you promote your business will continue to evolve with technology. Green energy and energy efficiency will offer a challenge as properties may need to be updated to meet new codes and supplies.

**What do you enjoy most about your job? What do you enjoy least about your job?**
I enjoy the independence of being able to schedule my own hours. If I want to go shorecasting before work, I go shorecasting instead of being in the office at 5:30 a.m.

What I enjoy least is people who abuse the system, and that includes both landlords and tenants. There are tenants—I prefer to call them residents—who destroy property. There are landlords out there who don't have the income to properly maintain a house. Landlords who want well-maintained, good housing are the ones I want to work with.

**Can you suggest a valuable "try this" for students considering a career in your profession?**

Get a job or internship with a property management company. Many companies have their own landscapers and maintenance personnel. See if you can take a course in property management or small business ownership at your local college or community college.

# Social/Community Service Manager

## Snapshot

**Career Cluster(s):** Government & Public Administration; Human Services

**Interests:** Human welfare; social assistance; charitable work

**Earnings (Yearly Average):** $67,150

**Employment & Outlook:** Much Faster Than Average Growth Expected

## OVERVIEW

### Sphere of Work

Social and community service managers coordinate and supervise programs and organizations that support public and animal well-being. They direct workers who provide these services to the public and may also own the organizations facilitating these services.

A woman leads her team at a local food bank. Photo via iStock.com/SDI Productions. [Used under license.]

### Work Environment

Social and community service managers primarily work in offices, but may also work in settings such as clinics, hospitals, and shelters. Most social and community service managers work full-time. Some work more than 40 hours per week. Owners may have irregular schedules depending on their role(s) within the organization and the nature of the services provided.

### Profile

**Interests:** People, Animals, Data
**Working Conditions:** Inside
**Education Needs:** Bachelor's Degree, Master's Degree
**Licensure/Certification:** Not Required
**Opportunities for Experience:** Internship, Volunteer Work
**Interest Score:** ES

### Occupation Interest

Social and community service managers have a strong desire to help others, whether people or animals. They also possess strong business skills to lead their organization and direct their employees.

### A Day in the Life—Duties and Responsibilities

Social and community service managers work for a variety of organizations. Some of these organizations focus on working with a particular demographic, such as children, people who are homeless, older adults, or veterans. Others focus on helping people with challenges, such as substance abuse, mental health needs, and chronic hunger. Still others focus on helping animals by providing shelter and rehoming services or overseeing special interests such as livestock.

A routine part of social and community service managers' job is to show that their programs and services are effective. They collect statistics and other information to evaluate the impact their programs have on the community or their target audience. They are usually required to report this information to administrators or funders. They may also use evaluations to identify opportunities to improve their programs, such as providing mentorship and assessments for their staff.

### Duties and Responsibilities

- Working with community members and other stakeholders to identify necessary programs and services
- Overseeing administrative aspects of programs to meet the objectives of the stakeholders
- Analyzing data to determine the effectiveness of programs
- Suggesting and implementing improvements to programs and services
- Planning and managing outreach activities for increased awareness of programs
- Writing proposals for social services funding

Although the specific job duties of social and community service managers may vary with the size and scope of the organization, most managers recruit, hire, and train new staff members. They also supervise staff, such as social workers, who provide services directly to clients. Additionally, they may perform some of the services of the workers they oversee.

In large agencies, social and community service managers tend to have specialized duties. They may be responsible for running only one program in an organization and reporting to the agency's upper management. They usually do not design programs but instead supervise and implement programs set up by administrators, elected officials, or other stakeholders.

In small organizations, social and community managers often have many roles. They represent their organization through public speaking engagements or in community-wide committees; oversee programs and execute their implementations; spend time on administrative tasks, such as managing budgets; and help with raising funds and meeting with potential donors.

Owners must be able to juggle these responsibilities with the day-to-day duties of running of a business, such as payroll and overseeing physical locations used by the organization.

## WORK ENVIRONMENT

### Immediate Physical Environment

Social and community service managers work for nonprofit organizations, for-profit social service companies, and government agencies. They also work in a variety of settings, including offices, clinics, hospitals, and shelters. Health and safety precautions must be followed when in the latter settings.

### Human Environment

By the very nature of their work, social and community service managers are in close contact with people throughout their workdays. They must have strong leadership abilities to oversee and direct their team and be comfortable reporting to senior administrators or stakeholders. They may also come into contact with the clients their organization supports, which could include people with challenges such as substance abuse and mental health needs. There could also be a fundraising component to their work, requiring them to meet with donors, or write and submit grant proposals.

### Technological Environment

Social and community service managers must be proficient at computer programs such as word processors and spreadsheet platforms, as well as databases, in order to prepare reports, track statistics, and perform administrative duties.

## EDUCATION, TRAINING, AND ADVANCEMENT

### High School/Secondary

High school students seeking a career in social or community services should take courses related to sociology and psychology, as well as English and other languages if offered. It is also highly beneficial to seek out volunteer work at the types of organizations they would one day like to work for and manage. It is worth noting that one's career path into nonprofit work does not have to be linear. An interest in journalism and communications can facilitate a path into nonprofit work, for instance, so students should pursue subjects that they are most interested in, with an eye for how that may one day translate into the desired nonprofit work.

**Suggested High School Subjects**

- Accounting
- Biology
- Civics
- Earth or Life or Physical Science
- Economics
- English
- Entrepreneurship
- History
- Psychology
- Statistics

**Related Career Pathways/Majors**

*Government & Public Administration Career Cluster*

- Planning Pathway
- Public Management & Administration Pathway

*Human Services Career Cluster*

- Counseling & Mental Health Services Pathway
- Early Childhood Development & Services Pathway
- Family & Community Services Pathway
- Personal Care Services Pathway

**Transferable Skills and Abilities**

**Analytical Skills**

- Understanding and evaluating data to provide strategic guidance
- Monitoring and assessing current programs as well as determining new initiatives

**Communication Skills**

- Speaking and writing clearly, including public speaking

**Managerial Skills**

- Administering budgets and responding to a variety of issues

**Problem-solving Skills**

- Addressing client, staff, and agency-related issues

**Time-management Skills**

- Prioritizing and handling numerous tasks, often in a short timeframe

### Postsecondary

Social and community service manager jobs typically require a bachelor's degree in social work, public or business administration, public health, or a related field. However, some positions also require a master's degree.

**Related College Majors**

- Business Administration
- Public Administration
- Public Health
- Social Work

### Additional Requirements

Workers usually need experience to become a social and community service manager, and it is essential for those with a bachelor's degree. Candidates can get this experience by working as a social worker, substance abuse counselor, or in a similar occupation. Volunteer positions are also a great way to gain experience and make contacts.

## EARNINGS AND ADVANCEMENT

Earnings of social and community service managers depend on the type of employer, the type of job, and the education and experience of the employee. Earnings also depend on whether the manager also owns the organization. The median annual wage for social and community service manager was $67,150 in 2019. The lowest 10 percent earned less than $41,220, and the highest 10 percent earned more than $112,480.

Social and community service managers may receive paid vacations, holidays, and sick days; life and health insurance; and retirement benefits. These are usually paid by an employer.

These types of organizations often prefer to hire internally, so students and workers can aim to climb the ladder through dedication and years of experience.

## EMPLOYMENT AND OUTLOOK

Social and community service managers held about 175,500 jobs nationally in 2019. Twenty-nine percent worked in individual and family services. The re-

## Fast Fact

**You've heard about the entrepreneur who started the business out of her dorm room? Here are some 2016 stats to back that up: 36 percent of student entrepreneurs started a business during studies, and 21 percent of graduates launched due to unemployment.**
Source: entrepreneurship.com

For industrious young entrepreneurs, it's possible to start your own business while still in college, working out of your dorm room. Photo via iStock.com/Prostock-Studio. [Used under license.]

mainder worked in areas such as religious, grantmaking, civic, professional, and similar organizations; nursing and residential care; local government; and community and vocational rehabilitation services.

Employment is expected to grow much faster than average through the year 2029, with a projected increase of 17 percent. Much of the job growth in this occupation is the result of an aging population. An increase in the number of older adults will result in a need for more social services, such as adult daycare and vocational services, creating demand for social and community service managers. Employment of social and community service managers is expected to increase the most in industries serving older adults.

In addition, employment growth is projected as people continue to seek treatment for their addictions and as people with substance abuse disorders are increasingly sent to treatment programs rather than to jail. As a result, managers who direct treatment programs will be needed.

### Related Occupations

- Health Educator/Community Health Worker
- Marriage/Family Therapist
- Medical/Health Services Manager
- Probation Officer/Correctional Treatment Specialist
- Rehabilitation Counselor
- School/Career Counselor
- Social/Human Service Assistant
- Social Worker
- Substance Abuse/Behavioral Disorder/Mental Health Counselor

## MORE INFORMATION

**Council on Social Work Education (CSWE)**
333 John Carlyle Street, Suite 400
Alexandria, VA 22314
703.683.8080
info@cswe.org
www.cswe.org

**National Association of Social Workers (NASW)**
750 First Street, NE Suite 800
Washington, DC 20002
800.742.4089
membership@socialworkers.org
www.socialworkers.org

**Network for Social Work Management (NSWM)**
c/o Special Service for Groups
905 E. 8th Street
Los Angeles, CA 90021
213.553.1870
info@socialworkmanager.org
socialworkmanager.org

*Stuart Paterson*

## *Conversation With...*

## STEPHANIE PEREIRA

Director, NEW INC
at the New Museum of Contemporary Art, Brooklyn, NY
Arts and culture business, 20 years

**What was your individual career path in terms of education/training, entry-level job, or other significant opportunity?**

School was tough for me; I didn't fit in to the traditional school model. For undergraduate studies, I went to art school because that felt like a place where I could go to college and still be happy. I went to the Mason Gross School of Arts at Rutgers University, flourished, and earned my BFA in Visual Art.

Art school was important because they teach you how to think like an artist, which is a creative and lateral way of thinking. It has really served me well. I love artists, have lived with artists, and want to spend the rest of my life helping artists make art.

I went to the School of the Art Institute of Chicago and earned an MA in Arts Administration. It was great. At that time, I wanted to work in a museum and did my thesis on how museums don't serve their local communities; they serve the art community. My thesis adviser told me museums were not interested in what I was talking about. But she knew someone who ran a nonprofit that placed working artists in schools, so I did a summer internship with them. The ethos was very much in the spirit of what I was writing and thinking about, and I worked two years for Chicago Arts Partnership in Education.

Then I returned to New York to do the same work for a larger organization. But I also realized I didn't want to be sitting in a cubicle so, at age 27 with no kids, no car, and deferred college loan debt, I quit my job and started doing volunteer projects that inspired me. I called up the curator of the New Museum who asked me to be an assistant. I started a CSA and worked on a festival. In the end, I earned $12,000 and lived on rice and beans for a year and a half, but it was one of the best experiences I could have had. By the time I landed a job at Eyebeam Art + Technology Center in New York, they hired me, in part, because of the projects I'd been working on. By the time I left, I was running all their youth and adult education programming. Then I went to Kickstarter, where I spent 6 years as the inaugural Director of Arts and left as Director of Creative Engagement with oversight of strategic growth and management of a global community of more than 100,000 people.

At NEW INC, our a-ha moment came because New York City graduates more artists and designers than anywhere else, but these people don't have a basic business education. What we've learned is that a basic business education doesn't center around the needs and values of creative people. They're not in it to make the most money. They're in it because they love what they do, they want to change the world, they want to have a sustainable practice. There's a long list of reasons, and making money is at the bottom. So, the question is: how do you create a business where you don't have to give up what you believe in?

In my current role, I handle everything from financial management to the integrity of our community programs and our partnerships. People at any stage of their careers can apply, from those who are just getting started to people who've been going for a while who come to us to learn new skills to support and advance a sustainable business. One example is a company founded by two young women who had been educators. They saw that black and brown youth ages 17 to 24 weren't getting the professional support and opportunities their white peers were getting, so their mission is to change that balance in the media-making field. Another is a production company called Scatter that made one hugely successful major virtual reality production. They also had half the toolkit necessary for making VR and volumetric filmmaking productions that they wanted to turn into a business. Depthkit is now a multi-million-dollar venture and Scatter is an Emmy award-winning studio.

**What are the most important skills and/or qualities for someone in your profession?**
Empathetic leadership. I spend most of my day listening to people and hearing them out. The trickier part is guiding, asking questions, and making sure things are moving along in a direction they need to be. We have a tiny team to do everything, and I need everyone on my team to feel agency and empowered.

Also, business acumen. I need to be able to look at a budget and understand how it adds up.

**What do you wish you had known going into this profession?**
I wish I'd known most people don't know what they're doing and are just making it up as they're going along. Keep plugging along, keep showing up, act like you know what you're doing and follow through. Have the swagger.

**Are there many job opportunities in your profession? In what specific areas?**
My area is such a niche. I think this intersection is really vital and important, between creativity and community and a formal business that is not just about making money. This work matters, and there's a lot of opportunity. A lot of people are easing out of museum leadership and retiring, so there is also accelerated transformation in the museum world.

**How do you see your profession changing in the next 5 years? How will technology impact that change, and what skills will be required?**
For my generation, there was a big tech explosion when we were growing up with an emphasis on tech literacy. I taught myself how to code a website. My generation had to figure out how to make it work for us, but now there are apps, products tools, and software to do everything. If you want to make a GIF, there's a thing that does it for you. So now, the generation coming up has had everything handed to them, and they're actually not as good at technology. However, we still expect new hires to possess overall literacy so they can figure out any particular software program or app.

**What do you enjoy most about your job? What do you enjoy least about your job?**
I enjoy working with people. I least enjoy processing invoices and check requests.

**Can you suggest a valuable "try this" for students considering a career in your profession?**
I've learned the most when I volunteered with another group of people to create a festival, or to run a program on emerging leaders in New York arts . . . when I banded together with people my age to create something. In college, get your hands into a project with friends and make things without anyone telling you what you can and cannot do. Dream. Decide if your projects are scalable or not scalable. You'll learn so much.

## Conversation With...

## KIM RHIM

Executive Director
The Training Source Inc., Seat Pleasant, MD
Nonprofit entrepreneur, 28 years

**What was your individual career path in terms of education/training, entry-level job, or other significant opportunity?**

I was born into a two-parent family with a stay-at-home mom. My father, a postal worker, had a heart attack and died when I was 5. Life quickly changed. During kindergarten, for instance, I stayed with an aunt and uncle during the week because school was only a half day, while my mother went to work full-time as a schoolteacher. I grew up imagining I would become a teacher. My grandmother was a principal, my aunt was a teacher. That's what we did in my family; we became educators.

I did well in high school, where my sister was a teacher and my principal sang in my church's choir, so there were guardrails. As it came time to start talking about careers, I heard that teachers weren't respected, and education doesn't pay. So, I went to University of Maryland-Baltimore County (UMBC) and chose law because I used to watch *Perry Mason.* The class sizes were huge. I hated it. A high school mentor introduced me to a Howard University recruiter, a man who later walked me down the aisle at my wedding. I transferred to Howard, in Washington, DC, changed my studies to business, and thrived. I had a full ride and graduated magna cum laude with a BBA in Business Administration & Insurance. I transitioned to Columbia University in New York City with a full ride and earned an MBA in Finance, Corporate Relations and Management.

During the summer break from Columbia, I interned at IBM in corporate training and loved it because I loved dealing with people. Due to a hiring freeze there, I started my career at C&P Telephone—now Verizon—after graduating. After a year and a half, the freeze was lifted, and I got a job at IMB's Bethesda, Maryland, office as a systems engineer. Life was great! I was newly married to my dream man, in my dream job; we had our two children and were building our new house. Seven years passed. Then the rumblings started that IBM was going to start getting rid of people. Other IT companies were coming in to compete.

One year later, IBM offered the Voluntary Transition Program. They wanted the older people who were making a lot of money to leave voluntarily to reduce the payroll. One year later came the day we were informed that IBM was laying off 100,000 people, a quarter of its workforce. It was a grueling process where everybody had to line up to meet with a manager and find out if they were deemed surplus or critical. It didn't take a rocket scientist to see what people had heard as they exited the managers' offices.

At the time I was a project manager, and my job was safe but that made the experience no less shocking. Three of us were left of a team of 14 people to finish an $8 million project. A lot of my friends took a hit. I started helping people write résumés and do what they needed to do to get past this because many people had been there a long time and weren't sure how to transition to a new job.

The more people I helped, the more I knew I had a gift. I wanted to help people transition in the job training arena. It was more exciting to me than any computer we sold to the government. I was a teacher.

My husband and I discussed me going out on my own to form a job training company and finally decided to go ahead. I negotiated a deal with IBM to be a consultant for a year, they gave me a computer to do the work, and I began the process of building a business.

I knew so little it wasn't even funny, but I knew I was going to figure it out. I started with a for-profit but dissolved that and incorporated as a nonprofit after I went to IBM's fire sale to buy furniture and equipment, and they told me they could donate it to me if I was a nonprofit. I took a training program on how to kick-start a business through my county's economic development program and told them I wanted to be close enough to my business to ride my bike from home. They asked me: "how many unemployed people live in my community? How many people ride buses?" I learned to do a demographic study and located the organization in the county's lowest income zip code. I found a free space for five years after driving around and deciding to go into a storefront community outreach organization to find out about the area. They welcomed me to share the space.

The Training Source, Inc. has grown from 15-week classes teaching students life skills, professional skills, and technical skills to an organization that has trained thousands of people. We have youth leadership programs, college, and career planning. We train employers to be more effective and inclusive in the workplace. People come in to get help getting clothing and food stamps. Just helping people get through COVID-19 has been huge.

I have six full-time employees, and we are funded by government and foundation grants. I'm not driven by the money; I'm driven by the impact. I love watching people change and achieve things they never thought they could.

And now my grown children—whose father was a consultant as they were growing up—have the entrepreneurial spirit. My daughter has taken her degree in cyber security, built a business, and travels the world. My son, with his finance background, has an e-commerce business.

**What are the most important skills and/or qualities for someone in your profession?**
Compassion is number one. If you don't have that, don't do it. You have to have helping skills, good writing skills to do grant writing, integrity, customer service, and sales skills. Listening and patience are critical, and you need math skills to track data. Many think if you're an entrepreneur you answer to no one, but the truth is we answer to everyone, whether it's the parents of the youth we serve or the foundations that award our grants.

**What do you wish you had known going into this profession?**
I wish I had known how different workforce development is from other nonprofits. It's its own separate entity from a funding standpoint, and I've learned our best approach is to seek corporate and foundation dollars.

**Are there many job opportunities in your profession? In what specific areas?**
I think there are. Starting with administrative and clerical work, we need people answering the phones, preparing class materials, and tracking time and attendance. In the professional realm, there are trainers, grant writers, case managers, career counselors, and job developers. In management, we need program managers, data managers, IT managers, and community relations managers. Plus, executive managers.

**How do you see your profession changing in the next 5 years? How will technology impact that change, and what skills will be required?**
COVID-19 already has made us pivot to more remote training. I foresee a hybrid model where we are preparing people for in-person and remote careers. I think a lot of industries will move in that direction.

**What do you enjoy most about your job? What do you enjoy least about your job?**
I enjoy most watching change happen positively in people's lives. Having a student who thinks he can never learn technology learn technology; letting a first-generation, college-bound student who thinks she can't go to college know there's more money out there for people who can't afford college than people who can. I could do that all day, every day.

I least like having to raise the money to do the work. I spend long hours writing proposals, and we have the administrative burden of reporting and requesting reimbursement for contracts. I also don't like working with anyone who has preconceived notions and stereotypes about the populations we serve.

**Can you suggest a valuable "try this" for students considering a career in your profession?**
Volunteer. Try to get your community service hours in an environment where you'd like to work. Try to get an internship, whether you are paid or not. Try a college practicum. A lot of nonprofit management classes require you to do work in the community in exchange for class credit. Also do informational interviews and tours.

# Software Developer

## Snapshot

**Career Cluster(s):** Business, Management & Administration; Human Services; Information Technology (IT)

**Interests:** Development; programming; computer code; software; technology

**Earnings (Yearly Average):** $107,510

**Employment & Outlook:** Much Faster Than Average Growth Expected

## OVERVIEW

### Sphere of Work

Software developers are the creative minds behind computer programs. Some develop the applications that allow people to do specific tasks on a computer or another device. Others develop the underlying systems that run the devices or that control networks. There are strong opportunities for entrepreneurship in this field, given the right ideas and execution of the programs or apps.

### Work Environment

In general, software development is a collaborative process, and developers work on teams with others who also contribute to designing, developing, and programming successful software. However, some developers work at home. Most software developers work full-time and additional work hours are common.

A software developer will design each piece of an application or system and plan how the pieces will work together. Photo via iStock.com/CreativeDJ. [Used under license.]

## Occupation Interest

Software developers have strong technical knowledge of computer code and programming and are able to translate that into the creation of functional computer programs ranging from mobile phone games to extraordinarily complex financial software. Every year the world becomes more reliant on computer systems, so the field is always in need of fresh talent and innovation. Successful programs can be worth millions of dollars, or more, so there is great interest in funding startup enterprises that might be the "next big thing."

### *Profile*

**Interests:** Data, Things, People
**Working Conditions:** Inside
**Education Needs:** Bachelor's Degree
**Licensure/Certification:** Usually Not Required
**Opportunities for Experience:** Internship
**Interest Score:** CIR

## A Day in the Life—Duties and Responsibilities

Software developers oversee the entire development process for a software program. They may begin by asking how the customer plans to use the software. They must identify the core functionality that users need from software programs. Software developers must also determine user requirements that are unrelated to the functions of the software, such as the level of security and performance needs. They design the program and then give instructions to programmers who write computer code and evaluate it.

If the program does not work as expected or if testers find it too difficult to use, software developers go back to the design process to fix the problems or improve the program. After the program is released to the customer, a developer may perform upgrades and maintenance.

Developers usually work closely with computer programmers. However, in some companies, developers write code themselves instead of giving instructions to programmers. This is also true of startup ventures, where the core developer may also serve as a programmer.

### *Duties and Responsibilities*

- Analyzing users' needs and then designing, testing, and developing software to meet those needs
- Recommending software upgrades for customers' existing programs and systems
- Designing each piece of an application or system and planning how the pieces will work together
- Creating a variety of models and diagrams (such as flowcharts) that show programmers the software code needed for an application
- Working with graphics and other designers to determine the website's layout
- Ensuring that a program continues to function normally through software maintenance and testing
- Documenting every aspect of an application or system as a reference for future maintenance and upgrades
- Collaborating with other computer specialists to create optimum software

Developers who supervise a software project from the planning stages through implementation sometimes are called information technology (IT) project managers. These workers monitor the project's progress to ensure that it meets deadlines, standards, and cost targets. Information technology project managers who plan and direct an organization's IT department or IT policies are included in the profile on computer and information systems managers.

## OCCUPATION SPECIALTIES

**Applications Software Developer**

Applications software developers design computer applications, such as word processors and games, for consumers. They may create custom software for a specific customer or commercial software to be sold to the general public. Some applications software developers create complex databases for organizations. They also create programs that people use over the Internet and within a company's intranet.

**Systems Software Developer**

Systems software developers create the systems that keep computers functioning properly. These could be operating systems for computers that the general public buys or systems built specifically for an organization. Often, systems software developers also build the system's interface, which is what allows users to interact with the computer. Systems software developers create the operating systems that control most of the consumer electronics in use today, including those used by cell phones and cars.

## WORK ENVIRONMENT

### Immediate Physical Environment

Software developers typically work in an office, whether as part of a corporate setting or at home. As they usually lead a team, they must be able to interact with team members either in-person or remotely. They may be required to work long hours to complete projects on deadline.

### Human Environment

Although some software development takes place solitarily, in many cases the developer leads a team of programmers. This most often takes place in a group-office setting, but as remote work becomes more the norm, all members of the team must be able to stay in touch if working from home or at a distance. This can include emails, phone, or video calls. Developers also must interact with clients as the software is being developed..

### Technological Environment

Although writing code is not their first priority, developers must have a strong background in computer programming. They usually gain this experience in school. Throughout their career, developers must keep up to date on new tools and computer languages.

Software developers also need skills related to the industry in which they work. Developers working in a bank, for example, should have knowledge of finance so that they can understand a bank's computing needs.

## EDUCATION, TRAINING, AND ADVANCEMENT

### High School/Secondary

High school students interested in a career as a software development should focus on computer science courses, math, and English to improve communication skills. Strong consideration should also be given to prospective colleges, as a degree is almost essential.

**Suggested High School Subjects**

- Algebra
- Biology
- Calculus
- Chemistry
- Computer Science
- Earth or Life or Physical Science
- Economics
- English
- Entrepreneurship
- Geometry
- History
- Political Science

### *Transferable Skills and Abilities*

**Analytical Skills**
- Analyzing users' needs and designing software to meet those needs

**Communication Skills**
- Giving clear instructions to others working on a project
- Explaining to customers how the software works and answer any questions that arise

**Creativity**
- Acting as the creative mind behind new computer software

**Detail-oriented**
- Working on many parts of an application or system at the same time

**Interpersonal Skills**
- Working well with others who contribute to designing, developing, and programming successful software

**Problem-solving Skills**
- Solving problems that arise throughout the design process

- Pre-Calculus
- Technical Reading
- Trigonometry

**Related Career Pathways/Majors**

*Business, Management & Administration Career Cluster*

- Business Information Management Pathway
- General Management Pathway

*Human Services Career Cluster*

- Consumer Services Pathway

*Information Technology Career Cluster*

- Network Systems Pathway
- Programming & Software Development Pathway
- Web & Digital Communications Pathway

## Postsecondary

Software developers usually have a bachelor's degree, typically in computer science, software engineering, or a related field. Computer science degree programs are the most common, because they tend to cover a broad range of topics. Students should focus on classes related to building software to better prepare themselves for work in the occupation. Many students gain experience in software development by completing an internship at a software company while in college. For some positions, employers may prefer that applicants have a master's degree.

**Related College Majors**

- Business Administration
- Computer Science
- Cyber Security
- Data Science
- Electrical Engineering
- Entrepreneurship
- Information Technology
- Mathematics
- Software Engineering

## Adult Job Seekers

Adults seeking employment as software developers should come from a related field or have significant experience with computer code and programming. Developing one's skills as a programmer over time is a good way to advance to becoming a developer.

## EARNINGS AND ADVANCEMENT

Earnings depend largely on the nature of the developer's work, the size of the software project, and whether the project is a startup or is overseen by a larger company. Startups may rely on funding to get off the ground, and not be a reliable source of income until the project is fully realized. Median annual earnings of web developers and designers were $107,510 in 2019. The lowest 10 percent earned less than $64,240, and the highest 10 percent earned more than $164,590.

Software developers may receive paid vacations, holidays, and sick days; life and health insurance; and retirement benefits. These are usually paid by an employer if the developer is not self-employed.

Software developers can advance to become IT project managers, also called computer and information systems managers, a position in which they oversee the software development process.

## EMPLOYMENT AND OUTLOOK

Software developers and software quality assurance analysts and testers held 1,469,200 jobs in 2019. Employment is expected to grow much faster than the average for all occupations through the year 2029, at a rate of 22 percent, as the need for new applications on smartphones and tablets help increase the demand for software developers.

The health and medical insurance and reinsurance carriers industry will need innovative software to manage new healthcare policy enrollments and administer existing policies digitally. As the number of people who use this digital platform increases over time, demand for software developers will grow.

Software developers are likely to see new opportunities because of an increase in the number of products that use software. For example, more computer systems are being built into consumer electronics and other products, such as cell phones and appliances.

Concerns over threats to computer security could result in more investment in security software to protect computer networks and electronic infrastructure. In addition, an increase in software offered over the Internet should lower costs and allow more customization for businesses, also increasing demand for software developers.

Job prospects will be best for applicants with knowledge of the most up-to-date programming tools and for those who are proficient in one or more programming languages.

### Related Occupations

- Computer Hardware Engineer
- Computer/Information Research Scientist
- Computer/Information Systems Manager
- Computer Network Architect
- Computer Programmer
- Computer Support Specialist
- Computer Systems Analyst
- Database Administrator
- Mathematician/Statistician
- Postsecondary Teacher
- Web Developer

## MORE INFORMATION

**Association for Computing Machinery (ACM)**
1601 Broadway, 10th Floor
New York, NY 10019-7434
212.869.7440
acmhelp@acm.org
www.acm.org

**Association of Software Professionals (ASP)**
c/o ASP Membership Manager
P.O. Box 1522
Martinsville IN 46151
asp-software.org

**CompTIA**
3500 Lacey Road, Suite 100
Downers Grove, IL 60515
866.835.8020
membership@comptia.org
www.comptia.org

**Computing Research Association (CRA)**
1828 L Street NW, Suite 800
Washington, DC 20036-4632
202.234.2111
info@cra.org
cra.org

**Computing Community Consortium (CCC):**
cra.org/ccc
Developer Alliance
525 Montgomery Street, Suite 574
Alexandria, VA 22314
www.developersalliance.org

**IEEE Computer Society**
2001 L Street NW, Suite 700
Washington, DC 20036-4928
202.371.0101
help@computer.org
www.computer.org

**International Game Developers Association (IGDA)**
1 Eglinton Avenue East, Suite 705
Toronto, ON M4P 3A1
Canada
info@igda.org
igda.org

**National Center for Women & Information Technology (NCWIT)**
NCWIT 1909 26th Street, 2nd Floor
Boulder, CO 80302
303.735.6671
info@ncwit.org
www.ncwit.org

**Network and Systems Professionals Association (NaSPA)**
214.771.8616
naspa.com

**Software & Information Industry Association (SIIA)**
202.289.7442
www.siia.net

---

*Stuart Paterson*

## *Conversation With...*
## BRIAN THARP

Principal and co-founder
ZENxd, HQ Santa Cruz, CA
Technology application design, 23 years

**What was your individual career path in terms of education/training, entry-level job, or other significant opportunity?**

I'm a principal and co-founder of a technology application design firm, but I didn't start in this field. I was a Fine Arts major at Arizona State University with an emphasis on printmaking. In the middle of my junior year, I left college. I was getting burned out because while a student I was working full-time to pay for school. I'd planned to take a break and return to college after earning more money to pay for it, but I never did. I realized there wasn't much opportunity in printmaking and instead I got a job designing circuit boards. I had a generous boss who taught me how to do the work. It was interesting, creative work that challenged me. Then I got a job testing software and networking equipment and learned about packet transfer and things I never expected to learn. I ended up setting up the company's intranet, and that's how I was introduced to web technology and design. As the industry evolved, so did a focus on human-centered design. That was my bridge back to my creative self. Before starting my company, I'd worked for more than a half dozen companies, designing systems that help people do things like comparison shop, or help businesses deploy campaigns faster, at lower costs and with higher interaction with their targeted audience.

In 2008, a colleague, Bill Daggett, and I partnered and founded ZENxd, a boutique UX Design firm. We are a distributed team, working from multiple locations, including Portland, Oregon, where I'm based, and Santa Cruz, California, where Bill is based. Bill and I had worked for a company called SideStep, Inc. where we designed the first application that allowed travelers to use a single website to search multiple sites for information on flights, lodging, car rental, guides, and deals. This was integrated into KAYAK's platform when KAYAK bought SideStep.

ZENxd designs applications for websites, mobile or any other type of device where there is human interaction required. We research users' needs, what they are looking for, how to engage them, and how long they interact with the applications. We focus on the human side, the users, and define strategies that help people solve a problem or reach a goal. Typically, a UX strategy defines several "digital touch points" that are needed to create a holistic experience. We just did a big project with Shutterfly. We helped redesign their manufacturing application by unifying it into a single platform so it's easier for their workers to learn and operate. We work on projects that could be something as big as a whole production platform, to as small as a smart watch application.

I've always loved tackling big design problems. When you work for a company, the meaty problems get solved, and you are left to "maintain" the experience. I would get the itch to jump ship and find a new problem to solve. So, I co-founded ZENxd to ensure I'd always have new challenges and get to wear a lot of hats.

**What are the most important skills and/or qualities for someone in your profession?**
Understanding the fundamental principles of design is key to knowing how a design is perceived, how people will learn from it, how to make it more appealing and useful.

You don't need to learn everything; it's a matter of starting with your strengths. If you understand good design principles—visual, color—start with those.

A good application design also involves research. If you're inquisitive and a people person, you may want to focus on research. Start there and begin to broaden.

Empathy, active listening, observation, and curiosity are important traits. Think about the lived experience of someone who will use the application and how they perceive or understand the design.

You have to collaborate with people, facilitate and bring in different views. It's critical to communicate clearly with people who perform different functions of work on the project.

**What do you wish you had known going into this profession?**
How nebulous the profession would prove to be. Even today it's hard for people to understand what I do. People say "you make it look good" or "you make it look simple," and there's more to it. Making something look simple is extremely hard. Making design decisions is a challenge because you have lots of needs and resources that are in conflict.

**Are there many job opportunities in your profession? In what specific areas?**
There are a ton of opportunities, and they're becoming more specialized and diverse due to advances in technology and the proliferation of disparate devices. There are jobs that focus on user research, experience design (UX), visual design (UI), service design, design strategy, design leadership, etc. Areas to specialize in include mobile applications, voice enabled devices, augmented reality, artificial intelligence.

**How do you see your profession changing in the next 5years? How will technology impact that change, and what skills will be required?**
It's harder for companies to differentiate on technology. Today's consumers have grown up in a digital world. Technology has changed expectations. If a customer has a bad experience, another option is just a tap away. To maintain market share, companies have shifted their focus to customer engagement. As a result, Experience Design has become a critical component to achieving long-term success.

Voice assistance, machine learning, and artificial intelligence are becoming more predictive. We are focused on developing relationships, learning about the customer, and anticipating the customer's needs.

There's growing emphasis on healthy experiences—understanding an application's impact on the individual's well-being. How well did the experience promote healthy habits, or does it inhibit healthy habits? Thinking about well-being is a big part of what we do because we're designing for humans.

There's an overdue emphasis on design justice and inclusive design. We are hyper-focused on improving our methods and practices to ensure our designs produce quality experiences for as many people as possible. If you neglect a segment of the population, you miss reaching potential customers. You also risk damaging your brand if you lack the care to ensure your products are usable and accessible.

**What do you enjoy most about your job? What do you enjoy least about your job?**
I get to speak with and learn about people from all walks of life. It's fun, enlightening, and even emotional at times. It's my job to improve their lives, and that enriches me.

I like learning about a variety of topics. We've designed experiences in health care, travel, legal, production accounting—all kinds of domains. You're really trying to understand the industries and it's never boring.

What I enjoy least is feeling in a constant state of critique. As a designer, everything you produce is subject to evaluation and criticism. You must be prepared to provide a rationale for your designs. While critique can be hard, it continually presents opportunities for growth and improvement, so you learn to embrace it.

**Can you suggest a valuable "try this" for students considering a career in your profession?**
We all have that product or application that we hate to use. Find something you think could be better. Ask other people how they feel about it. Identify a problem for you to solve. Write down as many solutions you can think of. Sketch out your favorite. Test it. Refine it. There's no better way to learn than to just put it in practice. You can go to school, or go online to learn about it, but unless you're putting it to practice, you're not going to hone those skills. Nothing beats observing a problem, trying to understand it, and trying to solve it with other people.

# Solar Photovoltaic Installers

## Snapshot

**Career Cluster(s):** Architecture & Construction; Business Management & Administration; Science, Technology, Engineering & Mathematics

**Interests:** Technology; renewable energy; installation; manual labor

**Earnings (Yearly Average):** $44,890

**Employment & Outlook:** Much Faster Than Average Growth Expected

## OVERVIEW

### Sphere of Work

Solar photovoltaic (PV) installers, also known as PV installers, assemble, set up, and maintain rooftop or other systems that convert sunlight into energy. Owners of these businesses may be self-employed, with a team of installers as employees.

### Work Environment

Although some installation work may take the installer inside spaces such as attics and crawl spaces, the bulk of the work is done outdoors, as solar panels are typically fixed to rooftops. Photovoltaic panels must have clear access to sunlight to function properly.

Installing solar panels on a roof. Photo via iStock.com/zstockphotos. [Used under license.]

## Occupation Interest

PV installers have an interest in the latest renewable energy technology and are well-suited to the sometimes-arduous manual labor required to install this equipment. They do not mind working outdoors in varying weather conditions and heights. They have an aptitude for math, in order to calculate angles, measurements, and areas.

### Profile

**Interests:** Things, Data, People
**Working Conditions:** Both Inside and Outside
**Physical Strength:** Heavy Work
**Education Needs:** On-The-Job Training, High School Diploma with Technical Education, Junior/Technical/Community College, Apprenticeship
**Licensure/Certification:** Varies By State
**Opportunities for Experience:** Apprenticeship
**Interest Score:** RC

## A Day in the Life—Duties and Responsibilities

At the jobsite, PV installers verify the measurements and design of the structure on which the PV system is being assembled. For PV systems on flat roofs, PV installers must first add a structure that allows the PV system to be mounted at an angle. PV installers set up new systems on support structures and place PV panels or PV shingles on top of them. Once the panels are in place, they sometimes connect the panels to electrical components. After the system is in place, PV installers must test the system and its components.

### Duties and Responsibilities

- Planning PV system configurations based on customer needs and site conditions
- Measuring, cutting, and assembling the support structure for solar PV panels
- Installing solar modules, panels, and support structures according to building codes and standards
- Connecting PV panels to the electrical system
- Applying weather sealant to equipment being installed
- Activating and test PV systems
- Performing routine PV system maintenance

Depending on the job and state laws, PV installers may connect the solar panels to the electrical grid, although electricians sometimes do this task. Once the panels are assembled, workers check the electrical systems for proper wiring, polarity, and grounding, and they also perform maintenance as needed.

# WORK ENVIRONMENT

## Immediate Physical Environment

Because photovoltaic (PV) panels convert sunlight into electricity, most PV installation is done outdoors. Residential installers work on rooftops but also sometimes work in attics and crawl spaces to connect panels to the electrical grid. PV installers who build solar farms work at ground level.

Solar photovoltaic installers risk falls from ladders and roofs, shocks from electricity, and burns from hot equipment and materials while installing and maintaining PV systems. To reduce the risk of injury, PV installers must wear safety equipment, such as harnesses, gloves, and hard hats.

### Human Environment

PV installers may work alone or as part of a team. Installation of solar panels may require the help of roofers and electricians. Installers may also interact with clients at the jobsite, and should always be courteous, especially when working on someone's private dwelling. The owner of the installation business must routinely interact with employees and is responsible for all staffing, including helping to resolve disputes.

### Technological Environment

PV installers use a variety of hand tools and power tools, including drills, wrenches, saws, and screwdrivers, to set up PV panels and connect them to frames, wires, and support structures. They must be well-acquainted with the latest in solar panel technology to keep pace with client demands and be able to both install and maintain the equipment.

## EDUCATION, TRAINING, AND ADVANCEMENT

### High School/Secondary

PV installers typically need a high school diploma. An emphasis on math, science, and courses related to trades work is beneficial. Business-related courses are also an asset, to prepare for one day being self-employed in the field.

**Suggested High School Subjects**

- Algebra
- Chemistry
- Construction Math
- Earth or Life or Physical Science
- Economics
- English
- Entrepreneurship
- Geometry
- History
- Physics

- Pre-Calculus
- Psychology
- Statistics
- Technical Writing
- Trigonometry

**Related Career Pathways/Majors**

*Architecture & Construction Career Cluster*

- Construction Pathway
- Design/Pre-Construction Pathway
- Maintenance/Operations Pathway

*Business, Management & Administration Career Cluster*

- General Management Pathway

*Science, Technology, Engineering & Mathematics Career Cluster*

- Engineering & Technology Pathway
- Science & Mathematics Pathway

### Transferable Skills and Abilities

**Ability to work at heights**
- Working on roofs, ladders, or lifts that are far above the ground

**Communication Skills**
- Conveying information effectively to clients, team members, and other workers

**Detail-oriented**
- Following instructions to ensure that the system works properly

**Math Skills**
- Calculating angles, measurements , and areas using algebra, geometry, and trigonometry

**Mechanical Skills**
- Working with complex electrical and mechanical equipment to build support structures for solar panels, connect the panels to the electrical system, and troubleshoot problems

**Physical Stamina**
- Carrying panels and other heavy equipment
- Climbing ladders many times throughout the day

**Physical Strength**
- Lifting heavy equipment and materials weighing up to 60 pounds

## Postsecondary

Some PV installers take courses at local community colleges or technical schools to learn about solar panel installation. Courses range from basic safety and PV knowledge to system design. Although course length varies, most usually last a few days to several months.

## Adult Job Seekers

Some candidates, especially those with construction experience, enter the field by taking online training courses.

## Professional Certification and Licensure

Some states require a license for PV installers. Contact your state's licensing board for more information.

PV installers must travel to jobsites, so employers may require them to have a driver's license.

Although not required for employment, certification demonstrates competency in solar panel installation. The Electronics Technicians Association, International

## Fast Fact

**One in 18 people world-wide owned their own business in 2016. Uganda led the way, with 28.1 percent entrepreneurs per capita.** Source: entrepreneur.com

The city of Kampala, Uganda. Photo by Simisa, CC BY-SA 3.0 <https://creativecommons.org/licenses/by-sa/3.0>, via Wikimedia Commons.

(ETA) and the North American Board of Certified Energy Practitioners (NABCEP) offer certification for PV installers. Some states require that for projects to qualify for solar-related subsidies, all PV installers working on the projects must have certification.

### Additional Requirements

Some PV installers learn their trade on the job by working with experienced installers. On-the-job training usually lasts between 1 month and 1 year. During training, PV installers learn about safety, tools, and PV system installation techniques.

Electrician and roofing apprentices and journey workers may complete photovoltaic-specific training modules through apprenticeships.

Solar PV system manufacturers may also provide training on specific products. Such training usually includes a system overview and proper installation techniques for the manufacturer's products.

Military veterans may benefit from the Solar Ready Vets program, which is funded by the US. Department of Energy (DOE) and prepares veterans to connect with training and jobs in the solar industry.

## EARNINGS AND ADVANCEMENT

Earnings depend on worker experience, whether they are self-employed, and the industry in which they work: electrical and other wiring installation; plumbing, heating, and air-conditioning; or utilities. Median annual earnings of PV installers were $44,890 in 2019. The lowest 10 percent earned less than $31,600, and the highest 10 percent earned more than $63,880.

PV installers may advance to become a project supervisor or project manager after gaining experience in the trade. PV installers may also transition to sales roles within the industry, given their knowledge of and experience with PV installation. They also may choose to start their own PV installation business.

## EMPLOYMENT AND OUTLOOK

PV installers held 12,000 jobs in 2019. Six percent were self-employed. Employment is expected to grow much faster than the average for all occupations through the year 2029, at a rate of 51 percent, due to the continued expansion and adoption of solar PV systems. As the cost of PV panels and shingles continues to decrease, more households are expected to take advantage of these systems, resulting in greater demand for the workers who install and maintain them. The increasing popularity of solar leasing plans—in which homeowners lease, rather than purchase, systems—should create additional demand, because homeowners no longer bear the upfront costs of installation. Demand may be greatest in states and localities that provide incentives to reduce the cost of PV systems.

About 2,300 openings for solar photovoltaic installers are projected each year, on average, over the decade. Many of those openings are expected to result from the need to replace workers who transfer to different occupations or exit the labor force, such as to retire.

Despite fast growth, this occupation is small and has limited employment; therefore, strong competition for jobs is expected. Job candidates who complete a course in photovoltaic systems at a community college or technical school should have the best opportunities. Those who enter apprenticeships also are expected to have extremely good job opportunities. Candidates with experience in construction occupations, such as laborers, roofers, and carpenters, should have better job opportunities than those without construction experience.

### Related Occupations

- Carpenter
- Construction Laborer/Helper
- Electrician
- Glazier
- Heating, Air Conditioning, & Refrigeration Mechanic/Installer
- Ironworker
- Masonry Worker

- Plumbers/Pipefitter/Steamfitter
- Roofer
- Sheet Metal Worker

## MORE INFORMATION

**American Solar Energy Society (ASES)**
2525 Arapahoe Avenue, Suite E4-253
Boulder, CO 80302
info@ases.org
ases.org

**Electrical Training Alliance**
5001 Howerton Way, Suite N
Bowie, MD 20715
888.652.4007
www.electricaltrainingalliance.org

**Electronics Technicians Association, International (ETA)**
5 Depot Street
Greencastle, IN 46135
800.288.3824
eta@eta-i.org
www.eta-i.org

**Interstate Renewable Energy Council (IREC)**
P.O. Box 1156
Latham, NY 12110-1156
518.621.7379
info@irecusa.org
irecusa.org

**National Center for Construction Education & Research (NCCER)**
13614 Progress Boulevard
Alachua, FL 32615
386.518.6500
www.nccer.org

**North American Board of Certified Energy Practitioners (NABCEP)**
56 Clifton Country Road, Suite 202

Clifton Park, NY 12065
800.654.0021
info@nabcep.org
www.nabcep.org

**Solar Energy Industries Association (SEIA)**
1425 K Street NW, Suite 1000
Washington, DC 20005
202.682.0556
info@seia.org
www.seia.org

**The Solar Foundation**
c/o Marcum
1899 L Street NW, Suite 850
Washington, DC 20036
202.469.3750
info@solarfound.org
www.thesolarfoundation.org

**Solar Training Network**
1110 Vermont Avenue NW
Washington, DC 20005
202.866.0924
info@americansolarworkforce.org
americansolarworkforce.org

---

*Stuart Paterson*

# Taxi Driver/ Ride-Hailing Driver/ Chauffeur

**Snapshot**

**Career Cluster(s):** Business, Management & Administration; Human Services; Transportation, Distribution & Logistics

**Interests:** Driving; passenger transportation

**Earnings (Yearly Average):** $25,980

**Employment & Outlook:** Much Faster Than Average Growth Expected

## OVERVIEW

### Sphere of Work

Taxi drivers, ride-hailing drivers, and chauffeurs drive people to and from the places they need to go, such as homes, workplaces, airports, and shopping centers. They must be familiar with city streets and locations to take passengers to their destinations. Self-employed ride-hailing drivers may utilize smartphone apps—sometimes more than one—to connect with customers and maximize profits.

A rideshare driver and customer. Photo via iStock.com/avdeev007. [Used under license.]

## Work Environment

Taxi drivers, ride-hailing drivers, and chauffeurs spend much of their day on the road, driving between pickup and dropoff locations and waiting for new fares. Work hours vary. Some work part-time. Evening and weekend work is common. Some drivers work late at night or early in the morning.

### Profile

**Interests:** People, Things, Data
**Working Conditions:** Both Inside and Outside
**Physical Strength:** Medium Work, Heavy Work
**Education Needs:** On-the-Job Training
**Licensure/Certification:** Driver's License, Licensure Varies by State and City
**Opportunities for Experience:** Part-Time Work
**Interest Score:** RE

Taxi and ride-hailing drivers work with little or no supervision, and their work schedules are flexible. They can take breaks for a meal or rest whenever they do not have a passenger.

Chauffeurs' work schedules are much more structured. They work hours based on client needs. Some chauffeurs must be ready to drive their clients at a moment's notice, so they remain on call throughout the day.

## Occupation Interest

Taxi drivers, ride-hailing drivers, and chauffeurs are people- and customer-oriented individuals who enjoy transporting others to their destinations. They have an aptitude for driving and are good communicators who like interacting with others. Mental alertness is crucial, as some work may be performed early in the morning or late at night, and in all types of weather.

### Duties and Responsibilities

- Driving taxicabs, limousines, company cars, or privately owned vehicles to transport passengers
- Picking up passengers and listening to where they want to go
- Helping passengers load and unload their luggage
- Obeying all traffic laws
- Checking the car for problems and do basic maintenance
- Keeping the inside and outside of their car clean
- Operating wheelchair lifts when needed
- Keeping a record of miles traveled

## A Day in the Life—Duties and Responsibilities

Taxi drivers, ride-hailing drivers, and chauffeurs must stay alert and watch the conditions of the road. They must take precautions to ensure their passengers' safety, especially in heavy traffic or bad weather. Taxi drivers and chauffeurs must also follow vehicle-for-hire or livery regulations, such as where they can pick up passengers and how much they can charge.

Good drivers are familiar with the streets in the areas they serve. They choose the most efficient routes, considering the traffic at that time of day. They know where the most often sought destinations are, such as airports, train stations, convention centers, hotels, and other points of interest. They also know where to find fire and police stations and hospitals in case of an emergency.

## OCCUPATION SPECIALTIES

**Chauffeur**

Chauffeurs take passengers on prearranged trips. They drive limousines, vans, or private cars. They may work for hire for single trips, or they may work for a person, a private business, or for a government agency. Customer service is important for chauffeurs, especially luxury vehicle drivers. Some do the duties of executive assistants, acting as driver, secretary, and itinerary planner. Other chauffeurs drive large vans between airports or train stations and hotels.

**Paratransit Driver**

Paratransit drivers transport people with special needs, such as the elderly or those with disabilities. They drive specially equipped vehicles designed to help people with various needs in nonemergency situations. For example, their vehicles may be equipped with wheelchair lifts, and the driver helps a passenger with boarding.

**Ride-hailing Driver**

Ride-hailing drivers pick up passengers who seek service through a smartphone app. The fare rate can fluctuate depending on demand; however, passengers are notified if the current fare rate is higher than usual. Passengers pay for rides through a credit card linked to the app. Drivers use their own private vehicles and set their own hours.

**Taxi Driver**

Taxi drivers, also called cabdrivers or cabbies, use a meter to calculate the fare when a passenger requests a destination. Many customers request a cab by calling a central dispatcher who then tells the taxi driver the pickup location. Some drivers pick up passengers waiting in lines at cabstands or in the taxi line at airports, train stations, and hotels. Cabbies drive around the streets looking for passengers in some large cities.

## WORK ENVIRONMENT

### Immediate Physical Environment

Some drivers contract with a dispatch company that refers passengers and allows the driver to use their service facilities for a fee. Drivers who do not own their taxicab may lease a dispatch company's car as part of the fee. Drivers usually pay for their own expenses such as fuel.

Driving for long periods, especially in heavy traffic, can be stressful for these workers. In addition, they often have to pick up heavy luggage and packages.

Taxi drivers, ride-hailing drivers, and chauffeurs sometimes get injured on the job. Most injuries result from traffic accidents.

### Human Environment

Human interaction is a key part of this work, as drivers must safely and respectfully transport paying passengers to their destinations. Drivers may have many fares per day and must always be attentive and courteous. Self-employed drivers who utilize smartphone apps often rely on ratings to maintain their business, and tips increase overall earnings.

### Technological Environment

Taxi drivers, ride-hailing drivers, and chauffeurs must be confident and knowledgeable behind the wheel. An understanding of car mechanics, even rudimentary, can be an asset if their vehicle encounters problems on the road. Self-employed drivers who use smartphone apps to facilitate their services must be able to use mobile technology to their advantage in order to maximize profits. Familiarity with Global Positioning System (GPS) and navigation software is also an asset.

## EDUCATION, TRAINING, AND ADVANCEMENT

### High School/Secondary

There are usually no formal education requirements, although many taxi drivers, ride-hailing drivers, and chauffeurs have a high school diploma or equivalent.

**Suggested High School Subjects**

- Algebra

- Biology
- Chemistry
- Civics
- Economics
- English
- Entrepreneurship
- Geometry
- History
- Physics
- Pre-Calculus
- Statistics
- Trigonometry

**Related Career Pathways/Majors**

*Business, Management & Administration Career Cluster*

- General Management Pathway

*Human Services Career Cluster*

- Consumer Services Pathway

*Transportation, Distribution & Logistics Career Cluster*

- Sales & Service Pathway
- Transportation Operations Pathway

### Transferable Skills and Abilities

**Customer-service Skills**

- Interacting with customers and representing their company positively, and ensuring passenger satisfaction
- Because passengers rate ride-hailing drivers after each trip, excellent customer-service skills can lead to a favorable review

**Hand-eye Coordination**

- Watching surroundings and avoiding obstacles and other hazards while driving a vehicle

**Initiative**

- Working with little or no supervision
- Being self-motivate and taking the initiative to earn a living

**Patience**

- Remaining calm and composed when driving through heavy traffic and congestion or dealing with rude passengers

**Reliability**

- Picking customers up on time and quickly transport them to their destination

**Visual Ability**

- Passing a state-issued vision and driver's license test

## Adult Job Seekers

Anyone with a good driving record, clean background check, access to a vehicle, and a smartphone can become a ride-hailing driver. Some taxi drivers start their own cab service by purchasing a taxi rather than leasing one through a dispatch company. Chauffeurs may work towards driving more important clients and different types of cars.

## Professional Certification and Licensure

All taxi drivers, ride-hailing drivers, and chauffeurs must have a regular automobile driver's license. States and local municipalities set other requirements; many require taxi drivers and chauffeurs to get a taxi or limousine license. This normally requires passing a background check, drug test, and a written exam about regulations and local geography.

Regulations for ride-hailing drivers vary by state and city. Check with your local area for more information.

The Federal Motor Carrier Safety Administration (FMCSA) requires limousine drivers who transport 16 or more passengers (including the driver) to hold a commercial driver's license (CDL) with a passenger (P) endorsement. Drivers must pass knowledge and driving skills tests to receive a CDL.

### Additional Requirements

Most taxi and limousine companies provide their new drivers with a short period of on-the-job training. This training usually takes from 1 day to 2 weeks, depending on the company and the location. Some cities require training by law.

Training typically covers local traffic laws, driver safety, and the local street layout. Taxi drivers also get training in operating the taximeter and communications equipment. Limousine companies, with an emphasis on customer service, usually train their chauffeurs. Ride-hailing drivers receive little to no training beyond how to work the electronic hailing app so they can pick up customers. Paratransit drivers receive special training in how to handle wheelchair lifts and other mechanical devices.

## EARNINGS AND ADVANCEMENT

Earnings depend on type of job, location, hours worked, and number of fares. Median annual earnings of taxi drivers, ride-hailing drivers, and chauffeurs were $25,980 in 2019. The lowest 10 percent earned less than $19,240, and the highest 10 percent earned more than $40,360.

These wage data include money earned from tips. Taxi drivers and chauffeurs who provide good customer service are more likely to receive higher tips on each fare.

Taxi drivers and chauffeurs may receive benefits from their employer, although this varies greatly. Self-employed ride-hailing drivers usually do not receive benefits, although third party ride-hailing apps may provide financial incentives to their drivers.

## EMPLOYMENT AND OUTLOOK

Taxi drivers, ride-hailing drivers, and chauffeurs held 370,400 jobs in 2019. Forty-three percent were self-employed. Employment is expected to grow much faster than average for all occupations through the year 2029, at a rate of 20 percent.

The growing demand for ride-hailing services, which use electronic hailing (also referred to as e-haling) through smartphone apps, should increase job growth. Specifically, employment of self-employed workers in this occupation is projected to grow 37 percent from 2018 to 2028.

Taxis and ride-hailing services generally operate in urban areas and complement public transit systems because people who regularly take a train or bus are more likely to use a taxi or ride-hailing service. Therefore, increasing demand for taxis and ride-hailing services should mostly occur in larger metropolitan areas.

Job prospects for ride-hailing drivers should be excellent. The occupation does not require any formal education and has low barriers to entry. Applicants who can pass a background check and have a clean driving record should have no problem contracting with a ride-hailing company.

### Related Occupations

- Automotive Service Technician/Mechanic
- Bus Driver
- Delivery Truck Driver/Driver/Sales Worker
- Heavy/Tractor-trailer Truck Driver
- Railroad Worker
- Water Transportation Worker

## MORE INFORMATION

**American Drivers Association**
P.O. Box 178
Winona, TX 75792
800.944.4948
americandriversassociation@gmail.com
americandriversassociation.com

**Federal Motor Carrier Safety Administration (FMCSA)**
United States Department of Transportation
1200 New Jersey Avenue SE
Washington, DC 20590
800.832.5660
cdlcompliance@dot.gov
www.fmcsa.dot.gov

**National Limousine Association (NLA)**
1002 Lincoln Drive West, Suite C
Marlton, NJ 08053
800.652.7007
info@limo.org
www.limo.org

**National Motorists Association (NMA)**
1001 Arboretum Drive, Suite 120
Waunakee, WI 53597
nma@motorists.org
www.motorists.org

**Rideshare Association**
855.964.3556
yo@yorideshare.com
www.yorideshare.com

**Rideshare Guy**
harry@therideshareguy.com
therideshareguy.com

**Transportation Alliance**
3200 Tower Oaks Boulevard, Suite 220
Rockville, MD 20852
301.984.5700
info@thetransportationalliance.org
www.thetransportationalliance.org

---

*Stuart Paterson*

# Telecommunications Equipment Installers/Repairers

### Snapshot

**Career Cluster(s):** Arts, A/V Technology & Communications; Architecture & Construction; Business Management & Administration; Information Technology; Human Services; Manufacturing; Science, Technology, Engineering & Mathematics

**Interests:** Technology; installation; telecommunications; consumer services

**Earnings (Yearly Average):** $57,910

**Employment & Outlook:** Decline Expected

## OVERVIEW

### Sphere of Work

A technician working and checking if all servers are up and running. Photo via iStock.com/PeopleImages. [Used under license.]

Telecommunications equipment installers and repairers, also known as telecom technicians, set up and maintain devices or equipment that carry communications signals, such as telephone lines and Internet routers. Technicians may work for a telecommunications organization, small business, or own their own installation and repair company. This sphere of work is also related to individuals who set up advanced systems such as smart-home networks.

## Profile

**Interests:** Data, Things, People
**Working Conditions:** Both Inside and Outside
**Physical Strength:** Medium Work, Heavy Work
**Education Needs:** Certificate, Associate Degree, On-the-Job Training
**Licensure/Certification:** Not Required
**Opportunities for Experience:** On-the-Job Training, Apprenticeship
**Interest Score:** RIC

### Work Environment

Telecom technicians often work in the field, physically installing and setting up the equipment in peoples' homes and businesses, which requires dexterity and physical strength. Others work in a central office. Most telecom technicians work full-time. Some businesses offer 24-hour repair services. Telecom technicians in these companies work shifts, including evenings, holidays, and weekends. Some are on call around the clock in case of emergencies.

### Occupation Interest

Individuals attracted to telecommunications have an interest in technology and customer service. They strive to provide the latest devices and connections to individuals, whether for home or business use, and to troubleshoot and fix components that are not working. As such, they are constantly keeping up with the latest advances in technology, such as smart-home systems. They must also be customer-oriented and courteous since much of the work takes place in peoples' homes or businesses. Technicians may choose to open their own company, relying on advertising, word-of-mouth, and contracts to generate business.

## Duties and Responsibilities

- Installing communications equipment in offices, private homes, and buildings that are under construction
- Setting up, rearranging, and replacing routing and dialing equipment
- Inspecting and servicing equipment, wiring, and phone jacks
- Repairing or replacing faulty, damaged, and malfunctioning equipment
- Testing repaired, newly installed, and updated equipment to ensure that it works properly
- Adjusting or calibrating equipment to improve its performance
- Keeping records of maintenance, repairs, and installations
- Demonstrating and explaining the use of equipment to customers

### A Day in the Life—Duties and Responsibilities

The specific tasks of telecom technicians vary with their specialization and where they work.

Central office technicians set up and maintain switches, routers, fiber-optic cables, and other equipment at switching hubs, called central offices. These hubs send, process, and amplify data from thousands of telephone, Internet, and cable connections. Telecom technicians receive alerts about equipment malfunctions from automonitoring switches and are able to correct the problems remotely.

Headend technicians perform work similar to that of central office technicians but work at distribution centers for cable and television companies. Headend technicians monitor signals for local cable networks through headend control centers.

Home installers and repairers—sometimes known as station installers and repairers—set up and repair telecommunications equipment in customers' homes and businesses. For example, they set up modems to install telephone, Internet, and cable television services. When customers have problems, home installers and repairers test the customer's lines to determine if the problem is inside the building or outside. If the problem is inside, they try to repair it. If the problem is outside, they refer the problem to line repairers.

Telecommunications equipment installers and repairers who work at a client's location must track hours worked, parts used, and costs incurred. Workers who set up and maintain lines outdoors are classified as line installers and repairers.

Technicians may also be required to attend classes and training sessions on an ongoing basis in order to stay apprised of the latest technology and installation techniques and requirements.

Technicians who own their own company must also be well-versed in how to run a business, especially if employing others.

## WORK ENVIRONMENT

### Immediate Physical Environment

Some telecom technicians provide in-home installation and repair services, while others work in central offices or electronic service centers. Equipment installation may require climbing onto rooftops and into attics and climbing ladders and telephone poles. Telecom technicians occasionally work in cramped, awkward positions, in which they stoop, crouch, crawl, or reach high to do their work. Sometimes they must lift or move heavy equipment and parts. They also may work on equipment while it is powered, so they need to take necessary precautions.

The work of telecom technicians can be dangerous. Telecommunications equipment installers and repairers have one of the highest rates of injuries and illnesses of all occupations. Common injuries include falls and strains. To reduce risk of injury, workers wear hard hats and harnesses when working on ladders or on elevated equipment. To prevent electrical shocks, technicians may lock off power to equipment that is under repair.

### Human Environment

Telecom technicians may conduct on-site visits by themselves, or with a small team of co-workers, depending on the size of the job. In many cases, they must be prepared to deal with clients face-to-face, and often in their private dwellings, requiring courteous behavior and attentiveness. If installing new equipment or services, the technician may need to teach the client how to operate it. If conducting installation or repair at a business during open hours, they may also have to work around customers of that business. Technicians who own their own businesses are also responsible for staffing and financial matters.

### Technological Environment

These workers use many different tools to inspect equipment and diagnose problems. For instance, to locate distortions in signals, they may employ spectrum analyzers and polarity probes. They also commonly use hand tools, including screwdrivers and pliers, to take equipment apart and repair it.

Many telecom technicians work with computers, specialized hardware, and other diagnostic equipment. They follow manufacturers' instructions or technical manuals to install or update software and programs on devices. They must keep pace with emerging technologies in order to provide clients with the latest systems they want, including advanced surveillance and wireless systems.

Technicians who own their own business should be familiar with standard word processing, recordkeeping, and accounting software.

## EDUCATION, TRAINING, AND ADVANCEMENT

### High School/Secondary

High school students interested in a career in telecommunications should become familiar with the latest phone and Internet technology, as well as evolving systems such a smart-homes. This can be done outside of school on a hobby basis, and by reading and viewing online tutorials. In class students should focus on math and science, as well as English to enhance communication skills.

**Suggested High School Subjects**

- Advanced Math
- Algebra
- Biology
- Chemistry
- Construction Math
- Earth or Life or Physical Science
- Economics
- English
- Entrepreneurship
- Geometry
- History
- Personal Finance
- Physics
- Political Science
- Pre-Calculus
- Psychology
- Statistics
- Trigonometry

### *Transferable Skills and Abilities*

**Color Vision**
- Telling apart color-coded wires

**Customer-service Skills**
- Being friendly and polite when in customers' homes and businesses
- Teaching people how to maintain and operate communications equipment

**Dexterity**
- Repairing small devices, connecting components, and using hand tools

**Mechanical Skills**
- Familiarity with devices installed and repaired, and with internal parts and appropriate tools
- Understanding manufacturers' instructions when installing or repairing equipment

**Troubleshooting Skills**
- Troubleshooting and devising solutions to problems that are not immediately apparent

**Related Career Pathways/Majors**

*Arts, A/V Technology & Communications Career Cluster*
- Telecommunications Pathway

*Architecture & Construction Career Cluster*
- Maintenance/Operations Pathway

*Business Management & Administration Career Cluster*
- General Management Pathway

*Human Services Career Cluster*
- Consumer Serviccs Pathway

*Information Technology Career Cluster*
- Information Support & Services Pathway
- Network Systems Pathway

*Manufacturing Career Cluster*
- Maintenance, Installation & Repair Pathway

*Science, Technology, Engineering & Mathematics Career Cluster*
- Engineering & Technology Pathway
- Science & Mathematics Pathway

**Fast Fact**

**Most self-employed professionals work in construction and trades. That number is 19.6 percent, followed by 10.9 percent in retail, 10.7 percent in real estate, and 10.3 percent in consulting.** Source: smallbizgenius.com

Installing a home security system. Photo via iStock.com/sefa ozel. [Used under license.]

## Postsecondary

Telecom technicians typically need postsecondary education in electronics, telecommunications, or computer networking. Generally, postsecondary programs include classes such as data transmission systems, data communication, AC/DC electrical circuits, and computer programming. Most programs lead to a certificate or an associate degree in telecommunications or related subjects. Some employers prefer to hire candidates with an associate degree.

### Related College Majors

- Computer Networking
- Electronics
- Telecommunications

## Adult Job Seekers

Adults seeking a career in telecommunications have the best chance if they come from a related discipline or have previous experience with telecom components, electronics, or computer networking. They can enhance their skills through individual classes or pursue full certificates or degrees if desired.

## Additional Requirements

Once hired, telecom technicians receive on-the-job training, typically lasting a few weeks to a few months. Training involves a combination of classroom instruction and hands-on work with an experienced technician. In these settings, workers learn the equipment's internal parts and the tools needed for repair. Technicians who have completed postsecondary education often require less on-the-job instruction than those who have not.

Some companies may send new employees to training sessions to learn about equipment, procedures, and technologies offered by equipment manufacturers or industry organizations.

**Fast Fact**

**Women are no strangers to entrepreneurship: the number of women-owned business in the US has increased by 114 percent in the last 20 years. Women own four out of ten businesses.**

Source: whattobecome.com

Women own four out of ten businesses. Photo via iStock.com/Ridofranz. [Used under license.]

Because technology in this field constantly changes, telecom technicians must continue learning about new equipment over the course of their careers.

## EARNINGS AND ADVANCEMENT

Earnings depend on the nature of the technician's work, and whether he or she works for a large company, small business, or runs his/her own business. Median annual earnings of farmers and farm managers were $57,910 in 2019. The lowest 10 percent earned less than $33,090, and the highest 10 percent earned more than $85,620.

Telecommunications equipment installers and repairers may receive paid vacations, holidays, and sick days; life and health insurance; and retirement benefits. These are usually paid by the employer if the business is not self-owned.

## EMPLOYMENT AND OUTLOOK

Telecom technicians held 215,700 jobs in 2019. Employment is expected to decline 3 percent through the year 2029, since consumers increasingly demand wireless and mobile services, which often require less installation, instead of landline-based services. This shift in demand means that telecommunications companies are expected to require fewer telecommunications equipment installers.

Some job opportunities should come from the need to replace workers who leave the occupation. Although job opportunities will vary by specialty, those with an associate degree and strong customer-service skills should have the best job prospects.

Technologies such as mobile video streaming and broadband Internet require high data transfer rates in telecommunications systems. Central office and headend technicians are likely to be needed to service and upgrade switches and routers to handle increased data usage, resulting in some job opportunities for them.

### Related Occupations

- Broadcast/Sound Engineering Technician
- Electrical and Electronics Installer/Repairer
- Line Installer/Repairers

## MORE INFORMATION

**International Society Broadband Experts (ISBE)**
140 Philips Road
Exton, PA 19341
610.363.6888
info@scte.org
www.scte.org

**National Alliance for Communications Technology Education and Learning (NACTEL)**
www.nactel.org

**NCTA—The Internet & Television Association**
25 Massachusetts Avenue NW, Suite 100
Washington, DC 20001
202.222.2300
info@ncta.com
www.ncta.com

**Society of Cable Telecommunications Engineers (SCTE)**
140 Philips Road
Exton, PA 19341
610.363.6888
info@scte.org
www.scte.org

**Telecommunications Industry Association (TIA)**
1310 North Courthouse Road, Suite 890
Arlington, VA 22201
703.907.7700
tiaonline.org

**USTelecom**
601 New Jersey Avenue NW, Suite 600
Washington, DC 20001
www.ustelecom.org

---

*Stuart Paterson*

## *Conversation With...*
## KEVIN MCCARTHY

Co-founder & President
X-Pert Communications, Inc., State College, PA
Electronics, 28 years

**What was your individual career path in terms of education/training, entry-level job, or other significant opportunity?**

I finished high school a year early because I was bored sitting at a desk in school. After I graduated, I didn't know what I wanted to do. My dad served in the US Navy, and he convinced me to talk to a Naval recruiter. The recruiter talked me into enlisting and going into the electronics division. I was always a gadget kind of guy, and it seemed interesting. As it turns out, they sent me to a Navy school for three years to become an electrical engineer. So, I was in school year-round, which was kind of ironic. But it was a mix of textbook and lab-based training, so I enjoyed it.

I spent eight years in the Navy—three in school, three onboard a ship, and two years at a naval air station, repairing radars and communication equipment. I loved it. I liked being in the Navy, in general, and I liked my job. I wasn't mentally ready for college, and I'm sure I would have dropped out if I tried to go.

After the Navy I worked for a company when high speed Internet was just coming to people's homes in the late 1990s. I worked with a good person, Christopher Gray. We had a lot in common—we were military veterans and had young kids—and we became good friends. But after a couple [of] years, we were laid off. We started working together doing side jobs on anything technology related. We discovered there was a real demand in our area for installing structured cabling in homes and businesses for better telecommunications connectivity. Structured cabling carries voice or data information from any device connected to the Internet. The cabling is designed to work for phones, computer networks, and other IP technology in use today and in the future. Think of the cables as a paved highway that carries traffic of a lot of different types of vehicles. The highways function as designed for cars and trucks that have been on the road for years, and they also function for new models of vehicles as those are released.

Chris and I started our technology and telecommunications company, X-Pert Communications, in 2002; he is vice president.

It took us two years to be able to hire an employee, and he's still with us. Those first two years were a struggle. One week we might do wiring, the next we might be cleaning gutters, anything to keep us going and build the business. Now, we have 22 employees.

We started out only installing structured cabling and soon branched out to include some of the advanced systems that were using the cabling. All of our work now is in commercial buildings.

We install surveillance systems, HVAC smart technology controls, card readers and facial recognition systems to control building access, and we do other specialty work for large commercial buildings. Everything is the latest technology, everything is IP-based. It all connects to your computer network. Specialty work has grown during the COVID-19 pandemic. We now install facial recognition for building access control and use thermal cameras to check people's temperatures before granting access to buildings. It works like this: you walk up to the door and look into the camera. It's set up to recognize if you have access to the building, then it takes your temperature. If you have a fever, it won't open the door for you. We have that installed in several factories.

Having a business partner with personality traits that are different from your own is beneficial. Not only do Chris and I have a solid friendship, we also trust each other and balance each other in business decisions. For example, I am cautious and methodical and benefit from Chris's eagerness and enthusiasm. A business partnership is similar to a marriage; it lasts and works best when built upon friendship, trust, and loyalty.

When we started the business, we got a lot of help from a Pennsylvania incubator program geared toward people who were laid off. The program provided business classes and hours with lawyers and other professionals at no charge. It basically cost us nothing to incorporate and get a set of books set up. We're also certified as a Veteran Owned Small Business, which has its advantages. The federal government requires a percentage of veteran participation in some of its contracts. There's not much federal work in our area, but Pennsylvania has a similar program, and we get a lot of work that way.

**What are the most important skills and/or qualities for someone in your profession?**
You have to be able to analyze data, solve problems, make decisions, and pay attention to details. You have to be a good listener to customers and to coworkers. You have to be trustworthy. We deal with a lot of sensitive information on people's computers and in their offices.

**What do you wish you had known going into this profession?**
I wish I'd known the importance of cash flow. We never worried about it until it became an issue. We learned some hard lessons. I wish I'd known more about managing employees. In the Navy I learned to lead people. Managing employees is different. In the navy it's about accomplishing a mission; with employees it's more about nurturing them.

**Are there many job opportunities in your profession? In what specific areas?**
There's definitely a shortage of qualified technicians. We have a hard time finding people who can program and troubleshoot advanced systems we install. There are technical schools that teach skills, and we do a lot of on-the-job training.

A lot of young people aren't getting into the construction industry. When we look for people to hire, we seem to be getting older people who are getting retrained. I'm hoping that as things get more technical, it may start to draw younger people. Our technicians' jobs involve working on a laptop in the field instead of swinging a hammer.

**How do you see your profession changing in the next 5 years? How will technology impact that change, and what skills will be required?**
The industry evolves quickly. We never know where it's going in the next few years, but we always try to adapt and go where the market takes us. The advanced systems side of our company will start to grow more, the surveillance systems, and wireless systems will become a bigger part of our business because they're starting to be required everywhere now. To work in this field, you'll need to keep your skills current as technology changes.

**What do you enjoy most about your job? What do you enjoy least about your job?**
I enjoy problem solving and troubleshooting. I love meeting new people, that my hours are flexible. There's always something new happening, and every day is different.

I don't like that I am always on call. On Christmas Day, I'm on call—even on vacation, no matter what. That's just part of the business.

There's also a certain amount of stress when you have employees. We get to know our workers and their families. I feel responsible for them and need to make sure our company has work so they keep their incomes. Work doesn't come to us. We have to look for it and bid it.

**Can you suggest a valuable "try this" for students considering a career in your profession?**
We've had, in the past, high school students work with us during the summers, as kind of a mini-internship where they are exposed to different aspects of the business. They get to see how we estimate, bid, and manage projects. We also have a big warehouse full of inventory that has to be maintained. Find a company like ours and ask to spend a couple of days, follow someone around to see what he or she does.

## *Conversation With...*

# JENNIFER MALLETT

Level Up Your Home/Level Up Automation
Northborough, MA
Home automation industry, 12 years; entrepreneur, 5 years

**What was your individual career path in terms of education/training, entry-level job, or other significant opportunity?**

My father started his own business when I was in high school, so I spent my summers working for his startup and got a taste of what being in a small business was like. I really loved the energy and the feel of the risk and what was on the line for his family. I picked up on that excitement. I went to Bentley University in Waltham, Massachusetts, with the intent of studying business, figured out I wanted to focus on marketing, and graduated with a BS in Marketing.

When I graduated, my dad set me up with twenty interviews, some informational, with his colleagues. That was one of the best things I did because it forced me to get out of a student role and interact with people in the workplace. I landed at Reebok International LLC as a marketing intern for their women's fitness group. I was there 18 months, had five different managers and was laid off twice. It was a public company, and I learned pretty quickly, "Wow, this isn't what I learned in college." I ended up at Bose Corporation, where I stayed for close to 15 years in a variety of roles. It was a fantastic experience.

The company's founder, Dr. Amar Bose, had a vision for the workplace: for people to reach their highest personal potential whatever their role. I traveled the country and ran a business unit for 7 years. However, I always wanted to start my own business. Six years ago, I started talking with Bose about outsourcing their US and Canadian home installation for audio business because they were looking to outsource, and I thought it would be a great way to roll into my new business. I left the company in order to negotiate that contract. I ended up not moving forward with it because, from a financial perspective, I was taking all the risk. We left it that I would be a Bose dealer, and they referred customers to me.

In the end, this allowed my business to broaden its reach to automation and smart and connected homes. I can be agnostic about brands we install and reach people that need help understanding home automation.

We want to be the go-to company for smart home automation in the United States and are working on franchising. We started by contracting with mom-and-pop installers, but 2 years in

I knew I wanted more control and a more branded experience including workers showing up in Level Up shirts and vans. It took about 2 years to find the right legal company to specialize in franchises, and we just started selling those in January. Our vision is 10 units by the end of this year and a goal of 150 units in 5 years.

We have one showroom in Massachusetts. The vision is for us to have micro-showrooms in different parts of the country.

COVID-19 has accelerated our business on the residential side. People have been investing in home improvement projects and that, along with the growth rate of connected products, is projected to double in 5 years. I do believe the numbers because past projections have come through. People are remodeling homes, bathrooms, looking to age in place. We've sold more audio and TV outdoor systems. The business side is growing more slowly during COVID because the workplace is currently different.

**What are the most important skills and/or qualities for someone in your profession?**
There's a lot of glamour around being an entrepreneur, but at the end of the day you have to have a lot of grit and resilience and the ability to pick yourself up and keep going where you need to go. Day to day is very stressful because not only are you creating your own income, you're responsible for other people's incomes.

You also have to be in a place where you're always evolving your business. If you stand flat-footed on success, it's not going to last very long.

**What do you wish you had known going into this profession?**
Even though I ran a business of similar size and scale at Bose, I wish I'd known that it would be entirely different running my own. I was very surprised when Bose rock stars came into this startup experience and were not a good fit at all.

**Are there many job opportunities in your profession? In what specific areas?**
Definitely. The term "smart home" was coined in the eighties but it's still early in this industry, and there's a tremendous need for people in the space. Part of our mission with our franchising program is to create the workforce of tradespeople to install and maintain smart systems. Think about plumbers and electricians. None of these people specialize in network-connected products. Smart thermostats have changed that to some degree in the HVAC industry, and there's certainly been more market penetration there and in plumbing. When our industry gets together to talk, we talk about how we are going to address what will be a huge labor shortage.

**How do you see your profession changing in the next 5 years? How will technology impact that change, and what skills will be required?**
The technology is moving at a lightning-fast pace right now. The things that are of real interest involve how to help people age in place. The technologies coming out, for example, include sensors that don't need to be worn and can be put throughout the house and can detect patterns, and whether someone has fallen. For example, say a person gets coffee at 8 a.m. but it's 10 o'clock, and they haven't moved. Someone can be notified. Those sensors also can check things like biometrics, and this also is very important for people aging in place. In addition, there are systems that control things like automated window shades, music, or security

so people can push a button and the home's doors lock and the security system goes on. This is going to become more mass market in the next 5 years. The workforce needs to be there.

**What do you enjoy most about your job? What do you enjoy least about your job?**
I love seeing where we're going to go next and trying to push the envelope of what's out there for us. Anything that's new, I love. It's super-energizing.

I don't like the day-to-day operations as much, such as an employee issue. Fortunately, after 5 years, I've found a great team member who can take a lot of that off my plate.

**Can you suggest a valuable "try this" for students considering a career in your profession?**
Get a connected product and work with it. Get hands-on and talk with people about it, what you learned, and share your experience and the benefits of that product.

# Top Executive

## Snapshot

**Career Cluster(s):** Business, Management & Administration

**Interests:** Business practices; operating own business; putting ideas into practice

**Earnings (Yearly Average):** $184,460 (Chief Executives); $100,780 (General and Operations Managers)

**Employment & Outlook:** As Fast As Average Growth Expected

## OVERVIEW

### Sphere of Work

Top executives plan strategies and policies to ensure that an organization meets its goals. They coordinate and direct work activities of companies and organizations. Top executives include general and operations managers, who oversee activities that are too diverse to be classified into one area of management or administration, and chief executive officers (CEOs), who provide overall direction for companies and organizations. Top executives may own a stake in, or the entirety of, the company they oversee. They may come from a variety of backgrounds, such as engineering or computer science, depending on their industry. Some fields, such as engineering, have a great deal of crossover and entrepreneurial potential.

Top executives must possess dedication, perseverance, and keen business and networking skills. Photo via iStock.com/gorodenkoff. [Used under license.]

### Work Environment

Top executives work in nearly every industry. They work for both small and large organizations, ranging from businesses in which they are the sole employee to firms with hundreds or thousands of employees. Because top executives often are held responsible for their organization's success, their work may be stressful. Travel for business purposes is common, as is interacting with other high-level executives during day-to-day business. Most top executives work full-time, and many work more than 40 hours per week, including evenings and weekends.

## Profile

**Interests:** Data, People, Things
**Working Conditions:** Inside
**Education Needs:** Bachelor's Degree, Master's Degree, Work Experience
**Licensure/Certification:** Varies
**Opportunities for Experience:** Growth within an Organization
**Interest Score:** EC

### Occupation Interest

Top executives are driven to succeed both personally and in terms of the business they oversee. In many cases they have climbed the corporate ladder over many years, with the goal of one day leading the organization. This takes dedication, perseverance, and keen business and networking skills. In other cases, the executive has played an integral role in founding the company, such as a tech startup or small business, building it from the ground up and taking a personal risk in order to see it succeed and grow. Still other top executives may inherit the role in a family business, but rarely does this happen without the person first working for the company, or at least preparing for the role through years of schooling and outside work experience.

## Duties and Responsibilities

- Establishing and executing departmental or organizational goals, policies, and procedures
- Directing and overseeing an organization's financial and budgetary activities
- Managing general activities related to making products and providing services
- Consulting with other executives, staff, and board members about general operations
- Negotiating or approving contracts and agreements
- Appointing department heads and managers
- Analyzing financial statements, sales reports, and other performance indicators
- Identifying places to cut costs and to improve performance, policies, and programs

### A Day in the Life—Duties and Responsibilities

The responsibilities of top executives largely depend on an organization's size. In small organizations, such as an independent retail store, an owner or manager often is responsible for hiring, training, quality control, and day-to-day supervisory duties. In large organizations, chief executives typically focus on formulating policies and planning strategies, while general and operations managers direct day-to-day operations.

Chief executive officers (CEO), who are also known by titles such as executive director, managing director, or president, provide overall direction for companies and organizations. Chief executive officers manage company operations, formulate and implement policies, and ensure that goals are met. They collaborate with and direct the work of other top executives and typically report to a board of directors. There may be other types of chief executives—such as chief operating officers (COOs), chief financial officers (CFOs), or chief human resources officers—who manage a specific part of the organization. The knowledge, skills, and job duties that these executives have differ, depending on which department they oversee.

General and operations managers oversee an array of activities relating to the management or administration of a company. Responsibilities may include formulating policies, directing daily operations, and planning the use of materials and human resources. These managers make staff schedules, assign work, and ensure that projects are completed. In some organizations, the tasks of CEOs may overlap with those of general and operations managers.

## OCCUPATION SPECIALTIES

**Mayor/City Manager/County Administrator/Governor**
Mayors, city managers, county administrators, and governors are chief executive officers of governments. They usually oversee budgets, programs, and the use of resources. Mayors and governors must be elected to office, whereas managers and administrators are typically appointed.

**School Superintendent/College or University President**
School superintendents and college or university presidents are chief executive officers of school districts and postsecondary schools. They manage issues such as student achievement, budgets and resources, general operations, and relations with government agencies and other stakeholders.

## WORK ENVIRONMENT

### Immediate Physical Environment

Top executives may work in a variety of locations, depending on the business they oversee. The CEO of a small business may be involved in many aspects of its day-to-day operations, while the leader of a large organization with thousands of employees may spend most of his or her time in an office and in meetings.

Travel occurs often, in order to attend meetings and conferences or to visit local, regional, national, or international offices of interest.

### Human Environment

Top executives often interact with other high-level executives, such as financial managers, human resource managers, or chief technology officers. By the nature of their position, executives must be comfortable interacting with others, including representing the company while attending conferences and trade shows, and possibly giving interviews to the media when the occasion calls for it. Further, many CEOs are beholden to a board of directors, so they must be comfortable accounting for the company's successes and failures during high-pressure meetings. General and operations managers must likewise report to superiors, consult with other managers, and oversee their team of employees.

### Technological Environment

It is beneficial for company leaders to be well-versed in numerous software programs, such as word processors and spreadsheet-makers, and accounting, human resources, and project management programs. Other technological requirements vary by the nature of the business—the CEO of a tech startup will likely have programming skills and be involved with the creation and evolution of the product, for instance.

## EDUCATION, TRAINING, AND ADVANCEMENT

### High School/Secondary

Top executives need to be well-rounded in their knowledge of language, math, and business practices in order to succeed. Many skills and traits are gained through years of work experience, but high school students with a desire to one day lead a company should focus on courses that prepare them for entry into the business world, such as English, economics, and history. Students should also start planning for their postsecondary studies, such as researching schools with strong business departments and reputations for worthwhile internships.

**Suggested High School Subjects**

- Algebra
- Biology
- Calculus
- Earth or Life Science

- Economics
- English
- Geometry
- History
- Physics
- Psychology
- Statistics
- Trigonometry

**Related Career Pathways/Majors**

*Business, Management & Administration Career Cluster*

- Business Information Management Pathway
- General Management Pathway
- Human Resources Management Pathway
- Operations Management Pathway

## Transferable Skills and Abilities

**Communication Skills**

- Conveying information clearly and persuasively
- Discussing issues and negotiating with others
- Directing staff
- Explaining policies and decisions to people within and outside the organization

**Decision-making Skills**

- Assessing different options and choosing the best course of action when setting policies and managing an organization

**Leadership Skills**

- Shaping and directing an organization by coordinating policies, people, and resources

**Problem-solving Skills**

- Identifying and resolving issues within an organization
- Recognizing shortcomings and implementing solutions

**Time-management Skills**

- Performing many tasks concurrently to ensure that their work gets done and that the organization meets its goals

## Postsecondary

Top executives typically need at least a bachelor's degree and considerable work experience to enter the occupation. Top executives of large corporations may have a master's degree in business administration (MBA). Postsecondary students should look for internships during or directly after schooling in order to become familiar with the business world outside of the classroom, build their résumés, and make important networking contacts.

**Related College Majors**

- Business Administration
- Law
- Liberal Arts
- Public Administration

## Adult Job Seekers

Many top executives advance within their own organizations, moving up from lower-level management occupations or supervisory positions. However, some companies may prefer to hire qualified candidates from outside their organization. Top executives who are promoted from lower-level positions may be able to substitute experience for education to move up in the organization.

**Fast Fact**

**If you want to be a billionaire, your best bet is to do it the self-made way. Of 585 billionaires in the US, according to 2016 research, only 20 percent got there via inheritance. A combination of inheritance and hard work got another 18 percent across the billion-dollar threshold.** Source: smallbizgenius.com

Benefits of a billionaire lifestyle. Photo via iStock.com/EXTREME-PHOTOGRAPHER. [Used under license.]

Chief executives typically need extensive managerial experience, and this experience is expected to be in the organization's area of specialty. Most general and operations managers hired from outside an organization need lower-level supervisory or management experience in a related field.

Some general managers move into higher-level managerial or executive positions. Executive training programs and development programs often benefit managers or executives.

### Professional Certification and Licensure

Some top executive positions may require the applicant to have a license or certification relevant to their area of management. For example, some employers may require their CEO to be a certified public accountant (CPA).

## EARNINGS AND ADVANCEMENT

Top executives are among the highest paid workers in the United States. However, salary levels vary substantially. For example, a top manager in a large corporation may earn significantly more than the mayor of a small town. Similarly, earnings for general and operations managers differ across industries because their responsibilities also vary by industry.

Median annual earnings of chief executives were $184,460 in 2019. The lowest 10 percent earned less than $62,290, and the highest 10 percent earned more than $208,000. Median annual earnings of general and operations managers were $100,780 in 2019. The lowest 10 percent earned less than $45,050, and the highest 10 percent earned more than $208,000.

**Fast Fact**

**Well-known companies that launched from an incubator include Airbnb and Dropbox. The five-year survival rate for incubator clients has been reported from 75 upwards to 87 percent.**

Source: ceigateway.com

Airbnb logo. Photo by DesignStudio via Wikimedia Commons. [Public Domain.]

Dropbox logo. Photo by Dropbox, Inc. via Wikimedia Commons. [Public Domain.]

Top executives may receive paid vacations, holidays, and sick days; life and health insurance; and retirement benefits. These are usually paid by the employer if the business is not self-owned. In addition to salaries, total compensation for corporate executives often includes stock options and other performance bonuses. These executives also may enjoy benefits such as access to expense allowances, use of company-owned aircraft and cars, and membership to exclusive clubs. Nonprofit and government executives usually receive fewer of these types of benefits.

## EMPLOYMENT AND OUTLOOK

Top executives held 2,774,300 jobs in 2019. Twenty-four percent of chief executives were self-employed. Overall employment of top executives is projected to grow 4 percent from 2019 to 2029, about as fast as the average for all occupations. Projected employment growth varies by occupation.

Employment of general and operations managers is projected to grow 6 percent from 2019 to 2029, faster than the average for all occupations. Organizations will continue to rely on these workers to help them operate successfully.

Employment of chief executives is projected to decline 10 percent from 2019 to 2029. Improving office technology and changing organizational structures have increased these workers' ability to perform tasks previously done by multiple chief executives. In addition, economic activity and employment has become increasingly concentrated in large, established companies, which may lead to fewer new jobs for these workers.

The high pay and prestige associated with these positions attract many qualified applicants. In addition to those arising from growth, openings are also expected to result from the need to replace workers who transfer to different occupations or exit the labor force, such as to retire. Those with an advanced degree and extensive managerial experience will have the best job prospects.

### Related Occupations

- Administrative Services Manager
- Advertising/Promotions/Marketing Manager
- Architectural/Engineering Manager
- Computer/Information Systems Manager
- Construction Manager
- Financial Manager
- Human Resources Manager
- Industrial Production Manager
- Medical/Health Services Manager
- Sales Manager

## MORE INFORMATION

**American Management Association (AMA)**
1601 Broadway
New York, NY 10019
877.566.9441
customerservice@amanet.org
www.amanet.org

**American Society of Association Executives (ASAE)**
1575 I Street NW
Washington, DC 20005
888.950.2723
ASAEservice@asaecenter.org
www.asaecenter.org

**Financial Executives International (FEI)**
89 Headquarters Plaza, Suite 1462
Morristown, NJ 07960
973.765.1000
membership@financialexecutives.org
www.financialexecutives.org

**Financial Management Association International (FMA)**
University of South Florida
Muma College of Business
4202 East Fowler Avenue, BSN 3403
Tampa FL 33620-5500
813.974.2084
fma@coba.usf.edu
www.fma.org

**International Executives Association (IEA)**
P.O. Box 49654
Charlotte, NC 28277
704.604.5599
director@ieaweb.com
ieaweb.com

**National Management Association (NMA)**
3055 Kettering Boulevard, Suite 210
Dayton, OH 45439
937.294.0421
nma1.org

**Senior Executives Association (SEA)**
4829 West Lane
Bethesda, MD 20814
202.971.3300
seniorexecs.org

---

*Stuart Paterson*

# *Conversation With...*

## DOUG BRENT

CEO and co-chairman
Brent Enterprises, LLC, Boulder, CO
Entrepreneur, 22 years

**What was your individual career path in terms of education/training, entry-level job, or other significant opportunity?**
I have a Bachelor of Commerce degree from the University of Toronto and a Master of Business Administration from Cornell University. I'd started college studying the sciences to be a doctor. But I was into sports, and I did a lot of socializing, and that was the end of my medical career. My degrees aren't necessary to be an entrepreneur; they just give you the confidence and jargon to deal in the financial arena.

Through the 1990s I ran a private equity and venture capital firm within a large investment bank. As that fund got bigger and more global, I realized I was spending too much time managing egos. My brother Hollis studied law and ran a small merchant bank, but we both wanted to get closer to managing our own businesses. In 1999, we formed a company, Brent Enterprises, LLC, to own and operate businesses. There are important legal protections that come from having a holding company between an individual and the businesses owned. We started our first small business in 2000, but it took what seemed a frustratingly long wait to close our second deal in 2003. Working together is great for us because we have quite different personalities, with complementary expertise; and when we disagree on things, it's never a question of whether one of us has an ulterior agenda—it's just a fundamental disagreement.

We've owned seven businesses; some we started, and some we bought. Some we've sold. We had a frozen pizza company, invested in it, and sold it to one of the largest frozen pizza companies in the United States. We had a specialty packaging company called The IntraPac Group. It consisted of nine packaging plants in the United States, Canada, and Costa Rica, making laminated, aluminum and tin tubes, plastic bottles, jars, and deodorant sticks. End markets were the pharmaceutical, personal care, and food industries. We sold it to someone else who saw it as a platform for a bigger strategy. The time to sell a business is when it's worth more to someone else than it is to you.

Our core businesses now are our organic snack food company, Made in Nature, LLC, and our grain fractionation and ethanol business, Permolex International. Made in Nature started in

1989 as a small, organic fresh produce and dried fruit company and eventually just sold dried fruit. We bought it in 2003 and transformed it into a healthy snack company.

Permolex mills flour and extracts the gluten to make a powder used in baked goods. We also produce food grade and pharmaceutical grade alcohols from our milling process to use in products such as hand sanitizers. The remaining grain is returned to the farmers for cattle feed. We have 250 employees between those two businesses.

Entrepreneurship is all about managing risk, and hopefully, those are calculated risks. There are two times in life where I think it is ideal to take that risk. Those times are when you are financially secure and can afford to lose, or when you are at a stage of life where you have nothing to lose. A great time is when you're young, have vim and vigor and don't know any better, and just want to get out there and give something a go. In my case, my kids were old enough and I had enough money set aside that if I failed, I could get up, dust myself off, and start again. We were fortunate enough that our failures were not enough to cripple the business, but as I say, an entrepreneur is always balancing risk, and hopefully those risks are well understood and thought through.

Sometimes you can make calculated decisions and be right in all of them and [then] something beyond your control can happen and upset the apple cart. Can you imagine starting a restaurant in 2019? I'm sure there are plenty of people who have strong business plans and a strong outlook, and then COVID comes along, and they lose everything.

**What are the most important skills and/or qualities for someone in your profession?**
The most important thing would be common sense. You're probably not going to find an answer in a textbook for most of the questions you're going to face in your career. You have to have a gut feeling—something just doesn't make sense, or something can be done a better way. If you don't have common sense to see opportunities or adapt, you don't have much chance succeeding as an entrepreneur. When COVID hit, we were producing ethanol at a grade to be used as a fuel additive, but suddenly people weren't driving anywhere. We moved fast and invested in upgrades to the plant to produce ethanol suitable for hand sanitizer. It was common sense to adapt to the new reality. Ninety-five percent is common sense, and five percent is confidence to sell your idea and resilience to keep going when facing initial hurdles.

**What do you wish you had known going into this profession?**
I have a unique perspective because I was fortunate enough to run an equity fund where I was sitting on the boards of companies run by entrepreneurs. I was always thinking: what's the common thread? There are all kinds of people who are entrepreneurs. We had every kind of leader—some who believed everything would just turn out right, and others who were detailed thinkers. I went in with the knowledge knowing there's not a formula, but the big awakening was when I was a private equity investor sitting on company boards, I would sit there and say, "why don't you outsource that," "why don't you consolidate that," "why don't you combine those two products"? It all seemed so obvious to me. But when you start running these businesses, you quickly realize that it's way harder than that. It's never as easy as you think it is in terms of finding the right people, implementation, and execution.

**Are there many job opportunities in your profession? In what specific areas?**
There are a broad array of types of entrepreneurial enterprises and almost infinite opportunities to get involved with them in some capacity. No matter what the industry, you need a good idea, a good business plan, to be able to justify it to others, and then go out and find the money.

**How do you see your profession changing in the next 5 years? How will technology impact that change, and what skills will be required?**
Technology disrupts everything and out of disruption comes opportunity. As technology applies to virtually any industry, it changes the characteristics of a winner and a loser. Take e-commerce. There are certain appealing elements to physically going to a store—I can browse; I can make impulse buys. People were willing to buy certain things online; but then all of a sudden COVID hits, and there's a huge growth in e-commerce. I don't think it's ever going to go back.

**What do you enjoy most about your job? What do you enjoy least about your job?**
No two days, no two hours are the same. You're dealing with the unpredictable all the time, and it's never boring. It's not always fun—but it's never boring.

What I like least is letting an employee go. We like to know our employees and create community within our businesses. You have to give people the tools they need to succeed, and believe they can succeed, and sometimes you're going to be disappointed because they just can't. Those personnel decisions are very difficult to make.

**Can you suggest a valuable "try this" for students considering a career in your profession?**
Right out of Nike: "Just do it." You can get a window into being an entrepreneur by just going and working in your local butcher shop. Try working in ten things, don't just try one thing. Nowadays, you can design and build something on a 3D printer and sell it exclusively on the Internet. Do whatever it takes to get up to bat. Because once you're up to bat you're going to hit the ball or you're not.

# *Conversation With...*

## RICK GARDNER

Director, Startup Ventures
University of Buffalo, Amherst, NY
Startup entrepreneur, 10 years; academia, one year

**What was your individual career path in terms of education/training, entry-level job, or other significant opportunity?**

I grew up in a little mining town in Colorado and became a professional bull rider after high school. I had a career-ending injury and didn't have a back-up plan, so I went to work: construction jobs, manual labor on a farm, in a meatpacking house, as an electrician. I realized I was pretty good at creating and designing things and that led me to engineering. At age 25, I entered Colorado State University where I earned a degree in mechanical engineering. I had a family and worked full-time to put myself through school, so I had to make sure my college paid off.

I worked for big Fortune 500 companies like Hewlett Packard, Schneider Electric, Lockheed Martin, and my career started to change toward the business side of product development. Then I moved into the startup space. I worked for four startups, one as co-founder. In all, I hold 31 US patents and many more foreign patents.

The first startup I worked for was Minute Key. At that time, if you wanted to get a key copied for your house you went to the hardware store, spent 30 minutes to find an associate, waited 20 minutes while they make the key and when you got home, there was a 25 percent chance the key was incorrectly cut and was not going to fit. I managed the development of a kiosk that, at the end of the day, could be adapted to large-scale use in grocery and big box stores. It can cut a key in 60 seconds with 99.9 percent accuracy. We created the market, then competition started.

I came to this job right as the pandemic started. This is the best job I could think of, to work in a place that funnels startups into the system. What they need is coaching, advice, and investment. I can help them not make the mistakes I made.

The number one mistake startups make is that they have a solution to a problem that doesn't matter. They get enamored of their solution. Make sure you are addressing a compelling problem.

The biggest challenge with a startup, which is a high-risk thing, is that even though you may think you are on to something, you have to balance that risk if you have a family. Really successful entrepreneurs can kind of compartmentalize that risk and not waiver.

One thing that's been really refreshing during COVID-19: these entrepreneurs see COVID as an opportunity, a new set of problems. The best entrepreneurs change their offerings. For example, we had a startup working on a software app, COVID happened, and they decided to shift and make an app where employees can say whether or not they tested positive or have symptoms. Employers could use that. Our entrepreneurs were right and got quite a bit of traction with it. Our drug development and bio sciences startups pivoted toward cheap ways to make masks, visors, or ventilators.

**What are the most important skills and/or qualities for someone in your profession?**
Entrepreneurs need determination and tenacity and to believe in their idea. As a mentor, I have to be empathetic. I have to be able to think about the perspective of the person I'm trying to help. I can give all the advice in the world; if that doesn't align with what they are trying to do, that's not much use.

**What do you wish you had known going into this profession?**
I went into engineering because I thought I was creative. But, had I known the direction my career would take, I would have focused more on business-related studies in parallel with engineering. I've also learned how to determine whether a problem is worth solving. That gets into problem-space vs. solution-space and how creativity works. In hindsight, I trained myself in some of those areas, but knowing up front how the creative process works would have been useful.

**Are there many job opportunities in your profession? In what specific areas?**
If you can hang with the risk and you're creative and aggressive, there's a lot of opportunity in the startup space. And I've been blown away by the number of opportunities for mentors and people who are willing to coach, although sometimes people are doing so to find their next opportunity. There are accelerators at universities all over the country.

**How do you see your profession changing in the next 5 years? How will technology impact that change, and what skills will be required?**
From an entrepreneur's perspective, I think you are going to see more and more opportunities for social impact-type ideas. When you look at what motivates millennials and the generation after that coming up, it's different from 20 or 30 years ago. They are interested in societal impact and positive change in the world, from diversity, inclusion, and racial equity to environmental impact. Technology comes and goes. Whether you are solving a compelling problem is the focus.

**What do you enjoy most about your job? What do you enjoy least about your job?**
Seeing young people energized and betting their life. They are onto something and helping them realize their dream—that's terrific. I least enjoy knowing not all are going to be successful, and I have to deliver the bad news and help them move to a different idea.

**Can you suggest a valuable "try this" for students considering a career in your profession?**

Get out and get real jobs doing real stuff—pouring concrete, roofing houses, building things. That is invaluable because you cannot fake real experience in the real world doing real stuff. It gave me perspective, and I wouldn't trade that for the world.

# Web Developer/Digital Designer

## Snapshot

**Career Cluster(s):** Business, Management & Administration; Information Technology

**Interests:** Design; technology; the Internet; customer service

**Earnings (Yearly Average):** $73,760

**Employment & Outlook:** Much Faster Than Average Growth Expected

## OVERVIEW

### Sphere of Work

Web developers create and maintain websites. They are also responsible for the site's technical aspects, such as its performance and capacity, which are measures of a website's speed and how much traffic the site can handle. In addition, web developers may create content for the site. Digital designers develop, create, and test website or interface layout, functions, and navigation for usability. They are responsible for the look and functionality of the website or interface.

Web designer creating and planning site with sketch and design parts. Photo via iStock.com/designer491. [Used under license.]

### Work Environment

Web developers and digital designers typically work in office settings, whether in a corporate or home office. This work can be done remotely in most cases, so the need for a developer to be present in an office building, for instance, depends on the company's needs. Web developers may also operate their own business and perform work for numerous clients located in different parts of the country, or around the world.

**Profile**

**Interests:** Data, Things, People
**Working Conditions:** Inside
**Education Needs:** Varies—High School Diploma, Bachelor's Degree
**Licensure/Certification:** Usually Not Required
**Opportunities for Experience:** Internship, Part-Time Work, Volunteer Work
**Interest Score:** CIR

## Occupation Interest

Individuals interested in web development and design have a passion not only for the technology behind it, but for creating something unique, eye-catching, and functional. Generally speaking, websites are not only visually appealing to the user, but allow them to access services or information about a company or product. Developers must have a creative mind, artistic talent, and be skilled in computer technology to bring ideas to life.

**Duties and Responsibilities**

- Meeting with clients or management to discuss the needs, design, and functionality of a website or interface
- Creating and testing applications, interfaces, and navigation menus for a website
- Writing code for the website, using programming languages such as HTML or XML
- Working with other team members to determine what information the site will contain
- Working with graphics and other designers to determine the website's layout
- Integrating graphics, audio, and video into the website
- Monitoring website traffic
- Creating prototypes and mockups of websites or applications
- Designing and developing graphics

## A Day in the Life—Duties and Responsibilities

Most web designers work full-time. When creating a website, developers and designers must strive to make their client's vision a reality. They build specific types of websites, such as e-commerce, news, or gaming sites, to fit clients' needs. Moreover, certain types of websites may require specialized applications. For example, a gaming site should be able to manage advanced graphics, whereas an e-commerce site would need a payment-processing application. The developer decides which applications and designs will best fit the site, and the designer focuses on the look and usability of these elements across browsers or devices.

## OCCUPATION SPECIALTIES

**Back-end Web Developer**

Back-end web developers are responsible for the overall technical construction of the website. They create the basic framework of the site and ensure that it functions as expected. Back-end web developers also establish procedures for allowing others to add new pages to the website and meet with management to discuss major changes to the site.

**Front-end Web Developer**

Front-end web developers create the technical features for a website's look. They develop the site's layout and integrate graphics, applications (such as a retail checkout tool), and other content. They also write web design programs in a variety of computer languages, such as HTML or JavaScript.

**Web and Digital Interface Designer**

Web and digital interface designers are responsible for creating the look and feel of a website or interface using photos, color, font type and size, graphics, and layout. They also are responsible for the functionality, usability, and compatibility of the website or interface.

**Webmaster**

Webmasters maintain and update websites. They ensure that websites operate correctly, and they test for errors such as broken links. Many webmasters respond to user comments as well.

## WORK ENVIRONMENT

### Immediate Physical Environment

Web designers primarily work in an office setting. They may be employed by a larger company or have their own business. Their working environment should be conducive to long periods of sitting, typing, and looking at a computer monitor. Industries typically employing web developers include: computer systems design and related services; publishing industries; management, scientific, and technical consulting services; and advertising, public relations, and related services.

### Human Environment

Web developers may work alone, or as part of a team on larger or more complex projects to combine specialties. If developers work in the same office, person-to-person collaboration may be part of the project. If developers work from home, communication by email, phone, or video chat is common. Such communication is also common when dealing with clients, and routine meetings may occur in order to ensure projects remain on schedule and on target.

### Technological Environment

Developers and designers need access to reliable, up-to-date computers to perform their duties effectively. Software varies by project, but may include development environment software, object or component-oriented development software, operating system software, and web platform development software.

Web developers need to have a thorough understanding of HTML programming. Many employers also want developers to understand other programming languages, such as JavaScript or SQL, and have knowledge of multimedia publishing tools, such as Flash. Throughout their career, web developers must keep up to date on new tools and computer languages.

## EDUCATION, TRAINING, AND ADVANCEMENT

### High School/Secondary

Educational requirements vary for web developers and digital designers, based on work setting and other factors, and can range from a high school diploma to a bachelor's degree. High school students interested in the field should take as many computer science courses as possible and consider joining extracurricular computer clubs if available. These students may also have such an interest in the field that they engage in web development and design projects on a hobby basis, and this is encouraged to build the necessary skill set.

**Suggested High School Subjects**

- Algebra
- Biology
- Calculus
- Chemistry
- Computer Science
- Earth or Life or Physical Science

- Economics
- English
- Entrepreneurship
- Geometry
- History
- Political Science
- Trigonometry

**Related Career Pathways/Majors**

*Business, Management & Administration Career Cluster*

- General Management Pathway

*Information Technology Career Cluster*

- Information Support & Services Pathway
- Programming & Software Development Pathway
- Web & Digital Communications Pathway

### Transferable Skills and Abilities

**Communication Skills**

- Communicate effectively with coworkers to coordinate work on projects

**Creativity**

- Creating the appearance of a website and ensuring that it is appealing as well as functional

**Customer-service Skills**

- Responding politely to user questions and requests

**Detail-oriented**

- Focusing for long periods on writing code precisely

**Mechanical Skills**

- Operating complex machinery and occasionally performing routine maintenance

**Problem-solving Skills**

- Checking for and fixing coding errors

## Postsecondary

Some employers prefer to hire web developer candidates who have a bachelor's degree in a specific field, such as computer science or programming. Employers of digital designers may prefer to hire candidates who have a bachelor's degree in a field such as web design, digital design, or graphic arts. Web developers and digital designers may not need specific education credentials if they can demonstrate their abilities through prior work experience or projects.

**Related College Majors**

- Computer Graphics
- Computer Networking & Telecommunications
- Digital Arts
- Digital Communications & Multimedia
- E-commerce
- Graphic Design
- Information Science

## Adult Job Seekers

Adults seeking employment as web developers and designers should have a solid background in IT or computer technology and should focus on building a portfolio of smaller projects. The Internet provides many forums where developers and designers can exchange work and ideas. It would be beneficial for adult job seekers to enhance their knowledge through classes on development and design. They must also be familiar with the latest tools and computer languages.

## EARNINGS AND ADVANCEMENT

Earnings depend on the size of the company for which the developer or designer works, whether they are self-employed, and the size of the projects undertaken. Median annual earnings of web developers and designers were $73,760 in 2019. The lowest 10 percent earned less than $39,550, and the highest 10 percent earned more than $142,080.

Web developers and designers may receive paid vacations, holidays, and sick days; life and health insurance; and retirement benefits. These are usually paid by an employer if the developer or designer does not run their own business.

Web developers and digital designers who have a bachelor's degree may advance to become project managers.

## EMPLOYMENT AND OUTLOOK

Web developers and designers held 174,300 jobs in 2019. Ten percent were self-employed. Employment is expected to grow much faster than the average for all occupations through the year 2029, at a rate of 8 percent, as e-commerce continues to expand. Online purchasing is expected to grow faster than the overall retail industry. As retail firms expand their online offerings, demand for these workers will grow. In addition, a rise in the use of mobile devices to search the web will lead to increased demand for web developers and digital designers. Instead of designing a website for a desktop computer, these workers will have to create sites and interfaces that work on mobile devices with many different screen sizes, leading to more work.

Because websites can be built from anywhere in the world, some developer and designer jobs could move to countries with lower wages. However, this practice may decline because the cost of managing workers in multiple countries can offset the savings to businesses. Furthermore, web developers and digital designers must understand cultural nuances that allow webpages to communicate effectively with users. US-based developers and designers are better suited to this task, curtailing the work that may be moved to other countries.

About 13,400 openings for web developers and digital designers are projected each year, on average, over the decade. Many of those openings are expected to result from the need to replace workers who transfer to different occupations or exit the labor force, such as to retire.

Job opportunities for web developers and digital designers are expected to be good. Those with knowledge of multiple programming languages and digital multimedia tools, such as Flash and Photoshop, will have the best opportunities.

### Related Occupations

- Computer/Information Systems Manager
- Computer Programmer
- Computer Support Specialist
- Computer Systems Analyst
- Database Administrator
- Graphic Designer
- Information Security Analyst
- Multimedia Artist/Animator
- Software Developer

## MORE INFORMATION

**American Webmasters Association (AWA)**
2977 Ygnacio Valley Road, Suite 132
Walnut Creek, CA 94598
info@aawebmasters.com
www.aawebmasters.com

**Association for Computing Machinery (ACM)**
1601 Broadway, 10th Floor
New York, NY 10019-7434
212.869.7440
acmhelp@acm.org
www.acm.org

**Computing Research Association (CRA)**
1828 L Street NW, Suite 800
Washington, DC 20036-4632
202.234.2111
info@cra.org
cra.org

**Computing Community Consortium (CCC):**
cra.org/ccc
IEEE Computer Society
2001 L Street NW, Suite 700
Washington, DC 20036-4928
202.371.0101
help@computer.org
www.computer.org

**International Web Association (IWA)**
556 S. Fair Oaks Ave. #101-200
Pasadena, CA 91105
626.449.3709
iwanet.org

**National Center for Women & Information Technology (NCWIT)**
1909 26th Street, 2nd Floor
Boulder, CO 80302
303.735.6671
info@ncwit.org
www.ncwit.org

**World Organization of Webmasters (WOW)**
P.O. Box 584
Washington, IL 61571-0584
662.493.2776
membership@webprofessionals.org
webprofessionals.org

---

*Stuart Paterson*

# Woodworker

## Snapshot

**Career Cluster(s):** Architecture & Construction; Business, Management & Administration; Manufacturing

**Interests:** Creativity; woodwork; working with one's hands

**Earnings (Yearly Average):** $32,690

**Employment & Outlook:** Decline Expected

## OVERVIEW

### Sphere of Work

Woodworkers manufacture a variety of products such as cabinets and furniture, using wood, veneers, and laminates. They often combine and incorporate different materials into wood. They may own their own business, often in very niche areas, or can transition their knowledge of woodwork into fields involving construction and/or repair.

### Work Environment

Working conditions vary with the specific job duties. At times, workers must handle heavy, bulky materials and may encounter noise and dust. As a result, they regularly wear hearing protection devices, safety glasses, and respirators or masks. Most woodworkers work full-time during regular business hours.

Carpenter working with an electric planer on a wooden plank. Photo via iStock.com/Monoliza21. [Used under license.]

### Occupation Interest

Woodworkers are skilled with their hands and have a strong grasp of math and design. Further, they are tech-savvy and know how to utilize the latest automated machinery to complete projects with increased accuracy. They are creative individuals with a desire to provide customers with artfully crafted wooden objects, often specializing in a particular niche, such as musical instruments.

**Profile**

**Interests:** Things, Data, People
**Working Conditions:** Both Inside and Outside
**Physical Strength:** Medium Work, Heavy Work
**Education Needs:** On-The-Job Training, High School Diploma with Technical Education
**Licensure/Certification:** Optional
**Opportunities for Experience:** Internship, Apprenticeship, Part-Time Work
**Interest Score:** RC

## A Day in the Life—Duties and Responsibilities

Despite the abundance of plastics, metals, and other materials, wood products continue to be an important part of our daily lives. Woodworkers make wood products from lumber and synthetic wood materials. Many of these products, including most furniture, kitchen cabinets, and musical instruments, are mass produced. Other products are custom made from architectural designs and drawings.

Although the term "woodworker" may evoke the image of a craftsman who uses hand tools to build ornate furniture, the modern woodworking trade is highly technical and relies on advanced equipment and highly skilled operators. Workers use automated machinery, such as computerized numerical control (CNC) machines, to do much of the work with great accuracy.

**Duties and Responsibilities**

- Understanding detailed architectural drawings, schematics, shop drawings, and blueprints
- Preparing and setting up machines and tooling for woodwork manufacturing
- Lifting wood pieces onto machines, either by hand or with hoists
- Operating woodworking machines, including saws and milling and sanding machines
- Listening for unusual sounds or detecting excessive vibration in machinery
- Ensuring that products meet industry standards and project specifications, making adjustments as necessary
- Selecting and adjusting the proper cutting, milling, boring, and sanding tools for completing a job
- Using hand tools to trim pieces or assemble products

Even specialized artisans generally use CNC machines and a variety of power tools in their work. Much of the work is done in a high-production assembly line facility, but there is also some work that is customized and does not lend itself to being performed on an assembly line.

Woodworkers set up, operate, and tend all types of woodworking machines, such as saws, milling machines, drill presses, lathes, shapers, routers, sanders, planers, and wood-fastening machines. Operators set up the equipment, cut and shape wooden parts, and verify dimensions, using a template, caliper, and rule. After the parts are machined, woodworkers add fasteners and adhesives and connect the parts to form an assembled unit. They also install hardware, such as pulls and drawer slides, and fit specialty products for glass, metal trims, electrical components, and stone. Finally, workers sand, stain, and, if necessary, coat the wood product with a sealer or topcoats, such as a lacquer or varnish.

Many of these tasks are handled by different workers with specialized training.

## OCCUPATION SPECIALTIES

**Cabinetmaker/Bench Carpenter**
Cabinetmakers and bench carpenters cut, shape, assemble, and make parts for wood products. They often design and create sets of cabinets that are customized for specific spaces. In some cases, their duties begin with designing a set of cabinets to specifications and end with installing the cabinets.

**Furniture Finishers**
Furniture finishers shape, finish, and refinish damaged and worn furniture. They may work with antiques and must judge how to preserve and repair them. They also do the staining, sealing, and top coating at the end of the process of making wooden products.

**Wood Sawing Machine Setter/Operator/Tender**
Wood sawing machine setters, operators, and tenders specialize in operating specific pieces of woodworking machinery. They may operate CNC machines.

**Woodworking Machine Setter/Operator/Tender (Except Sawing)**
Woodworking machine setters, operators, and tenders (except sawing) operate woodworking machines, such as drill presses, lathes, routers, sanders, and planers. They may operate CNC machines.

## WORK ENVIRONMENT

### Immediate Physical Environment

Woodworkers may work in a high-production assembly line facility, but some (especially those creating customized pieces) work in a woodshop instead. They set up, operate, and tend all types of woodworking machines to complete their projects.

Wood sawing machine setters, operators, and tenders have one of the highest rates of injuries and illnesses of all occupations. These workers use tools and equipment, such as saws and drill presses, which may be dangerous and can cause cuts or lacerations. Workers must wear proper safety equipment and be mindful of their surroundings to avoid injury.

Woodworkers are exposed to hazards such as harmful dust, chemicals, or fumes, and must often wear a respirator or mask. Others may be exposed to excessive noise and must wear hearing protection devices.

Most injuries involve sprains, back pain, carpal tunnel syndrome, and hernias. These injuries or illnesses come from excessive amounts of awkward bending, reaching, twisting, and overexertion or repetition.

### Human Environment

Woodworkers in manufacturing facilities interact with coworkers daily. They may or may not deal with customers directly. Woodworkers in smaller operations may not have as many support staff, but will likely interact directly with their customers, and may have multiple meetings with them to keep projects on track. Business owners are responsible for staffing and for settling disputes.

### Technological Environment

Woodworkers typically use CNC machines and a variety of power tools in their work. Machines include saws, milling machines, drill presses, lathes, shapers, routers, sanders, planers, and wood-fastening machines. Woodworkers must be well-acquainted with all available machinery in order to ensure high productivity and accuracy.

## EDUCATION, TRAINING, AND ADVANCEMENT

### High School/Secondary

A high school diploma or equivalent is typically required to become a woodworker. Although some entry-level jobs can be learned in less than 1 year, becoming fully proficient generally takes several years of on-the-job training. The ability to use computer-controlled machinery is becoming increasingly important, and people seeking woodworking jobs can enhance their employment prospects by getting training in computer applications and math.

**Suggested High School Subjects**

- Algebra
- Biology

- Chemistry
- Civics
- Earth or Life or Physical Science
- Economics
- English
- Entrepreneurship
- Geometry
- History
- Physics
- Pre-Calculus
- Psychology
- Statistics
- Trigonometry

**Related Career Pathways/Majors**

*Architecture & Construction Career Cluster*

- Design/Pre-Construction Pathway

*Business, Management & Administration Career Cluster*

- Manufacturing Production Process Development Pathway
- Production Pathway

*Manufacturing Career Cluster*

- General Management Pathway

### Transferable Skills and Abilities

**Detail-oriented**
- Meeting specifications and staying safe

**Dexterity**
- Precisely cutting with a variety of hand tools and power tools

**Math Skills**
- Understanding basic geometry in order to visualize how a three-dimensional wooden object, such as a cabinet or piece of furniture, will fit together

**Mechanical Skills**
- Using hand tools, such as screwdrivers and wrenches, to set up, adjust, and calibrate machines

**Physical Stamina**
- Enduring long periods of standing and repetitive movement

**Physical Strength**
- Lifting bulky and heavy pieces of wood

**Technical Skills**
- Understanding and interpreting design drawings and technical manuals for a range of products and machines

## Postsecondary

Some woodworkers obtain their skills by taking courses at technical schools or community colleges. Others attend universities that offer training in wood technology, furniture manufacturing, wood engineering, and production management. These programs prepare students for jobs in production, supervision, engineering, and management, and are becoming increasingly important as woodworking technology advances.

**Related College Majors**

- Furniture Manufacturing
- Production Management
- Wood Engineering
- Wood Technology

## Fast Fact

**Want to go into business building stringed instruments? Inside the USA, about 51 schools exist that can teach you how, according to the Guild of American Luthiers.**

Luthier. Photo by Christian Ericksen, CC BY-SA 4.0 <https://creativecommons.org/licenses/by-sa/4.0>, via Wikimedia Commons.

### Adult Job Seekers

Adults seeking employment as woodworkers have the best chance of success if they have previous experience with woodworking, such as on a hobby basis, or have worked in related fields or facilities such as assembly line plants.

### Professional Certification and Licensure

Although not required, becoming certified can demonstrate competence and professionalism. It also may help a candidate advance in the profession. The Woodwork Career Alliance of North America (WCA) offers a national certificate program, with five progressive credentials, which adds a level of credibility to the work of woodworkers.

### Additional Requirements

Education is helpful, but woodworkers are trained primarily on the job, where they learn skills from experienced workers. Beginning workers are given basic tasks, such as placing a piece of wood through a machine and stacking the finished product at the end of the process.

As they gain experience, new woodworkers perform more complex tasks with less supervision. In about 1 month, they learn basic machine operations and job tasks. Becoming a skilled woodworker often takes several months or even years. Skilled workers can read blueprints, set up machines, and plan work sequences.

## EARNINGS AND ADVANCEMENT

Earnings depend on the type of woodwork and the experience of the woodworker. Median annual earnings of woodworkers were $32,690 in 2019. The lowest 10 percent earned less than $22,310, and the highest 10 percent earned more than $50,070.

Woodworkers may receive paid vacations, holidays, and sick days; life and health insurance; and retirement benefits. These are usually paid by an employer if the business is not self-owned.

## EMPLOYMENT AND OUTLOOK

Woodworkers held 263,500 jobs in 2019. Seven percent were self-employed. Employment is expected to decline 4 percent through the year 2029. Some demand for woodworkers is expected in residential and commercial property repairs and renovations. However, automation, especially the use of computerized numerical controlled machines in wood product manufacturing, should reduce the overall need for these workers over the decade.

Woodworkers who know how to create and implement custom designs on a computer should have the best job opportunities in manufacturing industries.

Those who can demonstrate leadership, problem solving, and advanced math skills should also have the best job prospects.

Some job openings will result from the need to replace those who retire or leave the occupation for another job.

### Related Occupations

- Carpenter
- Computer Programmer
- Craft/Fine Artist
- Ironworker
- Jeweler/Precious Stone & Metal Worker
- Machinist/Tool & Die Maker
- Sheet Metal Worker

## MORE INFORMATION

**American Association of Woodturners (AAW)**
75 W 5th Street, 222 Landmark Center
St. Paul, MN 55102
877.595.9094
memberservices@woodturner.org
www.woodturner.org

**American Wood Council (AWC)**
222 Catoctin Circle SE, Suite 201
Leesburg, VA 20175
202.463.2766
membership@awc.org
www.awc.org

**Architectural Woodwork Institute (AWI)**
46179 Westlake Drive
Sterling, VA 20165
571.323.3636
info@awinet.org
www.awinet.org

**Association for Manufacturing Technology (AMT)**
7901 Jones Branch Drive, Suite 900
McLean, VA 22102-4206
800.524.0475
AMT@AMTonline.org
www.amtonline.org

**Association of Woodworking & Furnishings Suppliers (AWFS)**
2400 E Katella Ave Suite 340
Anaheim, CA 92806
800.946.2937
www.awfs.org

**Fabricators & Manufacturers Association (FMA)**
2135 Point Boulevard
Elgin, IL 60123
888.394.4362
info@fmanet.org
www.fmamfg.org

**International Wood Products Association (IWPA)**
4214 King Street
Alexandria, VA 22302
703.820.6696
info@iwpawood.org
www.iwpawood.org

**National Tooling & Machining Association (NTMA)**
1357 Rockside Road
Cleveland OH 44134
800.248.6862
ntma.org

**Wood Component Manufacturers Association (WCMA)**
P.O. Box 662
Lindstrom, MN 55045
651.332.6332
wcma@wcma.com
www.wcma.com

**Wood Machinery Manufacturers of America (WMMA)**
2331 Rock Spring Road
Forest Hill, MD 21050
443.640.1052
info@wmma.org
wmma.org

**Wood Products Manufacturers Association (WPMA)**
P.O. Box 761
Westminster, MA 01473-0761
978.874.5445
woodprod@wpma.org
www.wpma.org

**Woodwork Career Alliance of North America (WCA)**
info@woodworkcareer.org
woodworkcareer.org

**WoodWorkers Guild of America (WWGOA)**
2955 Xenium Lane N, Suite 10
Plymouth, MN 55441
855.253.0822
wwgoasubscription@program-director.net
www.wwgoa.com

**Woodworking Machinery Industry Association (WMIA)**
3025 Hamaker Court, Suite 460
Fairfax, VA 22031
571.279.8340
info@wmia.org
www.wmia.org

---

*Stuart Paterson*

## *Conversation With...*

## MICAH D. BRUCE

Owner
Bruce & Sons, Bellevue, NE
Luthier, 13 years

**What was your individual career path in terms of education/training, entry-level job, or other significant opportunity?**

I was interested in building and in music when I was young. I started playing guitar when I was 11 or 12. In seventh grade, I wrote a career report on luthiery, which is the craft of making and repairing stringed instruments. I remember thinking that would be fun, but probably not realistic because it sounded like there wasn't much money in it, and I didn't know anyone who did that.

As a kid I built tree forts and skateboard ramps. I built furniture in ninth grade woodshop, and in my senior year of high school I worked at a cabinet shop in a work-study program.

I always loved building things, working with my hands, seeing how things work. You get to see a direct cause and effect when working on something physical. I like the artistry of it, too, the creative element. Each piece of wood is unique. You can find joy in mundane, repetitive motion, too.

I started college at the University of Nebraska at Lincoln and studied construction management in my freshman year. It was not my favorite thing. The next semester I thought I would be a math major because it fit with building. But I left college because I wanted to build things. I started working at a music store repairing instruments. I was a good guitar player, knew how to use tools, and the store was willing to teach me from there. I was a pretty quick study.

I worked in trim and cabinetry work, and in guitar repair, before moving to Austin, Texas, and working for well-known custom guitar companies Bill Collings and John Allison, as a luthier and repair technician, and at Moniker Guitars as head of production.

I started Bruce & Sons eight years ago as a part-time job while working for another company because I enjoyed it, and it supplemented my income. As I became more capable and developed a reputation, more work started coming my way, and I could raise prices. Since my wife and I moved back to Nebraska to raise our family four years ago, I've operated Bruce & Sons full-time. I feel my skills exceeded the pay scale that I would make working for someone else.

I have customers from all over. I make instruments for people in Utah, Texas, New York. I built a guitar for someone in the United Kingdom. But primarily my customers are from places where I've lived—Texas and Nebraska, or nearby, like Iowa and South Dakota. I also work with a dealer in Hawaii who sells ukuleles that I build. You can sell your work through a wholesaler or a shop on consignment. You can also build an instrument customized for a particular user. You can charge more for the custom-built, so you make more on that arrangement than working through a wholesaler, but there are fewer orders for custom-builds. I try to do a blend of everything, and it all evens out in the end. I've hired a part-time employee to help mainly with repairs, but he also does some building.

**What are the most important skills and/or qualities for someone in your profession?**
You need to have an understanding of physical objects, geometry, and structure, but also troubleshooting. I do a lot of instrument repair work in addition to building instruments. You need tool competency. You need hand skills—dexterity and coordination. You can learn concepts from a book or a classroom, but can your hands do it?

**What do you wish you had known going into this profession?**
A lot of learning is just doing something. I'll always be a lifelong learner. I wish I'd been more aware of that: to try more things and not be intimidated or afraid of failing. You can't be a perfectionist. I've built some instruments looking back that aren't my proudest work, but I learned a lot. There are no secrets. It's just hard work and practice over time. You accumulate knowledge, skills, tools and reputation, and the sales aspects of the business. It's really just taking time to grow.

**Are there many job opportunities in your profession? In what specific areas?**
I wouldn't say it's a hot market. There's repair work, which in large part you'll either work at a music store or on contract to a music store. For building instruments, there are a lot of guitar factories you could work for. But it's not a huge growth industry.

**How do you see your profession changing in the next 5 years? How will technology impact that change, and what skills will be required?**
Selling instruments will continue to be more online, so you'll need better photos and video content. My customers in New York and the United Kingdom were found online through Instagram and my website. You never know who will come across your stuff and take interest!

For building instruments, I have computer-aided machinery, and that's getting more affordable every year, so it's lowering the bar for competition. That means I have to use it more advantageously, more efficiently than someone who has just bought it. For repairs, companies are always formulating new finishes, but it's not a landmark change. It's just a matter of keeping up with improvements.

In some ways we're doing the same thing we've been doing for centuries, maybe just with variations on the theme.

**What do you enjoy most about your job? What do you enjoy least about your job?**
I enjoy making a broken thing work again or restoring an old instrument. That's gratifying both in terms of the instrument itself and seeing a customer enjoy it. Building an instrument is a

whole other level. It's a work of art on its own but also will propagate art. That's a cool idea. Instruments are beautiful even when they are not being played but maybe partly because we intuit a potential.

What I like least is the business side. Usually, it's half a day a week for ordering parts and materials, answering e-mails, managing the financial side. I pay taxes monthly. Running a business that uses a lot of physical goods, there's a lot of upfront costs. I don't enjoy the business side; but as a sole entrepreneur, you have to wear different hats.

**Can you suggest a valuable "try this" for students considering a career in your profession?**

The interest in playing an instrument or in music, in general, is an essential starting point. Try playing an instrument. Or try building something for curves and form because there is an ergonomic aspect. Take woodworking courses at school or at a shop.

# What Are Your Career Interests?

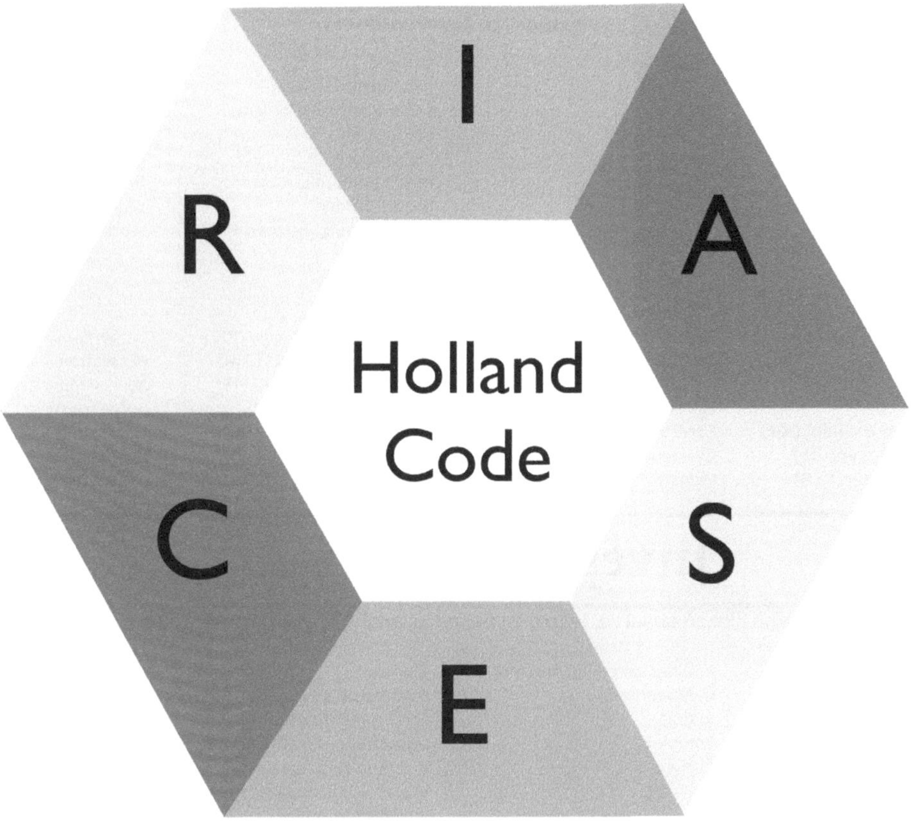


This is based on Dr. John Holland's theory that people and work environments can be loosely classified into six different groups. Each of the letters above corresponds to one of the six groups described in the following pages.

Different people's personalities may find different environments more to their liking. While you may have some interests in and similarities to several of the six groups, you may be attracted primarily to two or three of the areas. These two or three letters are your "Holland Code." For example, with a code of "RES" you would most resemble the Realistic type, somewhat less resemble the Enterprising type, and resemble the Social type even less. The types that are not in your code are the types you resemble least of all.
Most people, and most jobs, are best represented by some combination of two or three of the Holland interest areas. In addition, most people are most satisfied if there is some degree of fit between their personality and their work environment.

The rest of the pages in this booklet further explain each type and provide some examples of career possibilities, areas of study at MU, and co-curricular activities for each code. To take a more in-depth look at your Holland Code, take a self-assessment such as the SDS, Discover, or a card sort at the MU Career Center with a Career Specialist.

# Realistic *(Doers)*

**People who have athletic ability, prefer to work with objects, machines, tools, plants or animals, or to be outdoors.**

**Are you?**
practical
straightforward/frank
mechanically inclined
stable
concrete
reserved
self-controlled
independent
ambitious
systematic

Can you?
fix electrical things
solve electrical problems
pitch a tent
play a sport
read a blueprint
plant a garden
operate tools and machine

Like to?
tinker with machines/vehicles
work outdoors
be physically active
use your hands
build things
tend/train animals
work on electronic equipment

**Career Possibilities (Holland Code):**

Air Traffic Controller (SER)
Archaeologist (IRE)
Athletic Trainer (SRE)
Cartographer (IRE)
Commercial Airline Pilot (RIE)
Commercial Drafter (IRE)
Corrections Officer (SER)
Dental Technician (REI)
Farm Manager (ESR)
Fish and Game Warden (RES)
Floral Designer (RAE)
Forester (RIS)
Geodetic Surveyor (IRE)
Industrial Arts Teacher (IER)
Laboratory Technician (RIE)
Landscape Architect (AIR)
Mechanical Engineer (RIS)
Optician (REI)
Petroleum Geologist (RIE)
Police Officer (SER)
Practical Nurse (SER)
Property Manager (ESR)
Recreation Manager (SER)
Service Manager (ERS)
Software Technician (RCI)
Ultrasound Technologist (RSI)
Vocational Rehabilitation Consultant (ESR)

# Investigative *(Thinkers)*

**People who like to observe, learn, investigate, analyze, evaluate, or solve problems.**

Are you?
inquisitive
analytical
scientific
observant/precise
scholarly
cautious
intellectually self-confident
Independent
logical
complex
Curious

**Can you?**
think abstractly
solve math problems
understand scientific theories
do complex calculations
use a microscope or computer
interpret formulas

Like to?
explore a variety of ideas
work independently
perform lab experiments
deal with abstractions
do research
be challenged

**Career Possibilities (Holland Code):**

Actuary (ISE)
Agronomist (IRS)
Anesthesiologist (IRS)
Anthropologist (IRE)
Archaeologist (IRE)
Biochemist (IRS)
Biologist (ISR)
Chemical Engineer (IRE)
Chemist (IRE)
Computer Systems Analyst (IER)
Dentist (ISR)
Ecologist (IRE)
Economist (IAS)
Electrical Engineer (IRE)
Geologist (IRE)
Horticulturist (IRS)
Mathematician (IER)
Medical Technologist (ISA)
Meteorologist (IRS)
Nurse Practitioner (ISA)
Pharmacist (IES)
Physician, General Practice (ISE)
Psychologist (IES)
Research Analyst (IRC)
Statistician (IRE)
Surgeon (IRA)
Technical Writer (IRS)
Veterinarian (IRS)

# **Artistic** *(Creators)*

**People who have artistic, innovating, or intuitional abilities and like to work in unstructured situations using their imagination and creativity.**

**Are you?**
creative
imaginative
innovative
unconventional
emotional
independent
Expressive
original
introspective
impulsive
sensitive
courageous
complicated
idealistic
nonconforming

**Can you?**
sketch, draw, paint
play a musical instrument
write stories, poetry, music
sing, act, dance
design fashions or interiors

**Like to?**
attend concerts, theatre, art exhibits
read fiction, plays, and poetry
work on crafts
take photography
express yourself creatively
deal with ambiguous ideas

**Career Possibilities (Holland Code):**

Actor (AES)
Advertising Art Director (AES)
Advertising Manager (ASE)
Architect (AIR)
Art Teacher (ASE)
Artist (ASI)
Copy Writer (ASI)
Dance Instructor (AER)
Drama Coach (ASE)
English Teacher (ASE)
Entertainer/Performer (AES)
Fashion Illustrator (ASR)
Interior Designer (AES)
Intelligence Research Specialist (AEI)
Journalist/Reporter (ASE)
Landscape Architect (AIR)
Librarian (SAI)
Medical Illustrator (AIE)
Museum Curator (AES)
Music Teacher (ASI)
Photographer (AES)
Writer (ASI)
Graphic Designer (AES)

# **Social** *(Helpers)*

**People who like to work with people to enlighten, inform, help, train, or cure them, or are skilled with words.**

**Are you?**
friendly
helpful
idealistic
insightful
outgoing
understanding
cooperative
generous
responsible
forgiving
patient
kind

**Can you?**
teach/train others
express yourself clearly
lead a group discussion
mediate disputes
plan and supervise an activity
cooperate well with others

**Like to?**
work in groups
help people with problems
do volunteer work
work with young people
serve others

**Career Possibilities (Holland Code):**

City Manager (SEC)
Clinical Dietitian (SIE)
College/University Faculty (SEI)
Community Org. Director (SEA)
Consumer Affairs Director (SER)Counselor/Therapist (SAE)
Historian (SEI)
Hospital Administrator (SER)
Psychologist (SEI)
Insurance Claims Examiner (SIE)
Librarian (SAI)
Medical Assistant (SCR)
Minister/Priest/Rabbi (SAI)
Paralegal (SCE)
Park Naturalist (SEI)
Physical Therapist (SIE)
Police Officer (SER)
Probation and Parole Officer (SEC)
Real Estate Appraiser (SCE)
Recreation Director (SER)
Registered Nurse (SIA)
Teacher (SAE)
Social Worker (SEA)
Speech Pathologist (SAI)
Vocational-Rehab. Counselor (SEC)
Volunteer Services Director (SEC)

# Enterprising *(Persuaders)*

**People who like to work with people, influencing, persuading, leading or managing for organizational goals or economic gain.**

**Are you?**
self-confident
assertive
persuasive
energetic
adventurous
popular
ambitious
agreeable
talkative
extroverted
spontaneous
optimistic

**Can you?**
initiate projects
convince people to do things your way
sell things
give talks or speeches
organize activities
lead a group
persuade others

**Like to?**
make decisions
be elected to office
start your own business
campaign politically
meet important people
have power or status

**Career Possibilities (Holland Code):**

Advertising Executive (ESA)
Advertising Sales Rep (ESR)
Banker/Financial Planner (ESR)
Branch Manager (ESA)
Business Manager (ESC)
Buyer (ESA)
Chamber of Commerce Exec (ESA)
Credit Analyst (EAS)
Customer Service Manager (ESA)
Education & Training Manager (EIS)
Emergency Medical Technician (ESI)
Entrepreneur (ESA)
Foreign Service Officer (ESA)
Funeral Director (ESR)
Insurance Manager (ESC)
Interpreter (ESA)
Lawyer/Attorney (ESA)
Lobbyist (ESA)
Office Manager (ESR)
Personnel Recruiter (ESR)
Politician (ESA)
Public Relations Rep (EAS)
Retail Store Manager (ESR)
Sales Manager (ESA)
Sales Representative (ERS)
Social Service Director (ESA)
Stockbroker (ESI)
Tax Accountant (ECS)

# Conventional *(Organizers)*

**People who like to work with data, have clerical or numerical ability, carry out tasks in detail, or follow through on others' instructions.**

**Are you?**
well-organized
accurate
numerically inclined
methodical
conscientious
efficient
conforming
practical
thrifty
systematic
structured
polite
ambitious
obedient
persistent

**Can you?**
work well within a system
do a lot of paper work in a short time
keep accurate records
use a computer terminal
write effective business letters

**Like to?**
follow clearly defined procedures
use data processing equipment
work with numbers
type or take shorthand
be responsible for details
collect or organize things

**Career Possibilities (Holland Code):**

Abstractor (CSI)
Accountant (CSE)
Administrative Assistant (ESC)
Budget Analyst (CER)
Business Manager (ESC)
Business Programmer (CRI)
Business Teacher (CSE)
Catalog Librarian (CSE)
Claims Adjuster (SEC)
Computer Operator (CSR)
Congressional-District Aide (CES)
Cost Accountant (CES)
Court Reporter (CSE)
Credit Manager (ESC)
Customs Inspector (CEI)
Editorial Assistant (CSI)
Elementary School Teacher (SEC)
Financial Analyst (CSI)
Insurance Manager (ESC)
Insurance Underwriter (CSE)
Internal Auditor (ICR)
Kindergarten Teacher (ESC)
Medical Records Technician (CSE)
Museum Registrar (CSE)
Paralegal (SCE)
Safety Inspector (RCS)
Tax Accountant (ECS)
Tax Consultant (CES)
Travel Agent (ECS)

# GENERAL BIBLIOGRAPHY


Althoff, Susanne. *Launching While Female: Smashing the System that Holds Women Entrepreneurs Back.* Boston: Beacon Press, 2020.

Barringer, Bruce R. and R. Duane Ireland. *Entrepreneurship: Successfully Launching New Ventures*, 6th ed. New York: Pearson, 2019.

Bhargava, Rajat and Will Herman. *The Startup Playbook: Founder-to-Founder Advice from Two Startup Veterans.* Hoboken, NJ: Wiley, 2020.

Blank, Steve and Bob Dorf. *The Startup Owner's Manual: The Step-By-Step Guide for Building a Great Company.* Hoboken, NJ: Wiley, 2020.

Clifton, Jim. *Born to Build: How to Build a Thriving Startup, a Winning Team, New Customers, and Your Best Life Imaginable.* New York: Gallup Press, 2018.

Connor, Todd. *Third Shift Entrepreneur: Keep Your Day Job, Build Your Dream Job.* Hoboken, NJ: Wiley, 2021.

Dodgson, Mark and David Gann. *The Playful Entrepreneur: How to Adapt and Thrive in Uncertain Times.* New Haven: Yale UP, 2018.

Dru, Jean-Marie. *Thank You For Disrupting: The Disruptive Philosophies of the World's Great Entrepreneurs.* Hoboken, NJ: Wiley, 2019.

Feld, Brad and Ian Hathaway. *The Startup Community Way: Evolving an Entrepreneurial Ecosystem.* Hoboken, NJ: Wiley, 2020.

Galloway, Scott. *Post Corona: From Crisis to Opportunity.* New York: Portfolio, 2020.

Harrington, Kevin and Mark Tim. *Mentor to Millions: Secrets of Success in Business, Relationships and Beyond*. Carlsbad, CA: Hay House, 2021.

Heyworth-Dunn, Victoria, ed. *Entrepreneurs Who Changed History.* New York: DK Publishing, 2020.

Hoffman, Reid, Cohen, June, and Deron Triff. *Masters of Scale: Surprising Truths from the World's Most Successful Entrepreneurs.* New York: Currency, 2021.

Horowitz, Daniel. *Entertaining Entrepreneurs: Reality TV's* Shark Tank *and the American Dream in Uncertain Times*. Chapel Hill: The University of North Carolina Press, 2020.

Jacobi, Tamara. *Wildpreneurs: A Pratical Guide to Pursuing Your Passion as a Business.* New York: HarperCollins, 2020.

John, Daymond. *Rise and Grind: Outperform, Outwork and Outhustle Your Way to a More Successful and Rewarding Life.* New York: Currency, 2018.

Longenecker, Justin G., William J. Petty, Leslie E. Palich and Frank Hoy. *Small Business Management: Launching and Growing Entrepreneurial Ventures*, 19th ed. Boston, MA: Cengage, 2020.

Lytle, Carissa and Jara Kern. *The Infographic Guide to Entrepreneurs: A Visual Reference for Everything You Need to Know.* New York: Adams Media, 2019.

Madoff, B. Jeffrey. *Creative Careers: Making a Living with Your Ideas.* New York: Hachette, 2020.

Massa, Felipe G. *Entrepreneurship in the Wild: A Startup Field Guide.* Cambridge, MA: MIT Press, 2021.

McCracken, Grant. *Return of the Artisan: How America Went from Industrial to Handmade and You Can Too.* New York: Tiller Press, 2021.

McKelvey, Jim. *The Innovation Stack: Building an Unbeatable Business One Crazy Idea at a Time.* New York: Portfolio, 2020.

Pham, Tiffany. *You Are a Mogul: How to Do the Impossible, Do it Yourself, and Do it Now.* New York: Simon & Schuster, 2018.

Power, Rhett. *The Entrepreneur's Book of Actions: Essential Daily Exercises and Habits for Becoming Wealthier, Smarter and More Successful.* New York: McGraw-Hill, 2017.

Raz, Guy. *How I Built This: The Unexpected Paths to Success from the World's Most Inspiring Entrepreneurs.* New York: Houghton Mifflin, 2020.

Rickman, Cheryl D., ed. *How to Start Your Own Business...and Make it Work*. New York: DK Publishing, 2021.

Sax, David. *The Soul of an Entrepreneur: Work and Life Beyond the Startup Myth.* New York: PublicAffairs, 2020.

Smith, Daniel. *How to Think Like an Entrepreneur.* London: Michael O'Mara, 2021.

Steingold, Fred S. and David M. Steingold. *Legal Guide for Starting & Running a Small Business*, 17th ed. Berkeley: Nolo, 2021.

Tvede, Lars and Mads Faurholt. *Entrepreneur: Building Your Business from Start to Success.* Chichester, West Sussex, United Kingdom: Wiley, 2018.

Vaynerchuk, Gary. *Crushing It! How Great Entrepreneurs Build Their Business and Influence-and How You Can, Too.* New York: HarperCollins, 2018.

Yoo, Mina and Hilary Meyerson. *Be an InventHer: An Everywoman's Guide to Creating the Next Big Thing.* Seattle, WA: Sasquatch Books, 2019.

## LIST OF ORGANIZATIONS & RESOURCES

**Accreditation Board for Engineering and Technology, Inc. (ABET)**
415 North Charles Street
Baltimore, MD 21201
410.347.7700
www.abet.org

**Academy of Prosocial Learning (APL)**
860.262.1807
info@prosocialacademy.org
www.prosocialacademy.org

**Accrediting Commission for Community & Precollegiate Arts Schools (ACCPAS)**
11250 Roger Bacon Drive, Suite 21
Reston, VA 20190-5248
703.437.0700
info@arts-accredit.org
accpas.arts-accredit.org

**Advance CTE: State Leaders Connecting Learning to Work**
8484 Georgia Avenue, Suite 620
Silver Spring MD 20910
301.588.9630
careertech.org

**AIB International**
P.O. Box 3999
1213 Bakers Way
Manhattan, KS 66505-3999
www.aibinternational.com

**American Academy of Healthcare Interior Designers (AAHID)**
8735 W. Higgins Road, Suite 300
Chicago, IL 60631
847.375.6870
info@aahid.org
aahid.org

**American Advertising Federation (AAF)**
1101 K Street NW, Suite 420
Washington DC 20005
202.898.0089
www.aaf.org

**American Apparel & Footwear Association (AAFA)**
740 6th Street NW, 3rd and 4th Floors
Washington, DC 20001
202.853.9080
www.aafaglobal.org

**American Association for Laboratory Animal Science (AALAS)**
9190 Crestwyn Hills Drive
Memphis, TN 38125
901.754.8620
info@aalas.org
www.aalas.org
Offers testing and certification for animal technicians
www.aalas.org/certification/technician-certification

**American Association of Advertising Agencies (4A's)**
1065 Avenue of the Americas, 16th Floor
New York, NY 10018
212.682.2500
www.aaaa.org

**American Association of Engineering Societies (AAES)**
1801 Alexander Bell Drive
Reston, VA 20191
202.296.2237
orders@aaes.org
www.aaes.org

**American Association of Woodturners (AAW)**
75 W 5th Street, 222 Landmark Center
St. Paul, MN 55102
877.595.9094
memberservices@woodturner.org
www.woodturner.org

**American Bakers Association (ABA)**
601 Pennsylvania Avenue NW, Suite 230
Washington, DC 20004
202.789.0300
info@AmericanBakers.org
americanbakers.org

**American Bankers Association (ABA)**
1120 Connecticut Avenue NW
Washington, DC 20036
800.226.5377
www.aba.com

**American Bar Association (ABA)**
1050 Connecticut Avenue NW, Suite 400
Washington, DC 20036
202.662.1000
www.americanbar.org

**American Board of Funeral Service Education (ABFSE)**
992 Mantua Pike, Suite 108
Woodbury Heights, NJ 08097
816.233.3747
exdir@abfse.org
www.abfse.org

**American Craft Council (ACC)**
1224 Marshall Street NE, Suite 200
Minneapolis, MN 55413
612.206.3100
council@craftcouncil.org
www.craftcouncil.org

**American Culinary Federation (ACF)**
180 Center Place Way
St. Augustine, FL 32095
904.824.4468
acf@acfchefs.net
www.acfchefs.org

**American Drivers Association**
P.O. Box 178
Winona, TX 75792
800.944.4948
americandriversassociation@gmail.com
americandriversassociation.com

**American Farm Bureau Federation (AFBF)**
600 Maryland Avenue, SW, Suite 1000
Washington, DC 20024
202.406.3600
www.fb.org

**American Humane Association**
1400 16th Street NW, Suite 360
Washington, DC 20036
800.227.4645
info@americanhumane.org
www.americanhumane.org

**American Institute for Medical & Biological Engineering (AIMBE)**
1400 I Street NW, Suite 235
Washington, DC 20005
202.496.9660
info@aimbe.org
aimbe.org

**American Intellectual Property Law Association (AIPLA)**
1400 Crystal Drive, Suite 600
Arlington, VA 22202
703-415-0780
aipla@aipla.org
www.aipla.org

**American Management Association (AMA)**
1601 Broadway
New York, NY 10019
877.566.9441
customerservice@amanet.org
www.amanet.org

**American Marketing Association (AMA)**
130 E Randolph Street
Chicago, IL 60601
800.262.1150
customersupport@ama.org
www.ana.net

**American Mold Builders Association (AMBA)**
7321 Shadeland Station Way, #285
Indianapolis, IN 46256
317.436.3102
info@amba.org
amba.org

**American National Standards Institute (ANSI)**
330 E. Kilbourn Avenue, Suite 925
Milwaukee, WI 53202
414.501.5494
anabpd.ansi.org

**American Society for Engineering Education (ASEE)**
1818 N Street NW, Suite 600
Washington DC 20036
202.331.3500
www.asee.org

**American Society for the Prevention of Cruelty to Animals (ASPCA)**
424 East 92nd Street
New York, NY 10128-6804
212.876.7700
outreach@aspca.org
www.aspca.org

**American Society of Agricultural & Biological Engineers (ASABE)**
2950 Niles Road
St. Joseph, MI 49085
269.429.0300
www.asabe.org

**American Society of Agronomy (ASA)**
Career Development & Placement Services
5585 Guilford Road
Madison, WI 53711
608.273.8080
www.agronomy.org

**American Society of Association Executives (ASAE)**
1575 I Street NW
Washington, DC 20005
888.950.2723
ASAEservice@asaecenter.org
www.asaecenter.org

**American Society of Farm Managers & Rural Appraisers (ASFMRA)**
720 South Colorado Boulevard, Suite 360-S
Glendale, CO 80246-2664
303.758.3513
info@asfmra.org
www.asfmra.org

**American Society of Interior Designers (ASID)**
1152 15th Street NW, Suite 910
Washington, DC 20005
202.546.3480
membership@asid.org
www.asid.org

**American Society of Mechanical Engineers (ASME)**
Two Park Avenue
New York, NY 10016-5990
800.843.2763
CustomerCare@asme.org
www.asme.org

**American Solar Energy Society (ASES)**
2525 Arapahoe Avenue, Suite E4-253
Boulder, CO 80302
info@ases.org
ases.org

**American Trucking Associations (ATA)**
950 North Glebe Road, Suite 210
Arlington, VA 22203-4181
atamembership@trucking.org
www.trucking.org

**American Webmasters Association (AWA)**
2977 Ygnacio Valley Road, Suite 132
Walnut Creek, CA 94598
info@aawebmasters.com
www.aawebmasters.com

**American Wood Council (AWC)**
222 Catoctin Circle SE, Suite 201
Leesburg, VA 20175
202.463.2766
membership@awc.org
www.awc.org

**Alternative Farming Systems Information Center (AFSIC)**
National Agricultural Library
10301 Baltimore Avenue, Room 132
Beltsville, MD 20705
301.504.6559
www.nal.usda.gov/afsic

**Architectural Woodwork Institute (AWI)**
46179 Westlake Drive
Sterling, VA 20165
571.323.3636
info@awinet.org
www.awinet.org

**Art Dealers Association of America (ADAA)**
205 Lexington Avenue, Suite #901
New York, NY 10016
212.488.5550
adaa@artdealers.org
artdealers.org

**Association for Computing Machinery (ACM)**
1601 Broadway, 10th Floor
New York, NY 10019-7434
212.869.7440
acmhelp@acm.org
www.acm.org

**Association for Delivery Drivers (A4DD)**
P.O. Box 123
Gaylordsville, CT 06755
877.264.2433
a4ddteam@a4dd.org
www.a4dd.org

**Association for Manufacturing Technology (AMT)**
7901 Jones Branch Drive, Suite 900
McLean, VA 22102-4206
800.524.0475
AMT@AMTonline.org
www.amtonline.org

**Association of American Law Schools (AALS)**
1614 20th Street NW
Washington, DC 20009-1001
202.296.8851
info@aals.org
www.aals.org

**Association of Medical Illustrators (AMI)**
201 E. Main Street, Ste. 1405
Lexington, KY 40507
866.393.4264
hq@ami.org
ami.org

**Association of National Advertisers (ANA)**
155 E 44th Street
New York, NY 10017
212.697.5950
info@ana.net
www.ana.net
ANA Business Marketing: www.marketing.org

**Association of Nutrition & Foodservice Professionals (ANFP)**
406 Surrey Woods Drive
St. Charles, IL 60174
800.323.1908
info@ANFPonline.org
www.anfponline.org

**Association of Software Professionals (ASP)**
c/o ASP Membership Manager
P.O. Box 1522
Martinsville IN 46151
asp-software.org

**Association of Woodworking & Furnishings Suppliers (AWFS)**
2400 E Katella Ave Suite 340
Anaheim, CA 92806
800.946.2937
www.awfs.org

**Association of Zoos & Aquariums**
8403 Colesville Road, Suite 710
Silver Spring, MD 20910-3314
301.562.0777
generalinquiry@aza.org
www.aza.org
Sponsors professional development training and scholarships to attend training
www.aza.org/scholarships

**ASIS International**
1625 Prince Street
Alexandria, VA 22314-2882
703.519.6200
asis@asisonline.org
www.asisonline.org

**Biomedical Engineering Society (BMES)**
8201 Corporate Drive, Suite 1125
Landover, MD 20785
membership@bmes.org
301.459.1999
www.bmes.org

**BOMI International**
900 Bestgate Road, Suite 206
Annapolis, MD 21401
410.974.1410
service@bomi.org
www.bomi.org

**Child Care Aware of America**
703.341.4100
membership@usa.childcareaware.org
www.childcareaware.org

**College Art Association of America (CAAA)**
50 Broadway, 21st Floor
New York, NY 10004
212.691.1051
nyoffice@collegeart.org
www.collegeart.org

**Community Association Managers International Certification Board (CAMICB)**
6402 Arlington Blvd., Suite 510
Falls Church, VA 22042
703.970.9300
info@camicb.org
camicb.org

**Community Associations Institute (CAI)**
6402 Arlington Blvd., Suite 500
Falls Church, VA 22042
703.970.9220
cai-info@caionline.org
www.caionline.org

**CompTIA**
3500 Lacey Road, Suite 100
Downers Grove, IL 60515
866.835.8020
membership@comptia.org
www.comptia.org

**Computing Research Association (CRA)**
1828 L Street NW, Suite 800
Washington, DC 20036-4632
202.234.2111
info@cra.org
cra.org
Computing Community Consortium (CCC): cra.org/ccc

**Cookie & Snack Bakers Association (CASBA)**
jnewell@batoryfoods.com
mike@aecdierolls.com
casba.us

**Council for Interior Design Accreditation (CIDA)**
206 Grandville Avenue, Suite 350
Grand Rapids, MI 49503-4014
248.875.6705
info@accredit-id.org
www.accredit-id.org

**Council for Interior Design Qualification (CIDQ)**
225 Reinekers Lane, Suite 210
Alexandria VA 22314
202.721.0220
inquiries@cidq.org
www.cidq.org

**Council for Professional Recognition**
2460 16th Street NW
Washington, DC 20009-3547
800.424.4310
www.cdacouncil.org

**Council of Arts Accrediting Associations (CAAA)**
11250 Roger Bacon Drive, Suite 21
Reston, VA 20190-5248
703.437.0700
info@arts-accredit.org
www.arts-accredit.org
National Office for Arts Accreditation (NOAA):
www.arts-accredit.org/national-office-for-arts-accreditation

**Council of Fashion Designers of America (CFDA)**
65 Bleecker Street, 11th Floor
New York, NY 10012
212.302.1821
info@cfda.com
cfda.com

**Council on Social Work Education (CSWE)**
333 John Carlyle Street, Suite 400
Alexandria, VA 22314
703.683.8080
info@cswe.org
www.cswe.org

**Cremation Association of North America (CANA)**
499 Northgate Parkway
Wheeling, IL 60090-2646
312.245.1077
info@cremationassociation.org
www.cremationassociation.org

**Developer Alliance**
525 Montgomery Street, Suite 574
Alexandria, VA 22314
www.developersalliance.org

**Dictionary of Occupational Titles (DOT)**
occupationalinfo.org

**Electrical Training Alliance**
5001 Howerton Way, Suite N
Bowie, MD 20715
888.652.4007
www.electricaltrainingalliance.org

**Electronics Technicians Association, International (ETA)**
5 Depot Street
Greencastle, IN 46135
800.288.3824
eta@eta-i.org
www.eta-i.org

**Engineering Education Service Center (EESC)**
1411 Old Hardman Btms Road
Clarkesville, GA 30523
706-499-5011
www.engineeringedu.com

**Express Carriers Association (ECA)**
9532 Liberia Avenue, Suite 752
Manassas, VA 20110
703.361.1058
eca@expresscarriers.org
www.ecadeliveryindustry.org

**Fabricators & Manufacturers Association (FMA)**
2135 Point Boulevard
Elgin, IL 60123
888.394.4362
info@fmanet.org
www.fmamfg.org

**Fairchild Books Interior Design Library**
c/o Bloomsbury Publishing Inc.
1385 Broadway, 5th Floor
New York, NY 10018
212.419.5300
askacademic@bloomsbury.com
www.fairchildbooksinteriordesign.com

**Federal Bar Association (FBA)**
1220 North Fillmore Street, Suite 444
Arlington, VA 22201
571.481.9100
fba@fedbar.org
www.fedbar.org

**Federal Motor Carrier Safety Administration (FMCSA)**
United States Department of Transportation
1200 New Jersey Avenue SE
Washington, DC 20590
800.832.5660
cdlcompliance@dot.gov
www.fmcsa.dot.gov

**Financial Executives International (FEI)**
89 Headquarters Plaza, Suite 1462
Morristown, NJ 07960
973.765.1000
membership@financialexecutives.org
www.financialexecutives.org

**Financial Management Association International (FMA)**
University of South Florida
Muma College of Business
4202 East Fowler Avenue, BSN 3403
Tampa FL 33620-5500
813.974.2084
fma@coba.usf.edu
www.fma.org

**Home Baking Association (HBA)**
2931 SW Gainsboro Road
Topeka, KS 66614-4413
785.478.3283
hbapatton@aol.com
www.homebaking.org

**Humane Education Advocates Reaching Teachers (HEART)**
P.O. Box 738
Mamaroneck, NY 10543
347.766.7650
email@teachheart.org
teachheart.org

**Humane Education Coalition**
432 S. Juliana Street
Bedford, PA 15522
info@hecoalition.org
www.hecoalition.org

**Humane Education Network (HEN)**
650.851.8735
hen@hennet.org
www.hennet.org

**Humane Society of the United States**
Companion Animals Division
1255 23rd Street NW, Suite 450
Washington, DC 20037
202.452.1100
www.humanesociety.org

**IEEE Computer Society**
2001 L Street NW, Suite 700
Washington, DC 20036-4928
202.371.0101
help@computer.org
www.computer.org

**IEEE Engineering in Medicine and Biology Society (EMBS)**
445 Hoes Lane
Piscataway, NJ 08854
732.981.3433
www.embs.org

**Independent Bakers Association (IBA)**
316 F Street NE, Suite 206
Washington, DC 20002
202.333.8190
www.ibabaker.com

**Institute for Humane Education**
P.O. Box 260
Surry, ME 04684
info@humaneeducation.org
humaneeducation.org

**Institute of Biological Engineering (IBE)**
446 East High Street, Suite 10
Lexington, KY 40507
859.977.7450
info@ibe.org
www.ibe.org

**Institute of Real Estate Management (IREM)**
430 North Michigan Avenue
Chicago, IL 60611
800.837.0706
getinfo@irem.org
www.irem.org

**Intellectual Property Owners Association (IPOA)**
1501 M Street NW, Suite 1150
Washington, DC 20005
202.507.4500
info@ipo.org
ipo.org

**Interior Design Educators Council (IDEC)**
111 West Jackson Boulevard, 14th Floor
Chicago, IL 60604
630.544.5057
info@idec.org
www.idec.org

**International Advertising Association (IAA)**
511 Avenue of Americas, Suite 4017
New York, NY 10011
646.849.9908
iaa@iaaglobal.org
www.iaaglobal.org

**International Cemetery, Cremation & Funeral Association (ICCFA)**
107 Carpenter Drive, Suite 100
Sterling, VA 20164
800.645.7700
iccfa.com

**International Dairy Deli Bakery Association (IDDBA)**
8317 Elderberry Road
Madison, WI 53717-2603
608.310.5000
iddba@iddba.org
www.iddba.org

**International Design Continuing Education Council (IDCEC)**
4576 Yonge Street, Suite 405
Toronto, ON M2N 6N4
Canada
888.890.5515
admin@idcec.org
www.idcec.org

**International Executives Association (IEA)**
P.O. Box 49654
Charlotte, NC 28277
704.604.5599
director@ieaweb.com
ieaweb.com

**International Foodservice Distributors Association (IFDA)**
1660 International Drive, Suite 550
McLean, VA 22102
703.532.9400
www.ifdaonline.org

**International Foodservice Manufacturers Association (IFMA)**
Two Prudential Plaza
180 N. Stetson Ave., Suite 850
Chicago, IL 60601
312.540.4400
www.ifmaworld.com

**International Game Developers Association (IGDA)**
1 Eglinton Avenue East, Suite 705
Toronto, ON M4P 3A1
Canada
info@igda.org
igda.org

**International Interior Design Association (IIDA)**
111 E. Wacker Drive, Suite 222
Chicago, IL 60601
888.799.4432
iidahq@iida.org
iida.org

**International Nanny Association**
P.O Box 70496
Milwaukee, WI 53207
888.878.1477
info@nanny.org
nanny.org

**International Society of Automation (ISA)**
67 T.W. Alexander Drive
P.O. Box 12277
Research Triangle Park, NC 27709
919.549.8411
www.isa.org

**International Society of Broadband Experts (ISBE)**
140 Philips Road
Exton, PA 19341
610.363.6888
info@scte.org
www.scte.org

**International Web Association (IWA)**
556 S. Fair Oaks Ave. #101-200
Pasadena, CA 91105
626.449.3709
iwanet.org

**International Wood Products Association (IWPA)**
4214 King Street
Alexandria, VA 22302
703.820.6696
info@iwpawood.org
www.iwpawood.org

**Interstate Renewable Energy Council (IREC)**
P.O. Box 1156
Latham, NY 12110-1156
518.621.7379
info@irecusa.org
irecusa.org

**Latham Foundation for the Promotion of Humane Education**
1320 Harbor Bay Parkway, Suite 200
Alameda, CA 94502
510.521.0920
www.latham.org

**Law School Admission Council (LSAC)**
62 Penn Street
Newtown PA 18940
215.968.1001
LSACinfo@LSAC.org
www.lsac.org

**Logistics & Transportation Association of North America (LTNA)**
P.O. Box 426
Union, WA 98592
360.898.3344
www.ltna.org

**Maddie's Fund**
6150 Stoneridge Mall Road, Suite 125
Pleasanton, CA 94588
925.310.5450
info@maddiesfund.org
www.maddiesfund.org
Maddie's Tail Wag activities for children:
www.maddiesfund.org/maddies-tail-wag.htm

**Manufacturing Institute (MI)**
733 10th Street NW, Suite 700
Washington, DC 20001
202.637.3426
Institute@nam.org
www.themanufacturinginstitute.org

**Mortgage Bankers Association (MBA)**
1919 M Street NW, 5th floor
Washington, DC 20036
202.557.2700
membership@mba.org
www.mba.org

**NAIOP Commercial Real Estate Development Association**
2355 Dulles Corner Boulevard, Suite 750
Herndon, VA 20171
703-904-7100
www.naiop.org

**National Agri-Marketing Association (NAMA)**
11020 King Street, Suite 205
Overland Park, KS 66210
913.491.6500
agrimktg@nama.org
www.nama.org

**National Alliance for Communications Technology Education & Learning (NACTEL)**
www.nactel.org

**National Assembly of State Arts Agencies (NASAA)**
1200 18th Street NW, Suite 1100
Washington, DC 20036
202.347.6352
nasaa@nasaa-arts.org
nasaa-arts.org

**National Association for Law Placement (NALP)**
1220 19th Street NW, Suite 401
Washington, DC 20036-2405
202.835.1001
info@nalp.org
www.nalp.org

**National Association of Animal Breeders (NAAB)**
8413 Excelsior Drive, Suite 140
Madison, WI 53717
608.827.0277
naab-css@naab-css.org
www.naab-css.org

**National Association of Family Child Care (NAFCC)**
700 12 Street NW
Suite 700
Washington DC 20005
202.796.5700
nafcc@nafcc.org
nafcc.org

**National Association of Mortgage Brokers (NAMB)**
601 Pennsylvania Avenue NW, South Building
Washington, DC 20004
202.434.8250
membership@namb.org
namb.org

**National Association of Mortgage Underwriters (NAMU)**
Presidential Circle
4000 Hollywood Boulevard, Suite 555-South
Hollywood, FL 33021
800.865.8550
contact@mortgage-underwriters.org
www.Mortgage-Underwriters.org
National Association of Mortgage Processors (NAMP):
www.mortgageprocessor.org

**National Association of Patent Practitioners (NAPP)**
701 Exposition Place, Suite 206
Raleigh, NC 27615
919.230.9635
napp@napp.org
www.napp.org

**National Association of Power Engineers (NAPE)**
1 Springfield Street, Suite 1
Chicopee, MA 01013
413.592.9273
www.powerengineers.com

**National Association of Professional Pet Sitters (NAPPS)**
P.O. Box 362
Huron, Ohio 44839
856.439.0324
NAPPS@petsitters.org
www.petsitters.org
Offers online course that leads to certification:
petsitters.org/page/NAPPSCertificationCourse

**National Association of Realtors (NAR)**
430 N. Michigan Avenue
Chicago, IL 60611-4087
800-874-6500
www.nar.realtor

**National Association of Residential Property Managers (NARPM)**
1403 Greenbrier Parkway, Suite 150
Chesapeake, VA 23320
800.782.3452
info@narpm.org
www.narpm.org

**National Association of Schools of Art & Design (NASAD)**
11250 Roger Bacon Drive, Suite 21
Reston, VA 20190-5248
703.437.0700
info@arts-accredit.org
nasad.arts-accredit.org

**National Association of Social Workers (NASW)**
750 First Street, NE Suite 800
Washington, DC 20002
800.742.4089
membership@socialworkers.org
www.socialworkers.org

**National Center for Construction Education & Research (NCCER)**
13614 Progress Boulevard
Alachua, FL 32615
386.518.6500
www.nccer.org

**National Center for Women & Information Technology (NCWIT)**
NCWIT 1909 26th Street, 2nd Floor
Boulder, CO 80302
303.735.6671
info@ncwit.org
www.ncwit.org

**National Child Care Association (NCCA)**
P.O. Box 2948
Merrifield, VA 22116
877.537.6222
ncca@necpa.net
nationalchildcare.org

**National Conference of Bar Examiners (NCBE)**
302 South Bedford Street
Madison, WI 53703-3622
www.ncbex.org

**National Council of Examiners for Engineering & Surveying (NCEES)**
200 Verdae Boulevard
Greenville, SC 29607
800.250.3196
ncees.org

**National Endowment for the Arts**
400 7th Street SW
Washington, DC 20506
202.682.5400
www.arts.gov

**National FFA Organization**
P.O. Box 68960
6060 FFA Drive
Indianapolis, IN 46268-0960
317.802.6060
www.ffa.org

**National Funeral Directors & Morticians Association (NFDMA)**
6290 Shannon Parkway
Union City, GA 30291
800.434.0958
nfdma.com

**National Funeral Directors Association (NFDA)**
13625 Bishop's Drive
Brookfield, WI 53005
800.228.6332
nfda@nfda.org
nfda.org

**National Ground Delivery Association (NGDA)**
833.347.6863
info@grounddelivery.org
www.grounddelivery.org

**National Home Delivery Association (NHDA)**
P.O. Box 4141
Falls Church, VA 22044
703.931.6324
blecos@lecosandassociates.com
www.nationalhomedeliveryassociation.com

**National Institute for Metalworking Skills (NIMS)**
10565 Fairfax Boulevard, Suite 10
Fairfax, VA 22030
844.839.6467
www.nims-skills.org

**National Kitchen & Bath Association (NKBA)**
800.843.6522
info@nkba.org
nkba.org

**National Limousine Association (NLA)**
1002 Lincoln Drive West, Suite C
Marlton, NJ 08053
800.652.7007
info@limo.org
www.limo.org

**National Management Association (NMA)**
3055 Kettering Boulevard, Suite 210
Dayton, OH 45439
937.294.0421
nma1.org

**National Motorists Association (NMA)**
1001 Arboretum Drive, Suite 120
Waunakee, WI 53597
nma@motorists.org
www.motorists.org

**National Property Management Association (NPMA)**
3525 Piedmont Road
Building 5, Suite 300
Atlanta, GA 30305
404.477.5811
www.npma.org

**National Society of Professional Engineers (NSPE)**
1420 King Street
Alexandria, VA 22314
888.285.6773
www.nspe.org

**National Tooling & Machining Association (NTMA)**
1357 Rockside Road
Cleveland OH 44134
800.248.6862
ntma.org

**Nationwide Multistate Licensing System & Registry (NMLS) Resource Center**
855.665.7123
mortgage.nationwidelicensingsystem.org

**National Restaurant Association**
2055 L Street NW, Suite 700
Washington, DC 20036
202.331.5900
askus@restaurant.org
www.restaurant.org
National Restaurant Association Educational Foundation: chooserestaurants.org
Restaurant Law Center: restaurantlawcenter.org
ServSafe Accrediation: www.servsafe.com

**National Sustainable Agriculture Information Service**
P.O. Box 3838
3040 Continental Drive
Butte, MT 59702
800.346.9140
askanag@ncat.org
attra.ncat.org

**NCTA—The Internet & Television Association**
25 Massachusetts Avenue NW, Suite 100
Washington, DC 20001
202.222.2300
info@ncta.com
www.ncta.com

**Network & Systems Professionals Association (NaSPA)**
214.771.8616
naspa.com

**Network for Social Work Management (NSWM)**
c/o Special Service for Groups
905 E. 8th Street
Los Angeles, CA 90021
213.553.1870
info@socialworkmanager.org
socialworkmanager.org

**New York Foundation for the Arts (NYFA)**
20 Jay Street, Suite 740
Brooklyn, NY 11201
212.366.6900
help@nyfa.org
www.nyfa.org

**North American Board of Certified Energy Practitioners (NABCEP)**
56 Clifton Country Road, Suite 202
Clifton Park, NY 12065
800.654.0021
info@nabcep.org
www.nabcep.org

**North American Transportation Association (NTA)**
9120 Double Diamond Parkway, Suite 346
Reno, NV 89521-4842
800.805.0040
www.ntassoc.com

**O*NET OnLine**
onet@onetcenter.org
www.onetonline.org
My Next Move: www.mynextmove.org

**Out of Home Advertising Association of America (OAAA)**
1850 M Street, NW, Suite 1040
Washington, DC 20036
202.833.5566
oaaa.org

**Precision Machined Products Association (PMPA)**
6880 W Snowville Road
Brecksville, OH 44141
440.526.0300
gro.apmp@ofni
www.pmpa-national.com

**Precision Metalforming Association (PMA)**
6363 Oak Tree Boulevard
Independence, OH 44131-2500
216.901.8800
www.pma.org

**Promotional Products Association International (PPAI)**
3125 Skyway Circle North
Irving, TX 75038
888.426.7724
webmaster@ppai.org
www.ppai.org

**RedRover**
P.O. Box 188890
Sacramento, CA 95818
916.429-2457
info@redrover.org
redrover.org
Readers program: redrover.org/readers

**Retail Bakers of America (RBA)**
15941 S Harlem Avenue, Suite 347
Tinley Park, IL 60477
800.638.0924
info@retailbakersofamerica.org
retailbakersofamerica.org

**Rideshare Association**
855.964.3556
yo@yorideshare.com
www.yorideshare.com

**Rideshare Guy**
harry@therideshareguy.com
therideshareguy.com

**RPIA Group**
P.O. Box 803
Westfield, IN 46074
800.746.6551
rick.crawford@rpiausa.org
www.rpiausa.org

**Senior Executives Association (SEA)**
4829 West Lane
Bethesda, MD 20814
202.971.3300
seniorexecs.org

**Society of Biological Engineers (SBE)**
c/o American Institute of Chemical Engineers (AIChE)
120 Wall Street, FL 23
New York, NY 10005-4020
800.242.4363
www.aiche.org/sbe

**Society of Cable Telecommunications Engineers (SCTE)**
140 Philips Road
Exton, PA 19341
610.363.6888
info@scte.org
www.scte.org

**Society for Hospitality & Foodservice Management (SHFM)**
326 E. Main Street
Louisville, KY 40202
502.574.9931
shfm@hqtrs.com
www.shfm-online.org

**Software & Information Industry Association (SIIA)**
202-289-7442
www.siia.net

**Solar Energy Industries Association (SEIA)**
1425 K Street NW, Suite 1000
Washington, DC 20005
202.682.0556
info@seia.org
www.seia.org

**The Solar Foundation**
c/o Marcum
1899 L Street NW, Suite 850
Washington, DC 20036
202.469.3750
info@solarfound.org
www.thesolarfoundation.org

**Solar Training Network**
1110 Vermont Avenue NW
Washington, DC 20005
202.866.0924
info@americansolarworkforce.org
americansolarworkforce.org

**Technology Student Association (TSA)**
1904 Association Drive
Reston, VA 20191-1540
703.860.9000
general@tsaweb.org
tsaweb.org

**Telecommunications Industry Association (TIA)**
1310 North Courthouse Road, Suite 890
Arlington, VA 22201
703.907.7700
tiaonline.org

**Transportation Alliance**
3200 Tower Oaks Boulevard, Suite 220
Rockville, MD 20852
301.984.5700
info@thetransportationalliance.org
www.thetransportationalliance.org

**United States Bureau of Labor Statistics (BLS)**
Postal Square Building
2 Massachusetts Avenue NE
Washington, DC 20212-0001
202.691.5200
www.bls.gov
Occupational Outlook Handbook: www.bls.gov/ooh

**United States Fashion Industry Association (USFIA)**
1730 Rhode Island Avenue NW, Suite 312
Washington, DC 20036
202.419.0444
info@usfashionindustry.com
www.usfashionindustry.com

**United States Patent & Trademark Office (USPTO)**
USPTO Madison Building
600 Dulany Street
Alexandria, VA 22314
800.786.9199
www.uspto.gov

**USTelecom**
601 New Jersey Avenue NW, Suite 600
Washington, DC 20001
www.ustelecom.org

**Water Environment Federation (WEF)**
Public Education Manager-Career Information
601 Wythe Street
Alexandria, VA 22314
800.666.0206
csc@wef.org
www.wef.org

**Women In Trucking Association (WIT)**
P.O. Box 400
Plover, WI 54467-0400
888.464.9482
WIT@womenintrucking.org

**Wood Component Manufacturers Association (WCMA)**
P.O. Box 662
Lindstrom, MN 55045
651.332.6332
wcma@wcma.com
www.wcma.com

**Wood Machinery Manufacturers of America (WMMA)**
2331 Rock Spring Road
Forest Hill, MD 21050
443.640.1052
info@wmma.org
wmma.org

**Wood Products Manufacturers Association (WPMA)**
P.O. Box 761
Westminster, MA 01473-0761
978.874.5445
woodprod@wpma.org
www.wpma.org

**Woodwork Career Alliance of North America (WCA)**
info@woodworkcareer.org
woodworkcareer.org

**Woodworking Machinery Industry Association (WMIA)**
3025 Hamaker Court, Suite 460
Fairfax, VA 22031
571.279.8340
info@wmia.org
www.wmia.org

**WoodWorkers Guild of America (WWGOA)**
2955 Xenium Lane N, Suite 10
Plymouth, MN 55441
855.253.0822
wwgoasubscription@program-director.net
www.wwgoa.com

**World Organization of Webmasters (WOW)**
P.O. Box 584
Washington, IL 61571-0584
662.493.2776
membership@webprofessionals.org
webprofessionals.org

# INDEX

## A

## B



## C

## G



## H



## I

## N



## O



## P

## Q



## R



## S